WITTGENSTEIN AND THE PRACTICE OF PHILOSOPHY

WITTGENSTEIN AND THE PRACTICE OF PHILOSOPHY

MICHAEL HYMERS

BROADVIEW GUIDES to PHILOSOPHY

LIBRARY AND ARCHIVES CANADA CATALOGUING IN PUBLICATION

Hymers, Michael
Wittgenstein and the practice of philosophy / Michael Hymers.

(Broadview guides to philosophy)
Includes bibliographical references and index.
ISBN 978-1-55111-892-5

1. Wittgenstein, Ludwig, 1889-1951.
I. Title. II. Series: Broadview guides to philosophy

B3376.W564H95 2009 192 C2009-905154-0

Broadview Press is an independent, international publishing house, incorporated in 1985. Broadview believes in shared ownership, both with its employees and with the general public; since the year 2000 Broadview shares have traded publicly on the Toronto Venture Exchange under the symbol BDP.

We welcome comments and suggestions regarding any aspect of our publications—please feel free to contact us at the addresses below or at: broadview@broadviewpress.com / www.broadviewpress.com.

North America
Post Office Box 1243,
Peterborough, Ontario, Canada K9J 7H5

2215 Kenmore Ave.
Buffalo, New York, USA 14207

tel: (705) 743-8990; fax: (705) 743-8353

customerservice@broadviewpress.com

UK, Europe, Central Asia, Middle East, Africa, India and Southeast Asia
Eurospan Group
3 Henrietta St., London, WC2E 8LU, UK
tel: 44 (0) 1767 604972; fax: 44 (0) 1767 601640
eurospan@turpin-distribution.com

Australia and New Zealand
NewSouth Books
c/o TL Distribution, 15-23 Helles Ave.,
Moorebank, NSW, Australia 2170
tel: (02) 8778 9999 ; fax (02) 8778 9944
orders@tldistribution.com.au

Broadview Press acknowledges the financial support of the Government of Canada through the Book Publishing Industry Development Program (BPIDP) for our publishing activities.

Edited by Robert Martin

Cover design by Michel Vrana; interior design by Jennifer Blais, Black Eye Design.

This book is printed on paper containing 100% post-consumer fibre.

Printed in Canada

For Kathryn

CONTENTS

ACKNOWLEDGEMENTS

This book has its origins in my notes for a seminar on Wittgenstein that I taught at the University of Alberta in the fall of 1997. I thank my students in that class, especially Glenn Parsons whom I was not fooling for a moment. It was not until my first sabbatical leave from Dalhousie that I got around to writing what I had been thinking during that autumn, but in recent years numerous other students have been subjected to drafts of the material that follows, and I have been lucky to learn from many of them, especially Emily Bingeman, Stephanie Dick, Warren Heiti, Colin Hirano, Maja Jaakson, Caleb Lee, Rebecca Mason, Jeremy McMillan, Luke McNulty, Gillman Payette, Eve Roberts, Anna Sheridan-Jonah, David Suarez, and Graham Sullivan.

In the face of my flagging enthusiasm, my completion of the first draft of this book during the summer of 2005 was inspired by the good example, the good fellowship, the wit, and the intellectual stimulation of the hard-working and ever-thoughtful Edrie Sobstyl, who knows how to practice philosophy if anyone does.

I have presented versions of almost all this material to the Dalhousie Philosophy Department's weekly Friday colloquium, and I have benefited from the questions, criticisms and encouragement that I received on those occasions. This, more than any other, is the audience I write for.

David Braybrooke, Steven Burns, Andrew Fenton, and Letitia Meynell read a draft of the manuscript in its entirety, at Sheldon Wein's encouragement, and raised many difficult questions for my consideration. David G. Stern read the entire manuscript for Broadview and made a wealth of helpful suggestions. I am grateful to Rich Campbell for his comments on Chapter 1. Section 5.6 was shaped by conversations with Jack Canfield and with Bob Martin (who also copyedited the manuscript and offered many helpful philosophical comments). Section 7.6 profited enormously from comments and criticisms from Béla Szabados, Steven Burns, and Lynette Reid, and from conversations with Alyssa Robichaud. Section 7.7 is much better for comments and suggestions from Susan Sherwin.

In all of the above cases no automatic agreement should be assumed, and any errors or inadequacies that remain are my own to discover.

As well as providing philosophical feedback, my colleagues at Dalhousie and the University of King's College have been an invaluable source of emotional support and encouragement at times when I have needed it badly. I thank them all, but, especially, Duncan MacIntosh and Sue Campbell.

Wittgenstein thought that the task of philosophy was to remind us of things that, in some sense, we already know, but he also thought that it was impossible to be a good philosopher if one was not also a good human being. So I must also thank my friends Charles Davidson, Ward McBurney, Scott Owen, and Jayn Ritchie, and my sister Kathy Batstone for their philosophical reminders and for helping to save my sanity.

My greatest debt, as always, is to Kathryn Harvey, who proofread the penultimate draft, and to whom I owe more than I can say.

Michael Hymers
Halifax, NS

INTRODUCTION

Wittgenstein once wrote that "The philosopher's treatment of a question is like the treatment of an illness" (PI §255).[1] This remark and others regarding the practice of philosophy have occasioned a good deal of puzzlement. Surely Wittgenstein is not making a general factual claim to the effect that philosophers are actually engaged in the activity of trying to cure us of the urge to ask philosophical questions! To many philosophers it has seemed that the questions with which they are preoccupied are not ailments that need to be cured or palliated, but concerns of ultimate importance. What could matter more than understanding the nature of being and humanity's place within it? Answering such questions, moreover, may require unusual methods of careful analysis, thought-experiments, the generating of counterexamples, and rigid deductive reasoning—all aimed at discovering the truth, not alleviating our impulse to ask questions. Or perhaps philosophy is an extension of the natural sciences, which are surely concerned with answering genuine questions, not curing our desire to ask them. Philosophers, likewise, often

1 Ludwig Wittgenstein, *Philosophical Investigations*, 2nd ed., translated by G.E.M. Anscombe (Oxford: Basil Blackwell, 1968). As David Stern has emphasized to me, the translation of this passage is a matter of some controversy. See Garth Halett, *A Companion to Wittgenstein's Philosophical Investigations* (Ithaca, NY: Cornell University Press, 1977), 336 and Barry Stroud, "Wittgenstein's 'Treatment' of the Quest for 'a language which describes my inner experience and which only I myself can understand'" in *Meaning, Understanding, and Practice: Philosophical Essays* (Oxford: Oxford University Press, 2000), 67–79 at 73.

think of themselves as concerned with genuine questions for which there are correct answers, however difficult those answers might be to discover.

So it would seem that Wittgenstein's remark must be taken as a comment about his own methods in philosophy, or perhaps as a recommendation to other philosophers about how they ought to approach their subject-matter. But in that case, what exactly is Wittgenstein recommending? Is it a recommendation that applies to all philosophical questions? Or are there puzzles and problems of special interest to philosophers that do not fit the type foremost in Wittgenstein's mind when he makes his recommendations?

This book is an attempt to answer these questions in a way that should be accessible to anyone who has some familiarity with traditional philosophical problems. By examining Wittgenstein's pronouncements on the practice of philosophy and by looking at how these pronouncements come to life in his own philosophical practice, I aim to cast light on methodological commitments, a grasp of which seems to me to be an indispensable precondition for appreciating his work. In the process, I aim also to present a reasonably clear and plausible interpretation of Wittgenstein's views concerning some of the problems to which he applies his methods. I make no claims to comprehensiveness. Some of Wittgenstein's most interesting and provocative claims will go unmentioned here, but I think that a clear enough idea of how his techniques might be applied to the issues I neglect will be available once I have had my say about general methods and a few particular cases. I think, in fact, that the most important feature of Wittgenstein's contributions to philosophy is his metaphilosophy, though its value cannot, of course, be weighed independently of its success in particular instances.[2]

I begin in Chapter 1 by sketching some rival conceptions of the nature of philosophy, though, again, without making any claim to comprehensiveness. My focus will be, rather, on sketching slightly idealized versions of various accounts of philosophy which—unlike Wittgenstein's views, early or late—see its importance or status as defined in some way by its relation to natural science:

- Philosophy as a foundation for the sciences (Descartes);
- Philosophy as an under-labourer to the sciences (Locke);
- Philosophy as the queen of the sciences (Kant);
- Philosophy as logic (Russell and the Vienna Circle);
- Philosophy as inquiry continuous with the natural sciences (Quine).

2 I return to the metaphors of illness and therapy in Chapter 3, §3.10.

In Chapter 2 I turn to an examination of Wittgenstein's early views about philosophical method. I begin by offering an overview of major themes in the *Tractatus Logico-philosophicus*, some grasp of which is necessary in order to understand Wittgenstein's early metaphilosophical views and to compare and contrast them meaningfully with the views sketched in Chapter 1—especially those of Russell and the Vienna Circle. Understanding these themes is also important if the contrast I seek to defend in Chapter 3 between Wittgenstein's earlier and later work is to be made perspicuous. I focus in particular on Wittgenstein's logical atomism, his correlative commitment to the thesis of extensionality, and his picture theory of meaning. I compare and contrast his views with those of Frege and Russell particularly with regard to the so-called problem of "bearerless names" and the problem of ostensibly non-extensional contexts. Whereas Frege appealed to a theory of linguistic sense to solve these problems, and Russell introduced his theory of descriptions to deal with them, Wittgenstein thinks that the possibility of analyzing every empirical statement of natural language into a unique concatenation of simple names for simple objects eliminates the difficulties. His picture theory of meaning, in turn, tries to explain how such concatenations of simple names can serve as logical pictures of atomic facts by sharing their logical form with the facts depicted. But, as is well known, Wittgenstein holds that logical form itself cannot be represented, but only shown. I link this claim to the claim of TLP §6.41[3] that all value must lie outside the world, arguing that it should be taken to apply as much to *semantic* value—to meaning—as to ethical or aesthetic value. And this thesis about value, in turn, is reflected in Wittgenstein's contention that logic, like ethics and aesthetics in the *Tractatus*, is both *transcendental*—a condition of the possibility of meaning and of a world of facts—and *transcendent*—lying beyond the contingency of the world in an inexpressible realm of necessity. The task of philosophy, as a result, is to "mean the unspeakable by clearly displaying the speakable" (TLP §4.115).

Wittgenstein's transitional writings and lectures are the focus of Chapter 3, for it is in these works that Wittgenstein's mature conception of philosophy as a "therapeutic" practice begins to emerge—a conception that is spelled out further in a series of remarks in the later *Philosophical Investigations*. That emergence, I argue, against the views of so-called New Wittgensteinians, is intimately linked to his recognition of problems for the logical atomism of the *Tractatus* and to his subsequent rejection of the Tractarian thesis that all value lies outside the world. In its

3 Ludwig Wittgenstein, *Tractatus Logico-philosophicus*, translated by C.K. Ogden (London: Routledge & Kegan Paul, 1922).

place we find a kind of conventionalism about value and normativity,[4] according to which the possibility of meaning and value rests on our familiarity with tacit norms of behaviour. In turn, for Wittgenstein one of the key sources of philosophical confusion is the fact that we learn to employ concepts in accord with tacit conventions for their use without thereby learning to describe those conventions. The new task of philosophy, accordingly, is to make these conventional norms explicit when their implicitness leads us to fall into philosophical confusion—to remind us explicitly of what we already know implicitly. However, Wittgenstein's brand of conventionalism—as is hinted at by his focus on *implicit* norms—does not see conventions as arbitrary or whimsical. We cannot arbitrarily change our minds about norms that we grasp only tacitly, and if, when they are made explicit, we tend to see some of our linguistic conventions—for example, in mathematics—as expressions of hidden essences, of necessary truths, then that should serve as a reminder of the "deep need"[5] that we have for certain conventions—a deep need that Wittgenstein later hints is connected with the kind of organisms we are. In the sense that Wittgenstein abandons a supernatural view of value for a tacit conventionalism, bounded by our capacities as biological beings, his view might be described as a "naturalistic" one,[6] but it is by no means the Quinean view that philosophy is continuous with natural science, and it is not an attempt to *explain* the nature of necessity by appeal to conventions. Philosophy's task is the "synopsis of trivialities"[7]—that is, the explicit and "perspicuous representation" (PI §122) of conventional norms with which we are already implicitly acquainted.

Most of the remaining chapters—4 through 6—are devoted to examining how Wittgenstein applies his new conception of philosophy to an array of problems in metaphysics, the philosophy of language and mind, and epistemology. In Chapter 4

4 In a recent book Michael Luntley denies that Wittgenstein adopts any kind of conventionalism, but I think this view rests on too narrow a conception of conventionalism. See Michael Luntley, *Wittgenstein: Meaning and Judgment* (Oxford: Blackwell, 2003), 33.

5 Ludwig Wittgenstein, *Remarks on the Foundations of Mathematics*, rev. ed., edited by G.H. von Wright, R. Rhees, and G.E.M. Anscombe, translated by G.E.M. Anscombe (Cambridge, MA: MIT Press, 1978), 65.

6 For related suggestions see Marie McGinn, *Sense and Certainty: A Dissolution of Scepticism* (Oxford: Blackwell, 1989), 152 and Michael Williams, *Unnatural Doubts: Epistemological Realism and the Basis of Scepticism* (Princeton: Princeton University Press, 1996), 37. Williams describes Wittgenstein's naturalism as "methodological"—as focused on deriving a picture of our conceptual and normative commitments from our customary practices—and contrasts it with "substantive" or Humean naturalism, which is focused on explaining why we hold the beliefs we do by appealing to features of human nature. Quine's naturalism is perhaps neither of these exactly, but it clearly owes more to Hume than Wittgenstein's does.

7 Ludwig Wittgenstein, *Wittgenstein's Lectures—Cambridge, 1930–1932*, from the notes of John King and Desmond Lee, edited by Desmond Lee (Oxford: Blackwell, 1980), 26.

I examine the first ninety or so sections of the *Investigations*, paying particular attention to Wittgenstein's discussions of naming and family resemblances, each of which is elucidated by considering Wittgenstein's method of language-games. The key thought here is that we can avoid falling into philosophical puzzlement about naming, meaning, and general terms, if we examine the ways in which different kinds of words are taught and learned in very simple contexts. These simple kinds of linguistic interaction Wittgenstein calls "language-games," and they are interactions of the sort that we engage in when teaching young children their first language. Wittgenstein's use of the term 'language-game' becomes more expansive, including more sophisticated kinds of linguistic interaction, the further one reads into the *Investigations*, but for my purposes this initial use of the term at PI §7 is of fundamental importance. An examination of elementary language-games gets us closer to a perspicuous representation of our uses of words, which makes linguistic norms that are implicit in our practices explicit and open to view. Obtaining such a clear view of our linguistic practices undermines, for example, the temptation felt by the author of the *Tractatus* to postulate the necessary existence of simple objects to serve as the "substance of the world" (TLP §2.0231), and it likewise undermines the temptation to posit the existence of either transcendent or immanent universals to justify our employment of general terms in systems of classification.

What also becomes clear from an examination of the *Investigations* is that Wittgenstein does not write with a unified voice. His own doubts and philosophical temptations are as apparent in the text as are the synoptic overviews that are meant to alleviate them. This, I argue, need not prevent us from attributing particular views to Wittgenstein, but it does require us to be cautious.

I turn in Chapter 5 to Wittgenstein's discussions of rule-following and private language, which have received considerable attention in recent years in the wake of Saul Kripke's contention that Wittgenstein presents us with a new form of scepticism about the very possibility of meaning and rules.[8] I contend that Kripke is right when he argues that Wittgenstein rejects all likely proposals for a reductive theory of meaning, but wrong when he goes on to conclude that Wittgenstein is a meaning-sceptic. On the contrary, I take Wittgenstein's conclusion to be that meaning is not the sort of thing about which it makes any sense to have a reductive theory, *and* that the possibility of our grasping any norm or rule explicitly presupposes that at least some norms or rules are grasped *implicitly*. It is precisely because some of our norms *must* be implicit that we are vulnerable to the kind of philosophical confusion that Wittgenstein describes as "entanglement in our

8 Saul Kripke, *Wittgenstein on Rules and Private Language* (Cambridge, MA: Harvard University Press, 1982).

own rules" (PI §125), because in learning the application of a rule we may not—and in at least some cases, cannot—learn how to describe that application. The rule-following problem is itself a result of such entanglement and requires therapeutic treatment—the untying of "knots in our thinking"[9]—not solution.

Turning then to Wittgenstein's discussion of private language, I take Wittgenstein to be arguing that our best understanding of how naming customarily works—our most perspicuous representation of the implicit norms of naming—leaves it mysterious how there could ever be a language in which naming was something *private*. However, this does not constitute a refutation of the logical possibility of private naming, and we should not expect to find any such refutation in Wittgenstein's work if he is being true to his later conception of philosophical method. His task is simply to assemble "reminders for a particular purpose" (PI §127)—in this case reminders about how naming ordinarily proceeds and how we ordinarily decide that someone has come to understand a name.

The central concern of Chapter 6 is to pursue the twin themes of implicit norms and the alleviation of philosophical confusion into Wittgenstein's reflections on knowledge in *On Certainty*. We find in this late work, not a theory of knowledge or of epistemic justification, but an (incomplete) attempt to provide a synoptic view of the roles played by the concepts of knowledge and justification in our daily lives—to elucidate the often implicit norms that govern ascriptions of knowledge. Despite apparent affinities with Quine, Wittgenstein is not a holist about epistemic justification, but neither is he a foundationalist. If we must apply a term to his view, then perhaps the closest approximation would be "contextualism" in a sense of that word that has recently been defended by Michael Williams.[10] This is just to say that Wittgenstein does not think there is anything non-trivial that can be said about knowledge or justification in general. Moreover, I do not think that Wittgenstein is best thought of as trying to give what Williams calls a "definitive refutation"[11] of epistemological scepticism, though he may feel the temptation to, any more than I think he is trying to refute the very possibility of a private language in the *Investigations*. Passages in which Wittgenstein seems to be saying that sceptical doubts literally make no sense are better thought of as attempts to shift the burden of proof onto the shoulders of the sceptic—to demand that the sceptic give us some reason to think that, given our ordinary practices of

9 Ludwig Wittgenstein, *Zettel*, 2nd ed., translated by G.E.M. Anscombe (Oxford: Basil Blackwell, 1981), §452.

10 Michael Williams, *Problems of Knowledge* (New York: Oxford University Press, 2001).

11 Williams, *Unnatural Doubts* (Princeton: Princeton University Press, 1996), 32. In fact Williams finds several different strains of thought about scepticism in *On Certainty*, but he seems to suggest that this is one of them. See Williams (1996), 180–81.

language-learning, sceptical doubts about the external world could be expressed without having learned a language. Wittgenstein is again reminding us of conventional grammatical norms with which we are implicitly familiar, in an attempt to dissolve the problem of scepticism, not solve it.

In this chapter I also undertake to defend Wittgenstein against the worry that in *On Certainty* he returns to the view of the *Tractatus* that if any norms are to be possible, there must be some norms that lie outside the world—that value must be, in some sense, *transcendent* as it was in the *Tractatus*, even if logical atomism is not to be embraced again. I contend that Wittgenstein does arrive at something like the view that there are some *transcendental* norms—norms that are conditions of the possibility of any intelligible discourse or reasoning at all. However, I argue that we need not expect the list of such norms to be very long, and that commitment to some transcendental norms does not entail commitment to *transcendent* norms—to the view that value must ultimately lie outside the world in something absolutely necessary. Wittgenstein's view, I think, is similar to Hilary Putnam's contention that there must be at least one *a priori* truth, such as the very weak "minimal" principle of non-contradiction, which tells us that *not every proposition can be simultaneously and unambiguously both true and false.*[12] Weak logical principles of this sort are what I think Wittgenstein has in mind when he speaks of the "hard rock" of the "river-bed of thought," which is to be contrasted with both the less stable sandy bottom of the river and the water that flows over it.[13]

The task of Chapter 7 is to consider briefly a number of worries and criticisms that Wittgenstein's therapeutic vision of philosophy are likely to engender. I respond briefly to the charges that Wittgenstein is recommending that we give up doing philosophy, that he unjustifiably privileges ordinary language over philosophical language, that he is unduly pessimistic about philosophical progress, and that his philosophy is politically conservative. I believe that none of these charges is reasonable. However, it is a more serious concern how general Wittgenstein's method can plausibly be seen to be. I contend that by his own lights he cannot reasonably insist that a therapeutic conception of philosophy captures the essence or true nature of philosophy because "philosophy" is itself a family-resemblance concept. There is no one feature that justifies us in applying the term 'philosophy' to an intellectual practice, but rather a "network of similarities, overlapping and criss-crossing" (PI §66). I insist, however, that the exercise of obtaining a synoptic

12 Hilary Putnam, "There Is at Least One *A Priori* Truth" in *Realism and Reason* (Cambridge: Cambridge University Press, 1983), 98–114.

13 Ludwig Wittgenstein, *On Certainty*, translated by Denis Paul and G.E.M. Anscombe (New York: Harper Torchbooks, 1972), §§97–99.

view of the relevant linguistic conventions is an essential first step in deciding what kind of philosophical problem one is dealing with and how to deal with it—whether by dissolution or by attempted solution.

A related question about the scope of Wittgenstein's method concerns moral philosophy. Wittgenstein's early view treats value as something that must lie outside the world and about which nothing can be said, so that ethics as most philosophers conceive of it has no place in philosophy. When Wittgenstein abandons the thesis that all value and normativity must lie outside the world, he ought, by rights, to leave this mystical view of ethics behind, but he expresses a lingering attachment to it, and he says very little about the consequences of his new conventionalism for ethics, even though he spells them out in great detail for meaning, mind, and mathematics. I propose that the natural way to extend Wittgenstein's thinking in this neglected area is to spell out the consequences of seeing moral vocabulary as full of family-resemblance terms. This entails, at the meta-ethical level, that there are no non-trivial unified theories of the nature of moral goodness, and, at the normative ethical level, that moral rules and principles are to be seen as tentative, revisable generalizations based on comparisons of particular cases in a manner roughly analogous to legal reasoning.

I conclude by taking up once again the thread of science and philosophy, briefly returning to some respects in which Wittgenstein's views differ from those of Quine. In particular, I contend that Quine's behaviourism, his radical holism about meaning and confirmation, his wholesale rejection of the analytic-synthetic distinction, and, above all, his scientistic version of naturalism, are all in significant tension with important features of Wittgenstein's view. But the differences, as is perhaps the case with anything of philosophical interest, are not simple ones.

1

PHILOSOPHY AND SCIENCE

In this chapter I shall focus on a number of views that see philosophy as getting its significance from its relation to natural science, whether as its overseer, its subordinate, or its partner in a shared endeavour. Each of these views has been historically influential, and each differs in important ways from the more autonomous conception of philosophy that Wittgenstein goes on to develop, in spite of the fact that Wittgenstein's view develops in the course of his interactions with Russell and the Vienna Circle, and in spite of the fact that there are certain *prima facie* similarities between Wittgenstein's mature views and the naturalistic view of philosophy later promoted by Quine—also in response to Russell and the Vienna Circle.

1.1 A FOUNDATION FOR THE SCIENCES

Western philosophy and science share their historical roots. In the *Timaeus* Plato offers us not merely a philosophical dialogue, but a comprehensive cosmology—albeit one that does not stand up very well to current empirical scrutiny. We owe to Aristotle not just the *Nicomachean Ethics* and the *Metaphysics*, but *De Caelo* (*The Heavens*) and *De partibus Animalium* (*On the Parts of Animals*), as well. During the Middle Ages, students of nature were guided by the writings of "the Philosopher," and it was Aristotle and his influence that Galileo and Descartes alike felt compelled to challenge at the outset of the European scientific revolution. The project of mathematizing nature was, likewise, a shared passion for these thinkers, who are often portrayed as the founders of modern science and modern philosophy respectively.

With the rapid rise of natural science in the seventeenth century, the idea that science and philosophy might be separate disciplines began to take shape, though in its early articulations it appeared as a concern with discovering or formulating what René Descartes called a "*Method of rightly conducting one's reason and seeking the truth in the sciences.*"[1] As Descartes envisioned it, science could make no systematic headway unless it could free itself from error and accept only those things that an individual inquirer could know with objective certainty. Without this propadeutic, it would not be possible to "establish anything at all in the sciences that was stable and likely to last" (MED II 12).[2] That goal of certainty was to be reached, Descartes thought, by employing two related techniques: the method of doubt and the method of analysis. The former of these advises us that we must accept as true only those things that admit of no possible doubt whatsoever. It does not matter whether such doubts seem unmotivated or arbitrary. As long as they are possible—as long as no contradiction or incoherence is engendered by such doubts—they must be taken seriously. The method of analysis teaches us that complexity is frequently a source of error and possible doubt, and, so, if one seeks to minimize what can be coherently doubted amongst one's beliefs, then one would do well to break the objects of possible knowledge into their simplest parts, for subjects such as arithmetic and geometry "which deal only with the simplest and most general things, regardless of whether they really exist in nature or not, contain something certain and indubitable" (MED II 14). However, even such simple objects of thought as the natural numbers and basic arithmetic are not entirely immune from doubt, for, despite their intrinsic clarity, they may also be subjected to a deeper "metaphysical"[3] kind of doubt. Thus Descartes imagines himself deceived by God or by an evil demon so that whenever he tries to add two and three together, he is tricked into getting a wrong result. Basic arithmetic may admit of no uncertainty taken in itself, but the possibility of a malevolent deceiver provides an extrinsic reason for thinking that doubt is possible even here.

1 The full title of René Descartes's *Discourse* is "*Discourse on the Method of Rightly Conducting One's Reason and Seeking the Truth in the Sciences.*" In *The Philosophical Writings of Descartes*, Vol. I, translated by John Cottingham, Robert Stoothoff, and Dugald Murdoch (Cambridge: Cambridge University Press, 1984).

2 Descartes, *Meditations on First Philosophy* in *The Philosophical Writings of Descartes*, Vol. II, 1–62.

3 Descartes, *Objections and Replies* in *The Philosophical Writings of Descartes*, Vol. II, 63–397 at 308.

What the evil demon cannot do, thinks Descartes, is cause him to be deluded in his belief that he himself exists: "let him deceive me as much as he can, he will never bring it about that I am nothing so long as I think that I am something" (MED II 17). Doubt here seems self-defeating, for I seem to be vulnerable to demonic deception only if I actually exist. Nor, it seems, can I doubt that I doubt without undermining that original doubt, for if I doubt that I doubt, then I surely doubt. I can be certain, therefore, that I exist and that I doubt.

Commentators, since Descartes's own time, have doubted that Descartes has really taken his method of doubt as far as it can go by its own lights and have questioned his contention to have found at least one thing that he can know with objective certainty—that is, one thing concerning which he cannot possibly be mistaken. How can I be certain that it is *I* who doubt and that there is not merely free-floating doubt, unattached to any doubting subject? In English we say, "It is raining"; in French, "*Il pleut.*" But no one supposes that there is an "it" or an "*il*" that does the raining. Descartes, Nietzsche was later to write, has failed to "free [himself] from the seduction of words."[4] Nonetheless, Descartes fancies that he has secured his result and that he can use it as a foundation on which to reconstruct the edifice of his knowledge. And that edifice includes prominently the findings and theoretical hypotheses of what we now customarily think of as empirical science. When his *Discourse* was published anonymously in 1637, it appeared together with three essays, *Optics*, *Meteorology*, and *Geometry*, each of which was supposed to display Descartes's method in extensive practical application. These are the results "in the sciences that [are] stable and likely to last" (MED II 12) in Descartes's view, and their stability he takes to rest directly on the method.[5] Philosophy, in this conception of it, thus plays the role of certifying or rejecting candidates for scientific knowledge, and science can proceed with justifiable confidence only given an adequate "first philosophy."

4 Friedrich W. Nietzsche, *Beyond Good and Evil*, translated by Walter H. Kaufmann (New York: Vintage Books, 1966), §16.

5 Some of his results, such as his independent derivation of Snell's Law in optics and his employment of what are now known as Cartesian axes in analytical geometry, have, indeed, proved lasting, though it is a further question whether this has much to do with the method to which Descartes attributes them.

1.2 THE QUEEN OF THE SCIENCES

Many philosophers find the details of Descartes's reconstruction of his knowledge unconvincing, but the foundationalist conception of justification that he advocates has remained popular to the present day—though, as we shall see below, forms of foundationalism are compatible with a more modest outlook on the importance of philosophy for science. By contrast, Immanuel Kant was no foundationalist about justification, but there is a clear sense in which Kant also thought of philosophy as the master discipline, as having a special privilege in pronouncing on the epistemic status of the rest of culture, including science.

Kant's project in the *Critique of Pure Reason* is not to develop a method for all of science, nor—directly and explicitly—to give certification to the sciences. Rather, he describes his purpose as that of determining the proper method and scope of metaphysics, lamenting the fact that reason "in its non-empirical application" (A xii)[6] has a way of falling into contradiction and paradox, with the result that metaphysics either slips into dogmatic system-building or loses all credibility in the eyes of those who resist such dogmatism:

> Time was when metaphysics was entitled the Queen of all the sciences; and if the will be taken for the deed, the pre-eminent importance of her accepted tasks gives her every right to this title of honour. Now, however, the changed fashion of the time brings her only scorn ... (A viii)

Critics of metaphysics, thinks Kant, are right to be suspicious of the unrestrained use of pure reason, but in rejecting metaphysics completely, they ignore the legitimate application of pure reason and overlook the key importance for human beings of such metaphysical concepts as "*God*, *freedom*, and *immortality*" (B xxx):

> But it is idle to feign indifference to such enquiries, the object of which can never be indifferent to our human nature. Indeed, these pretended *indifferentists*, however they may try to disguise themselves by substituting a popular tone for the language of the Schools, inevitably fall back, in so far as they think at all, into those very metaphysical assertions which they profess so greatly to despise. (A x)

6 Immanuel Kant, *Critique of Pure Reason*, translated by Norman Kemp Smith (New York: St. Martin's Press, 1965).

Caught between the prospect of dogmatic commitment to a metaphysical position and the apparent impossibility of escaping metaphysical debate, philosophy, says Kant, is charged with the task of instituting "a tribunal which will assure to reason its lawful claims, and dismiss all groundless pretensions, not by despotic decrees, but in accordance with its own eternal and unalterable laws" (A xi-xii).[7] Such a "*critique of pure reason*" must "decide as to the possibility or impossibility of metaphysics in general, and determine its sources, its extent, and its limits—all in accordance with principles" (A xii). The results of this tribunal are grand indeed, if Kant is to be taken at his word, for he contends that "there is not a single metaphysical problem which has not been solved, or for the solution of which the key at least has not been supplied" (A xiii).

The model that Kant appeals to in this critique is one that he borrows from the formal and natural sciences. Both mathematics and physics, he thinks, have enjoyed progress and maturity as the result of "a single and sudden revolution" (B xvi) in each, whereby it was realized that knowledge of its objects consisted in recovering what reason itself had put into them:

> A new light flashed upon the mind of the first man ... who demonstrated the properties of the isosceles triangle. The true method, so he found, was not to inspect what he discerned either in the figure, or in the bare concept of it, and from this, as it were, to read off its properties; but to bring out what was necessarily implied in the concepts that he had himself formed *a priori*, and had put into the figure in the construction by which he presented it to himself. (B xii)

Similarly, in physics,

> When Galileo caused balls, the weights of which he had himself previously determined, to roll down an inclined plane; when Torricelli made the air carry a weight which he had calculated beforehand to be equal to that of a definite volume of water; or in more recent times, when Stahl changed metals into oxides, and oxides back into metal, by withdrawing something and then restoring it, a light broke upon all students of nature. They learned that reason has insight only into that which it produces after a plan of its own, and that it must not allow itself to be kept, as it were, in nature's leading-strings, but must itself show the way with principles of judgment

7 That such laws are eternal and immutable is itself, of course, a metaphysical claim.

> based upon fixed laws, constraining nature to give answer to questions of reason's own determining. (B xii-xiii)

The examples of these sciences, Kant thinks, suggest that "We must therefore make trial whether we may not have more success in the tasks of metaphysics, if we suppose that objects must conform to our knowledge" (B xvi), rather than that our knowledge must conform to the ways that objects are in themselves. Objects, he goes on to argue at great length, are known to us only as they appear to us, and they appear to us in a structured way made possible by our *a priori* synthesis of the manifold of experience in accordance with the pure concepts of understanding. Objects as they are in themselves are forever unknowable to us, and the mistakes of metaphysics have lain in confusing appearances with things in themselves.

But none of this suggests that metaphysics is *not* the Queen of the sciences after all. She was merely "*despotic*" (A ix) in her dogmatism and overly ambitious in her attempts to annex territory over which she could claim no legitimate rule. Indeed, in the course of his critique, Kant purports to show how *a priori* knowledge of synthetic truths concerning space and time is possible, thereby certifying Euclidean geometry and arithmetic respectively. He then goes on to certify our knowledge of objects and events in space and time generally by showing how such knowledge is made possible by our *a priori* grasp of twelve concepts of pure understanding, including, for example, *unity*, *plurality*, *existence*, and *causality*. These twelve fundamental categories are further subdivided into four groups: Quantity, Quality, Relation, and Modality.

The tidiness of this scheme is striking, but even more remarkable is the way in which this conceptual structure is mirrored in Kant's discussion of physical theory in his *Metaphysical Foundations of Natural Science*. There, Kant insists that his table of categories provides the metaphysical basis for the Newtonian concepts of matter and motion:

> The *Metaphysical Foundations of Natural Science* may be brought, then, under four main chapters. The first may be called *Phoronomy*; and in it motion is considered as pure quantum, according to its composition, without any quality of the matter. The second may be termed *Dynamics*, and in it motion is regarded as belonging to the quality of the matter under the name of an original moving force. The third emerges under the name *Mechanics*, and in it matter with this dynamical quality is considered as by its own motion to be in relation. The fourth is called *Phenomenology*; and in it matter's motion or rest is determined merely with reference to the

> mode of representation, or modality, i.e., as an appearance to the external senses. (MFNS 14–15)[8]

Quantity, Quality, Relation, and Modality all prove to be key pillars in the foundations of physics, and Kant proceeds in the remainder of the book to try to show that Newtonian physics has discovered once and for all the true principles governing the nature of matter. The derivation here is not strictly *a priori*, Kant is quick to point out, for it relies crucially on empirical observations to secure concepts of "the special nature of this or that kind of things" (MFNS 6). Even so, the confidence with which Kant "proves" that matter is infinitely divisible (MFNS 49–50) and that forces of attraction act at a distance through empty space (61–62), and the conviction with which he derives Newton's laws of motion is enough to make us wonder how it could have been so difficult for natural philosophers in the seventeenth century to finally arrive at Newton's results. Natural science may supply the results, but it is philosophy that tells us why they *must* be so.

Indeed, it is philosophy that tells us what gets to count as a science and what does not: "A rational doctrine of nature ... deserves the name of natural science only when the natural laws that underlie it are cognized a priori and are not mere laws of experience" (MFNS 4). Physics, Kant thinks, passes this test, but chemistry does not. It is merely a "systematic art rather than science" (MFNS 4) because, in Kant's day at least, "no law of the approach or withdrawal of the parts of matters can be stated according to which (as, say, in proportion to their densities and such-like) their motions together with the consequences of these can be intuited and presented a priori in space (a demand that will hardly ever be filled)" (MFNS 7).[9] So much, we might say, for avoiding dogmatism!

---

8 Immanuel Kant, *Metaphysical Foundations of Natural Science* in *Philosophy of Material Nature*, translated by James W. Ellington (Indianapolis: Hackett Publishing, 1985).

9 It is a bit puzzling how Kant can (a) say that chemistry is not yet a science, if it ever will be, and yet use it as an example on the same footing as physics and geometry of how reason finds in nature what it itself has put there, and (b) change his mind about what *a priori* principles structure the would-be science of chemistry if he is so confident about the example of Stahl. I am tempted to say that Kant is getting carried away by his own rhetoric here. Eric Watkins suggests that Kant's view leaves open the possibility that chemistry is a science "in some sense," if not quite the sense applicable to physics, and that Kant came to reject Stahl's view in favour of Lavoisier's theory of combustion some time between the mid-1780s (between the two editions of the *Critique of Pure Reason*) and the late 1790s. (See Eric Watkins, "Kant's Philosophy of Science," *The Stanford Encyclopedia of Philosophy* (Winter 2003), edited by Edward N. Zalta, <http://plato.stanford.edu/archives/win2003/entries/kant-science/>.)

1.3 PHILOSOPHY AS AN UNDER-LABOURER TO THE SCIENCES

I remarked earlier that something like Descartes's foundationalist conception of justification remains popular amongst philosophers—or at least amongst influential epistemologists. Contemporary versions of foundationalism typically eschew the project of finding any belief or other cognitive state that is invulnerable to Descartes's metaphysical doubts, and they similarly reject the demand that in order for a belief to be justified it must be derivable by a valid deductive argument from premises that are certain.[10] Non-deductive reasoning may also bestow justification, and so-called moderate foundationalists do not even insist that foundational beliefs be certain in the way that Descartes describes the subject matter of arithmetic and geometry. But they remain committed to the idea that some beliefs are intrinsically better justified than others and that these "basic" beliefs can serve as reasons, either deductive or non-deductive ones, for any non-basic belief that gets to count as justified. In contemporary foundationalist epistemology, then, there remain echoes of the Cartesian view that philosophy has the task of providing a foundation for scientific knowledge—a set of basic beliefs that can serve as justification for all other, non-basic beliefs.

Many foundationalists, however, do not regard these echoes as of fundamental importance. The view that philosophy can give science its rational foundations contributes to the reputation of philosophy as a self-designated "master discipline," charged—too conveniently, perhaps—with the task of pronouncing on all other disciplines. But a slightly more modest conception of the task of philosophy and its relation to the sciences in particular also arose late in the seventeenth century. According to this view, philosophy cannot pronounce on the ultimate legitimacy of science, but it can be of service to science by helping to eliminate confusions and by clarifying concepts. Such a view is widely associated with John Locke.

1.4 LOCKE, THE UNDER-LABOURER

Locke, like Descartes, was a foundationalist about epistemic justification, and there is much in his approach and the problems that preoccupy him in his *Essay concerning Human Understanding* that owes a debt to Descartes. But Descartes's project of employing hyperbolic doubt in order to uncover the certain foundations

10 It would probably be anachronistic to attribute the view rejected here to Descartes inasmuch as he did not think of himself necessarily as reasoning from beliefs or other cognitive states that are expressible in propositional form.

of all knowledge struck Locke as, at best, unnecessary. It is abundantly clear, he thinks, what we can be certain of. There are, in particular, three different categories of human knowledge, with diminishing degrees of certainty:

> For if we will reflect on our own ways of thinking, we shall find that sometimes the mind perceives the agreement or disagreement of two ideas *immediately by themselves*, without the intervention of any other; and this I think we may call *intuitive knowledge*.... Such kinds of truths the mind perceives at the first sight of the ideas together by bare intuition, without the intervention of any other idea; and this kind of knowledge is the clearest and most certain that human frailty is capable of. (ECHU IV, II, §1)[11]

Slightly less certain than intuitive knowledge is what Locke calls "demonstrative" knowledge, in which we reason from premises intuitively known. Each step of such reasoning is intuitively certain, but only after one has completed the demonstration is the conclusion certain, and the length of some chains of reasoning requires us to trust our memories and to work harder to grasp the complexity that is absent from ideas intuitively known. The third kind of knowledge available to us, according to Locke, is "*sensitive*" knowledge, which, he says, goes "beyond bare probability, and yet [does] not [reach] perfectly to either of the foregoing degrees of certainty" (ECHU IV, II, §14). This is the knowledge that we have by way of our senses of objects and events "actually present" (ECHU IV, II, §14) to us (our beliefs about absent objects or past events count only as "*faith* or *opinion*" (ECHU IV, II, §14)). Whereas Descartes pretends that he cannot tell the difference between his waking experience and his dreams, Locke takes the distinction to be "past doubting" (ECHU IV, II, §14). Like Descartes, Locke is an infallibilist about knowledge, strictly so-called. That is, both think that knowledge requires certainty. However, Locke seems to allow that certainty comes in degrees, and that there is a threshold below which we are no longer dealing with knowledge, but mere probable opinion.[12] This slightly more relaxed attitude toward the conditions necessary for knowledge is mirrored in a more relaxed attitude toward the significance of philosophy for scientific inquiry. Locke expresses his view in "The Epistle to the Reader" of his *Essay*:

11 John Locke, *An Essay concerning Human Understanding*, abridged and edited by A.D. Woozley (New York: Meridian, 1974), Book IV, Chapter II, §1.

12 Whether objective certainty is the sort of thing that can come in degrees is by no means clear, but it is better not to stray too far down that path here.

> [I]t is ambition enough to be employed as an under-labourer in clearing ground a little, and removing some of the rubbish that lies in the way to knowledge; which certainly had been very much more advanced in the world, if the endeavours of ingenious and industrious men had not been much cumbered with the learned but frivolous use of uncouth, affected, or unintelligible terms, introduced in the sciences, and there made an art of, to that degree that philosophy, which is nothing but the true knowledge of things, was thought unfit or incapable to be brought into well-bred company and polite conversation. (ECHU 58–59)

The "master-builders," according to Locke, were not what we would now regard as philosophers, but such natural scientists as Robert Boyle, Thomas Sydenham, Christian Huygens, and Isaac Newton. Helping along the efforts of "such masters" by searching out and exposing "Vague and insignificant forms of speech, and abuse of language" (ECHU 59) is the appropriate task of the philosopher.

This is a task that Locke applies himself to with considerable enthusiasm, attempting to clarify our thinking about innate ideas (Book I), about ideas in general (Book II), and about knowledge and opinion (Book IV), and it leads naturally to his preoccupation with philosophical questions about language in Book III of the *Essay*—"Of Words." Here Locke presents a version of what is often known as the "idea-theory" of meaning, according to which every meaningful word gets its meaning by standing for some associated idea in the mind of the speaker. When we acquire a language, Locke thinks, each of us forms a series of arbitrary associations between external signs and internal ideas, and communication occurs between you and me when the word with which I associate a particular idea excites in your mind a similar idea.

There are some difficult questions raised by such a view. If I cannot have direct access to the contents of your mind, how am I to know that any idea in your head is similar to any idea in mine? Indeed, how can I know that any idea in your head *can* be similar to any idea in mine? If there is no way in principle of making the comparison, we might wonder whether it is even meaningful to talk about "similarity" or "difference" here. (Compare this case with the case in which someone claims that Mendelssohn's violin concerto is green, or is three metres long, or smells like berries. Barring synaesthesia, such claims have to be regarded as metaphorical if they are to make any sense at all because no comparison can be made between the concerto and metre-stick or a colour sample, for example.) Such a comparison, it seems, is comprehensible only by imagining a kind of God's-eye-view that would enable us to look into each other's consciousnesses.

Assuming that this even makes sense, it seems that our practical lot falls far short. It seems entirely possible that we might never really be communicating at all on this view, because each of us might associate a different idea with a given word.

Of course, Locke might argue that if two people have enough in common, enough shared experience, then similarities that we try to capture with talk of human nature are enough to make communication possible, even if there are occasional breakdowns. But there is a further puzzle here concerning how my association of an idea with a sound-pattern can constitute my *understanding* of a word. How does the association license my applying the word in a new case? How can an idea serve as a general representation of a whole class of things, each of which may vary in some detail from all the others? This is a problem that I shall return to in Chapter 4, when I discuss Wittgenstein's attempt to dissolve the problem of what it is to understand and follow a rule.

Whatever the merits of Locke's theory of meaning, Locke thinks that it allows him to isolate for study the various kinds of "imperfection of words" (ECHU III, IX), as well as the abuses to which words are subject (ECHU III, X). This, in turn, allows him to formulate a set of rules that will remedy these imperfections and abuses (ECHU III, XI), thereby making it possible to avoid the "frivolous use of uncouth, affected, or unintelligible terms" (ECHU 58) that he complains about in his Epistle. As we shall see, the idea that philosophy should serve science by carefully clarifying its terms and concepts gets its most acute expression in the views defended by Bertrand Russell and members of the Vienna Circle of logical positivists, led by Moritz Schlick.

1.5 PHILOSOPHY AS LOGIC: RUSSELL

Russell's conception of philosophy is a direct descendant of Locke's treatment of philosophy as an under-labourer of the sciences, and like Locke, Russell has an account to offer of the sources of the confusion and misunderstanding that plague philosophy. Russell contends that philosophy has always arisen from two different motives: religious and ethical ones, on one hand, and scientific ones, on the other. The former sort of motive has been "a hindrance to the progress of philosophy" (OSMP 57),[13] much as it was, according to Russell, also a hindrance to the progress of science:

---

13 Bertrand Russell, "On Scientific Method in Philosophy" in *The Collected Papers of Bertrand Russell*, Vol. 8, edited by John G. Slater (London: George Allen and Unwin, 1983), 57–73.

> Human ethical notions ... are essentially anthropocentric, and involve, when used in metaphysics, an attempt, however veiled, to legislate for the universe on the basis of the present desires of men. In this way they interfere with that receptivity to fact which is the essence of the scientific attitude towards the world. (OSMP 63)

Like David Hume,[14] on most readings, Russell accepts a sharp divide between fact and value and seems to hold that interference from human values is an obstacle to apprehending the facts in their proper purity. "[A]ll ethics, however refined, remains more or less subjective" (OSMP 63) and so a hindrance to making contact with that which is objective. Ethics may well impart "some new way of feeling toward life and the world" (OSMP 64), which Russell claims to value as much as any of us, but it can tell us nothing about the "nature of the world" and remains entirely "with practice and not with theory" (OSMP 64).

We are left with the remaining scientific motive for philosophy, the motive of "understanding the world" (OSMP 64). But even this motive can lead philosophy astray if the relevance of science for philosophy is not correctly understood. "Much philosophy inspired by science has gone astray through preoccupation with the *results* momentarily supposed to have been achieved" (OSMP 57). Kant, for example, seemed prepared to argue that we could have *a priori* knowledge of synthetic truths concerning the Euclidean nature of space, and his inspiration seems to have been the remarkable achievements of Newtonian physics, which took Euclidean geometry for granted. It is not, however, the results of science that mark the significance of science for philosophical inquiry, but the methods of science, thinks Russell.[15] At first glance it may seem as though Russell is advocating something like the radical empiricism that Quine would later defend, according to which there is no principled barrier between science and philosophy. However, Russell has something different in mind. There are points of comparison and contrast between science and philosophy.

Let us begin with the comparisons. First, as we have already seen, philosophy should not allow human values to intervene in the course of its inquiry. Its concern is with objective fact (or more carefully, *possible* fact), not with subjective value.

---

14 Hume might plausibly be seen as another proponent of the under-labourer conception of the philosopher's task, though his scepticism might be taken to mitigate the applicability of that description.

15 Russell's commitment to this principle was not long-lasting enough to prevent him from going on seven years later to argue that psychological behaviourism had laid the path for a proper understanding of philosophical questions concerning the nature of mind. See his *Analysis of Mind* (London: Allen & Unwin, 1921).

Secondly, philosophy should not be systematic, but "piecemeal and tentative like other sciences" (OSMP 66):

> Most philosophies hitherto have been constructed all in one block, in such a way that, if they were not wholly correct, they were wholly incorrect, and could not be used as a basis for further investigations. It is chiefly owing to this fact that philosophy, unlike science, has hitherto been unprogressive, because each original philosopher has had to begin the work again from the beginning, without being able to accept anything definite from the work of his predecessors. (OSMP 66)[16]

Philosophy, like science in Russell's view, should be concerned with achieving better and better approximations to the truth—a view about science now known as convergent realism.

Thirdly, the tentative character desirable in philosophy suggests that it should not be preoccupied with establishing anything like certain results. The philosopher must borrow from the scientist the method of hypothesis. "A scientific philosophy ... will be able to invent hypotheses which, even if they are not wholly true, will yet remain fruitful after the necessary corrections have been made" (OSMP 66).

Nevertheless, Russell does think that one of the features of philosophy that distinguishes it from science is its concern with *a priori* propositions. However tentative the philosopher's results may be, the evidence for or against them is not to be gleaned from sense experience. "A philosophical proposition must be such as can neither be proved nor disproved by empirical evidence" (OSMP 65). Moreover, a further point of contrast, the propositions of philosophy must be completely general. They are not to "deal specially with things on the surface of the earth, or with the solar system, or with any other portion of space and time" (OSMP 64). Propositions of science, by contrast, even if they are general laws, deal specially with the properties and behaviour of kinds of things that actually exist. Because philosophical propositions are supposed to have this sort of generality, they are also, thinks Russell, propositions concerning what is *possible*, not just what is actual. The possible and the general, says Russell, "are indistinguishable" (OSMP 65).

The claim that philosophy is to deal with general propositions is not meant to suggest that philosophy takes the universe as a whole as its object of inquiry. That, Russell is eager to point out, was the mistake of absolute idealism, which held that

16 Russell's portrait of philosophy here seems to anticipate Kuhn's portrait of immature science. See Thomas Kuhn, *The Structure of Scientific Revolutions*, 2nd ed. (Chicago: University of Chicago Press, 1970).

everything was really a manifestation of the absolute and that it was the proper business of philosophy, not of science, to pronounce on the nature of the universe as a unified whole—a view that resonates with the conception of philosophy as a master discipline, considered above.

The consequence of these requirements, Russell thinks, is that philosophy "becomes indistinguishable from logic as that word has now come to be used" (OSMP 65), for logic, he holds, has two branches: the study of "general statements which can be made concerning everything without mentioning any one thing or predicate or relation" and "the analysis and enumeration of logical forms" (OSMP 65), which is to be carried out by the formulation of hypotheses that admit of no empirical confirmation or disconfirmation.

Such a view can allow us, for example, to see how Kant was led astray by his question "How is synthetic *a priori* knowledge of space possible?" A careful analysis of this question, Russell contends, reveals that it actually conflates three different problems, one of logic, one of physics, and one of epistemology. The problems of logic and physics become misleadingly intertwined, thinks Russell, because Kant fails to distinguish pure geometry from physical geometry. Pure geometry is concerned with the study of various idealized spaces defined by axiomatized assumptions about the ways in which points comprising such a space are related to each other. Euclidean space is just one kind of space, defined by one set of axioms, and other spaces with the "same logical coherence and the same title to respect as the more familiar Euclidean" (OSMP 67) space are possible by adjusting or replacing those Euclidean axioms. One may, for example, consider spaces which, unlike Euclidean space, are characterized by the fact that parallel lines may meet—as is the case in spherical geometry. Reasoning about such pure spaces, says Russell, is "purely deductive and purely logical" (OSMP 68).[17] Physical geometry, by contrast, is concerned with the very empirical task of saying which geometry comes closest to describing the actual space of the universe we inhabit. It is not given that it has to be Euclidean geometry, because there are many possible geometries, and whichever geometry fares the best in the face of the empirical evidence will still be an idealization. Geometrical points, for example, have no real existence in physical space.

The third problem—the epistemological one—says Russell, arises straight away from the confusion of the logical and physical problems. Pure geometry deals

17 Oddly, Russell seems to allow that there may be epistemological problems regarding "our knowledge concerning the axioms in some given space" (OSMP 68). This is odd, because it would seem that these axioms are to be stipulated, not discovered. Discoveries in geometry are always the result of reasoning from the stipulated axioms.

with *a priori* reasoning. Physical geometry deals with synthetic propositions about space—propositions not true simply in virtue of the meanings of their terms. If we fail to distinguish pure from physical geometry, then, like Kant, we shall be tempted to think that it must be possible to have *a priori* knowledge of synthetic propositions concerning space. But a philosophy that is concerned with the enumeration and analysis of logical forms, according to Russell, saves us from repeating this error.

Taking up a "scientific" method in philosophy has the effect of circumscribing philosophy's proper field of endeavour. Russell, in this respect, is like Kant, who wanted to discover the "bounds of sensibility" (B XXV) for pure reason and to delineate the proper sphere within which metaphysics might be pursued without resulting in paradox and contradiction:

> The adoption of scientific method in philosophy, if I am not mistaken, compels us to abandon the hope of solving many of the more ambitious and humanly interesting problems of traditional philosophy. Some of these it relegates, though with little expectation of a successful solution, to special sciences, others it shows to be such as our capacities are essentially incapable of solving. But there remain a large number of the recognized problems of philosophy in regard to which the method advocated gives all those advantages of division into distinct questions, of tentative, partial, and progressive advance, and of appeal to principles with which, independently of temperament, all competent students must agree. (OSMP 73)

1.6 PHILOSOPHY AS LOGIC: THE VIENNA CIRCLE

In the informal manifesto of the Vienna Circle, its authors celebrate the names of three "Leading representatives of the scientific world-conception":[18] Albert Einstein, Ludwig Wittgenstein, and Bertrand Russell. I shall have nothing to say about Einstein here, but Russell and Wittgenstein are obviously of central importance to my discussion.

The logical positivists agreed with Russell that philosophy is essentially logic, and that the task of philosophy is to clarify the terms and concepts of significance to science, but their conception of logic was profoundly different from Russell's.

---

18 Hans Hahn, Otto Neurath, and Rudolf Carnap, "The Scientific Conception of the World: The Vienna Circle," translated by P. Foulkes and M. Neurath, in *Otto Neurath: Empiricism and Sociology*, edited by M. Neurath and R.S. Cohen (Dordrecht: D. Reidel, 1973), 318.

This difference is readily attributable to the influence of Wittgenstein's *Tractatus Logico-philosophicus*.

Russell, recall, held that the propositions of logic were "those general statements which can be made concerning everything without mentioning any one thing or predicate or relation, such for example as 'if x is a member of the class α and every member of α is a member of β, then x is a member of the class β, whatever x, α, and β may be'" (OSMP 65). Or, to take a briefer example, "Something is related somehow to something."[19] By contrast, in the *Tractatus* Wittgenstein advanced the view that, far from being completely general propositions with content, the propositions of logic were one and all "tautologies":

6.1 The propositions of logic are tautologies.

6.11 The propositions of logic therefore say nothing. (They are the analytical propositions.)

6.111 Theories which make a proposition of logic appear substantial are always false.[20]

Tautologies or logical truths are quite literally empty ("senseless" Wittgenstein likes to say, but this does not mean *nonsensical*), and, accordingly, they are all logically equivalent. If they *seem* to say different things, then this is because the fact that a given tautology *is* a tautology is a different fact from the fact that some other tautology is a tautology. The fact, for example, that '$p \supset p$' is a tautology is not the same as the fact that '$p \vee {\sim}p$' is a tautology. One might allow that '$p \supset p$' is a tautology without allowing that '$p \vee {\sim}p$' is a tautology, as logical intuitionists do.[21] This advance over Russell was considered by members of the Vienna Circle to be a "decisive turning point" (TPP 54)[22] in philosophy. Rudolf Carnap described it as "the most important insight" of Wittgenstein's work that "the truth of logical statements is based only on their logical structure and on the meaning of the terms. Logical statements are true under all conceivable

19 P.M.S. Hacker, *Wittgenstein's Place in Twentieth Century Analytic Philosophy* (Oxford: Blackwell, 1996), 15.

20 Ludwig Wittgenstein, *Tractatus Logico-philosophicus*, translated by C.K. Ogden (London: Routledge & Kegan Paul, 1922), §§6.1–6.111.

21 See Ludwig Wittgenstein, *Wittgenstein's Lectures, Cambridge, 1932–1935*, edited by Alice Ambrose (Amherst, NY: Prometheus Books, 2001), 137–38.

22 Moritz Schlick, "The Turning Point in Philosophy," translated by David Rynin, in *Logical Positivism*, edited by A.J. Ayer (Glencoe, IL: The Free Press, 1959).

circumstances; thus their truth is independent of the contingent facts of the world. On the other hand, it follows that these statements do not say anything about the world and thus have no factual content."[23] And earlier, Moritz Schlick credited Wittgenstein with having been the first to understand "the nature of logic itself" (TPP 55), which was to be "purely *formal*" (TPP 54). That understanding alone, thought Schlick, was sufficient grounds for thinking that "an end has come to the fruitless conflict of systems" (TPP 54), against which Kant and Russell alike had railed. Schlick thought that all those problems traditionally categorized as the proper subject-matter of epistemology, for example, could now be seen really to be either a part of empirical psychology or a part of the logical task of clarifying our forms of expression.

This represents much the same division as Russell thought followed from taking a scientific approach in philosophy, and the logical positivists pushed Russell's exclusion of ethical and religious motives from philosophy even further. According to the Verification Theory of Meaning, which received numerous different formulations as the members of the Circle tried to modify it in response to internal and external criticism, a proposition qualified as meaningful if and only if it was (a) an analytic truth or falsehood or (b) a synthetic (i.e., non-analytic) proposition for which there might be some kind of confirming or disconfirming evidence to be gleaned from sense experience. The meaning of such a synthetic proposition, in turn, was said to be its method of confirmation and disconfirmation—the series of sense experiences that would provide evidence for thinking either that it was true or that it was false.

Propositions of ethics, such as 'Torture is wrong', and propositions of religion, such as 'God will reward the virtuous in the afterlife', did not satisfy this criterion, according to the positivists. No sense experience could possibly count for or against either claim, they maintained, and since neither claim is tautologous or contradictory, both must be meaningless. At best, they count as attempts to express one's attitude toward particular practices or toward life in general.

Metaphysics, too, fell into the well of meaninglessness, according to this view. Debates between realists and idealists, for example, turn on the impossibility of any sense experience's ever deciding for or against the claim that the world of objects and events exists independently of some mind or minds that experience it. Accordingly, the whole dispute is meaningless—a mere *pseudoproblem*. Carnap offered a trenchant assessment of metaphysics. Not only was metaphysics devoid

---

23 Rudolf Carnap, "Intellectual Autobiography" in *The Philosophy of Rudolf Carnap*, edited by P.A. Schilpp (LaSalle, IL: Open Court, 1963), 25.

of theoretical content, serving only "for the *expression of the general attitude of a person towards life*" (EM 78),[24] it was an inadequate means of such expression:

> Metaphysicians are musicians without musical ability. Instead they have a strong inclination to work within the medium of the theoretical, to connect concepts and thoughts. Now, instead of activating, on the one hand, this inclination in the domain of science, and satisfying, on the other hand, the need for expression in art, the metaphysician confuses the two and produces a structure which achieves nothing for knowledge and something inadequate for the expression of attitude. (EM 80)

We may hear echoes of both Kant and Russell here, but for Carnap, metaphysical questions do not merely need careful circumscription, as they did for Kant, and they are not merely questions that "our capacities are essentially incapable of solving" (OSMP 73), to use Russell's words. As Schlick puts it, "metaphysics collapses not because the solving of its tasks is an enterprise to which the human reason is unequal (as for example Kant thought) but because there is no such task" (TPP 57). And the collapse of metaphysics does not leave philosophy with a body of *a priori* propositions, as Russell seemed to think—a corollary of his conviction that logic deals with the most general of statements that can be made about everything without mentioning anything in particular. The only propositions knowable *a priori*, according to the logical positivists, are analytic propositions—those true simply in virtue of their meanings and independently of their content. But philosophy, according to Schlick, is not the sum of all these propositions: "The great contemporary turning point is characterized by the fact that we see in philosophy not a system of cognitions, but a system of *acts*; philosophy is that activity through which the meaning of statements is revealed or determined" (TPP 56).[25] "Philosophy," Wittgenstein had remarked in the *Tractatus*, "is not a theory but an activity" (TLP §4.112).

---

24 Rudolf Carnap, "The Elimination of Metaphysics Through Logical Analysis of Language," translated by Arthur Pap, *Logical Positivism*, edited by A.J. Ayer (Glencoe, IL: The Free Press, 1959), 60–81; originally published as "*Überwindung der Metaphysik durch Logische Analyse der Sprache*," *Erkenntnis* 2 (1932).

25 Schlick seems to think that this activity is enough to call philosophy the Queen of the Sciences once again, but he thinks that this does not entail that philosophy is itself a science.

1.7 QUINE'S NATURALISM

The Verification Theory of Meaning on which logical positivism rests holds, remember, that the only meaningful statements fall into the category of being (a) analytic truths or falsehoods or (b) synthetic (i.e., non-analytic) propositions for which there might be some kind of confirming or disconfirming empirical evidence—which, in turn is supposed to give us the meaning of a synthetic statement. Take the first category first. Analytic truths divide into two kinds (as do analytic falsehoods): tautologies or logical truths, and statements that can be transformed into tautologies by substituting appropriate synonyms. Thus

(1) All vixens are vixens

is said to be a tautology, because its truth does not depend on the meanings of any of the non-logical terms that it contains.

(2) All vixens are female foxes

is not a tautology. One must understand more than just the logical terms it contains in order to understand the statement as a whole. However, what is supposed to make such a statement analytic, nonetheless, is the fact that 'vixen' and 'female fox' are synonymous with each other. Thus, one can substitute 'vixen' for 'female fox' in (2), and the result is (1)—a tautology. To vary the point slightly, (1) and (2) are synonymous statements, and every non-tautologous analytic statement is synonymous with some tautology. Similar considerations apply to an analytic falsehood, such as

(3) No vixen is a female fox,

which is synonymous with the contradiction

(4) No vixen is a vixen,

into which it can be transformed by substituting for 'female fox' its synonym 'vixen'.

By contrast, synthetic propositions, such as

(5) Vixens have litters of three or four

are not tautologies, and they cannot be turned into tautologies by substituting synonyms. The meaning of 'have litters of three or four' is quite different from the meaning of 'vixen'. That is why (5) can be informative to someone who discovers it to be true (if it is true). At most, (2) informs someone only of the meaning of the word 'vixen', not of any empirical fact about vixens.

So goes the standard story about the analytic-synthetic distinction. It is a story that Quine will have no truck with, and his critique of the distinction is closely linked with his view that philosophy is neither the Queen of the Sciences nor an under-labourer for them, but continuous with natural science.

In the first four sections of his influential essay "Two Dogmas of Empiricism," Quine offers numerous technical criticisms of the analytic-synthetic distinction, particularly as it is developed and employed by Carnap. How successful these criticisms are is controversial, but they are less important for my purposes here than the criticisms that appear in sections 5 and 6, which are aimed directly at the Verification Theory of Meaning. So I shall focus on these later criticisms.

It is best, I think, to read Quine as advancing two distinct criticisms of the attempt to bolster the analytic-synthetic distinction by reference to the Verification Theory of Meaning. However, both of the criticisms are inspired by Quine's holistic attitude toward empirical confirmation and disconfirmation.

The first of these holistic criticisms is roughly as follows. The Verification Theory of Meaning tells us that the meaning of a synthetic statement is its method of verification. The meaning of an analytic statement can be seen as a limiting case of the meaning of a synthetic statement, insofar as a tautology is a statement that is confirmed by every experience—nothing counts as evidence against it. Non-tautologous analytic statements, in turn, are synonymous with particular tautologies, as we have seen, which is to say that they have the same methods of confirmation and disconfirmation. This view presupposes, however, that it makes sense to pair up individual statements uniquely with individual methods of confirmation and disconfirmation, and it is precisely this presumption that Quine casts doubt on. "My countersuggestion," he writes, "is that our statements about the external world face the tribunal of sense experience not individually but only as a corporate body" (TDE 41).[26] It is easy to see why this must be so. Individual scientific hypotheses are never advanced in complete isolation, but always in the context of a broader theory about some part of the natural world, and it is only against the background of this broader theoretical context that any hypothesis can be meaningfully tested. Consider, for example, the hypothesis that if the sun is powered by nuclear fusion

26 W.V. Quine, "Two Dogmas of Empiricism" in *From a Logical Point of View*, 2nd ed. (Cambridge, MA: Harvard University Press, 1980), 20–46.

reactions, then level *L* of neutrinos should be observable passing through a given region of space near to the surface of the Earth. When this hypothesis was first tested in the late 1960s, the observed neutrino-flux was substantially lower than stellar evolution theory predicted.[27] If hypotheses are tested in isolation, then the following argument should have persuaded physicists to give up the hypothesis that the sun is powered by nuclear fusion:

> (T1) If the sun is powered by nuclear fusion, then level *L* of neutrinos will be observed passing through region *R* of space near to the surface of the Earth.
>
> (O1) Level *L* of neutrinos is not observed passing through region *R*.
>
> (C1) Therefore, the sun is not powered by nuclear fusion.

However, no such conclusion was seriously entertained. Instead, physicists went in search of auxiliary assumptions whose falsehood would explain the recalcitrant observations. A great many proposals were made. Here are just a few:

> (T2) If the sun is powered by nuclear fusion, and if the experimenter is competent, and if the neutrino detector is properly calibrated, and if the value of *L* has been properly calculated, and if the sun was not contaminated by heavy metals early in its development, and if cooler material at the surface of the sun does not mix with hotter material in the interior, and if neutrinos do not "oscillate" among their three states, etc., then level *L* of neutrinos will be observed passing through region *R* of space near to the surface of the Earth.
>
> (O1) Level *L* of neutrinos is not observed passing through region *R*.
>
> (C2) Therefore, the sun is not powered by nuclear fusion, or the experimenter is incompetent, or the neutrino detector is improperly calibrated, or....

27 For a thorough account of this experiment and the ensuing controversy see Harry Collins and Trevor Pinch, *The Golem: What Everyone Should Know about Science* (Cambridge: Cambridge University Press, 1993), 121–39. As a result of work at the Sudbury Neutrino Observatory, it is now thought that solar neutrinos oscillate among several different states, not all of which were detectable in the original experiment.

All that the unexpected observation demonstrated was that at least one of the hypotheses—the target hypothesis or one of the many background hypotheses—was mistaken. It did not settle which one, and it certainly did not show that stellar evolution theory was egregiously mistaken about the sun's being powered by nuclear fusion. The theory as a whole had to confront the evidence, and there was no tidy one-to-one pairing of hypotheses with methods of confirmation and disconfirmation. This, however, is the normal course of events in the testing of scientific hypotheses, and so there is no reason to think that the Verification Theory of Meaning is right. Indeed, it seems clearly mistaken. But if the Verification Theory of Meaning is mistaken, then it offers no ground for making sense of the analytic-synthetic distinction by telling us that synonymous statements share methods of confirmation and disconfirmation.

The preceding criticism targets the viability of saying that a non-tautologous analytic statement is synonymous with some tautology, but it poses no threat to the notion of a tautology. Quine's second holistic criticism is more controversial and more far-reaching. Even if we can identify tautologies on grounds that they are true in virtue of their logical form, they fail to have the status of being knowable *a priori*, if Quine is right. For a claim to be knowable *a priori*, it must be the case that no experience could count as a reason for giving up that claim. The *a priori* for Quine, and for many philosophers since, is just that which is rationally unrevisable in the face of experience. But, according to Quine, no belief or claim is rationally unrevisable in the face of all possible experience:

> The totality of our so-called knowledge or beliefs, from the most casual matters of geography and history to the profoundest laws of atomic physics or even of pure mathematics and logic, is a man-made fabric which impinges on experience only along the edges. Or, to change the figure, total science is like a field of force whose boundary conditions are experience. A conflict with experience at the periphery occasions readjustments in the interior of the field. (TDE 42)

This much gets us the result, already encountered, that "No particular experiences are linked with any particular statements in the interior of the field, except indirectly through considerations of equilibrium affecting the field as a whole" (TDE 43). But Quine thinks that an even more dramatic consequence follows:

> Any statement may be held true come what may, if we make drastic enough adjustments elsewhere in the system. Even a statement very close to the periphery may be held true in the face of recalcitrant experience

> by pleading hallucination or by amending certain statements of the kind called logical laws. Conversely, by the same token, no statement is immune to revision. (TDE 43)

So the most casual and tentative of observation claims, if one is prepared to make the appropriate redistribution of assigned truth-values, has as much title to unrevisability as a tautology, and a tautology is as vulnerable to revision of its assigned truth-value as any tentative empirical claim. Quine's view is antithetical to the whole idea of *a priori* knowledge.

Quine takes this result to show that there is no interesting boundary to be drawn between philosophy and the natural sciences:

> [M]y position is a naturalistic one; I see philosophy not as an *a priori* propadeutic or groundwork for science, but as continuous with science. I see philosophy and science as in the same boat—a boat which, to revert to Neurath's figure as I so often do, we can rebuild only at sea while staying afloat in it. There is no external vantage point, no first philosophy. All scientific findings, all scientific conjectures that are at present plausible, are therefore in my view as welcome for use in philosophy as elsewhere. (OR 126–27)[28]

Such a view is clearly at odds with the treatment of philosophy as a master discipline, but where does it stand relative to the view that philosophy should be an under-labourer for science? Russell, who regards philosophy as concerned with the clarification of logical forms and with completely general propositions that can be known *a priori* would not be able to accept Quine's view. Indeed, he would regard it as a view that mistakes the relevance of science for philosophy by focusing on scientific results instead of on scientific methods.

> In utilizing these results as the basis of a philosophy, we sacrifice the most valuable and remarkable characteristics of scientific method, namely, that, although almost everything in science is found sooner or later to require some correction, yet this correction is almost always such as to leave untouched, or only slightly modified, the greater part of the results which have been deduced from the premiss subsequently discovered to be faulty. The prudent man of science acquires a certain instinct as to the kind of uses which may be made of present scientific beliefs without incurring the

28 W.V. Quine, *Ontological Relativity and Other Essays* (New York: Columbia University Press, 1969).

> danger of complete and utter refutation from the modifications likely to be introduced by subsequent discoveries. Unfortunately, the use of scientific generalizations of a sweeping kind as the basis of philosophy is just that kind of use which an instinct of scientific caution would avoid, since, as a rule, it would only lead to true results if the generalizations upon which it is based stood in *no* need of correction. (OSMP 60)

But Quine would respond that Russell's complaint is premised on the assumption that philosophy is concerned fundamentally with unrevisable results—that philosophy traffics in *a priori* propositions—precisely the feature of traditional philosophy that Quine purports to be rejecting. Scientific results are a problem in philosophy, on his view, only if they are arbitrarily insulated from recalcitrant experience, but to do that is to treat them as *a priori* propositions.

What of logical positivism? Because Quine articulates his view as part of a critique of the logical positivists, it seems obvious that his conception of philosophy must be incompatible with theirs. However, although Schlick, for example, endorses the analytic-synthetic distinction and allows the possibility of *a priori* knowledge of analytic propositions, he does not think of philosophy as a body of *a priori* knowledge, as we saw earlier:

> Every science, (in so far as we take this word to refer to the content and not to the human arrangements for arriving at it) is a system of cognitions, that is, of true experiential statements. And the totality of sciences, including the statements of daily life, is the system of cognitions. There is, in addition to it, no domain of "philosophical" truths. Philosophy is not a system of statements; it is not a science. (TPP 56)

The claim that there is no domain of "philosophical" truths strikes a chord with Quine's rejection of the possibility of any "first philosophy" whose job it is to lay the foundations for the sciences. Yet Schlick explicitly distances philosophy from science. Perhaps this is because he categorizes science as a system of statements, instead of attending to the activities that scientists engage in, which might well include, at times, attempting to clarify their own concepts and assertions. If so, then a tentative rapprochement of Schlick's and Quine's positions might suggest itself. However, when Schlick goes on to characterize philosophy as an activity, he does so in terms that Quine would be wary to accept:

> But what is [philosophy] then? Well, certainly not a science, but nevertheless something so significant and important that it may henceforth, as

> before, be honored as the Queen of the Sciences. For it is nowhere written that the Queen of the Sciences must itself be a science. The great contemporary turning point is characterized by the fact that we see in philosophy not a system of cognitions, but a system of *acts*; philosophy is that activity through which the meaning of statements is revealed or determined. By means of philosophy statements are explained, by means of science they are verified. The latter is concerned with the truth of statements, the former with what they actually mean. (TPP 56)

The under-labourer seems to have ambitious designs in this passage, though perhaps we should not be too distracted by Schlick's rhetoric.

We should, however, be distracted by Schlick's stark contrast between the tasks of verifying statements and determining what they mean, for this is a contrast that Quine would be no more willing to acknowledge than the analytic-synthetic distinction or the possibility of *a priori* knowledge. The holistic arguments of "Two Dogmas" suggest that in order to determine the meaning of a statement one must invariably rely on a background of empirical beliefs. Changes of meaning cannot be sharply distinguished from changes of background beliefs, and no statement's meaning can be held fixed in the face of changing empirical beliefs. This is because Quine retains a kind of Verification Theory of Meaning:[29] the meaning of a statement *is* its method of verification, but because there is no exclusive one-to-one mapping of statements onto methods of verification, we must view such methods as making a potential contribution to the meanings of all our statements. Thus the decision to give up an assumption when faced with recalcitrant evidence is as easily seen as a decision about how to distribute the fund of empirical meaning among the statements of one's theory, and a new decision to give up a different assumption would as easily count as a redistribution of meanings. So in Quine's opinion there is no way of saying what a statement means apart from making revisable assumptions about which statements have been well confirmed and which ones have not. The tasks of philosophy and science cannot be so neatly hived off from each other as Schlick suggests, if Quine is right.

---

29 "The Vienna Circle espoused a verification theory of meaning but did not take it seriously enough. If we recognize with Peirce that the meaning of a sentence turns purely on what would count as evidence for its truth, and if we recognize with Duhem that theoretical sentences have their evidence not as single sentences but only as larger blocks of theory, then the indeterminacy of translation of theoretical sentences is the natural conclusion.... Should the unwelcomeness of the conclusion persuade us to abandon the verification theory of meaning? Certainly not" (OR 80–81).

2

PHILOSOPHY AND SCIENCE IN THE *TRACTATUS*

I intend to argue that however exactly we should interpret Wittgenstein's attitude toward philosophy in his early work, we should not understand it as falling into any of the categories that I outlined in the preceding chapter. This suggestion conforms with what most major interpreters of Wittgenstein's work contend, but it stands in opposition to a reading of the *Tractatus* that has nonetheless been widely influential. According to that reading, the *Tractatus* is best thought of as supporting the logical positivists' version of philosophy as an under-labourer to the sciences, setting philosophy the task of clarifying the concepts of science by providing a proper logical analysis of them that will "make propositions clear" (TLP §4.112).[1] We saw in Chapter 1 that Schlick's conception of philosophy as "a system of *acts*... through which the meaning of statements is revealed or determined" (TPP 56)[2] was inspired by Wittgenstein's view in the *Tractatus* that "Philosophy is not a theory but an activity" of "logical clarification" (TLP §4.112). In spite of this clear line of influence, I think that Wittgenstein's early conception of philosophy—like his later conception, to which I shall turn in later chapters—is profoundly at odds with the under-labourer conception of philosophy that I have attributed to Russell

1 Ludwig Wittgenstein, *Tractatus Logico-philosophicus*, translated by C.K. Ogden (London: Routledge & Kegan Paul, 1922), §4.112.

2 Moritz Schlick, "The Turning Point in Philosophy," translated by David Rynin, in *Logical Positivism*, edited by A.J. Ayer (Glencoe, IL: The Free Press, 1959), 56.

and the Vienna Circle alike. The interpretation that assimilates Wittgenstein's views to those of Schlick and his colleagues ignores the most puzzling and perplexing passages of the *Tractatus*, which seem clearly to be incompatible with the "scientific world-conception" advocated by the Vienna Circle.[3] It dismisses as an eccentric aberration the serious paradox that Wittgenstein presents at the end of the *Tractatus*, when he tells us that his own propositions are "nonsense" (TLP §6.54). Like it or not, this paradox must be confronted head-on.

However, determining just what to say about these puzzling and perplexing passages is not easy. In the past two decades an influential line of interpretation has emerged, according to which the *Tractatus* presents a view of philosophy that is in no significant way different from the view of philosophy that is presented in Wittgenstein's post-Tractarian writings. This line of interpretation has the virtue of discouraging the temptation to see Wittgenstein's early work and later work as separated by a huge gulf. However, against it, I contend that there remains an important difference between Wittgenstein's early work and his transitional and later work regarding how we ought to think about normativity. According to the reading that I shall present in this chapter and the next, this difference has important consequences for his conception of the nature of philosophical problems and the task of philosophy.

In order to make sense of any of these lines of interpretation, we first need to examine briefly some of the salient details of the *Tractatus*.

2.1 THE *TRACTATUS*

It is customary to distinguish Wittgenstein's early work (primarily the *Tractatus Logico-philosophicus* and the *Notebooks* that he kept in preparation for the *Tractatus*) from his later work (especially the *Blue and Brown Books*, *Philosophical Investigations*, and *On Certainty*), although there are also works that are clearly transitional (*Philosophical Remarks*, *Philosophical Grammar*) and works that amalgamate writings from over a long and variable course of time (*Remarks on the Foundations of Mathematics*). Furthermore, as I have noted, it is a disputed question how much continuity there is to be found between Wittgenstein's early views and his later views.

---

3 Hans Hahn, Otto Neurath, and Rudolf Carnap, "The Scientific Conception of the World: The Vienna Circle," translated by P. Foulkes and M. Neurath, in *Otto Neurath: Empiricism and Sociology*, edited by M. Neurath and R.S. Cohen (Dordrecht: D. Reidel, 1973), 318.

The *Tractatus* was the fruit of philosophical thinking that Wittgenstein, the youngest son of one of the wealthiest families in Europe, had begun on his own while working as a research student in aeronautics at the University of Manchester from 1908 to 1911. A deepening interest in pure mathematics led him to read Russell and Frege and eventually to travel to Cambridge, where he sought Russell's evaluation of his potential as a philosopher. After some initial doubts provoked by Wittgenstein's intense personality (he would follow Russell back to his rooms and argue with him late into the night), Russell decided that Wittgenstein was well-suited to carrying on where Russell's work in logic had left off. After studying with Russell and spending some time writing in isolation in Norway, Wittgenstein enlisted in the Austro-Hungarian army at the start of the Great War, taking his ideas about logic into the trenches and emerging with a profoundly altered view of the world and a masterwork of twentieth-century philosophy.[4]

The *Tractatus* is a startling book, both because of the spareness and elegance of its form, and because of its extraordinary difficulty. Some, indeed, have thought it too difficult. J. Alberto Coffa, for example, remarks that no one can be reasonably criticized for *mis*understanding the *Tractatus* because "no one can seriously claim to understand clearly what the *Tractatus* says about anything."[5] I think this assessment is needlessly pessimistic (though it does make for a good joke). There are many obscure passages in the *Tractatus*, but it is not completely opaque.

On the face of it, the *Tractatus* is a book about language, logic, metaphysics, and the relation between mind and world. It comments in passing on, among other things, free will, solipsism, scepticism, realism, idealism, induction, probability—as well, of course, as the relation of science to philosophy. (But, as we shall see, its apparently straightforward treatment of these traditional topics is given a jarring twist in the final pages of the book.) Ostensibly, it is a presentation of seven numbered propositions, six of which Wittgenstein thinks require extensive elaboration by means of a complicated system of decimal-numbered propositions. Here are those central six.

> 1. The world is everything that is the case.
>
> 2. What is the case, the fact, is the existence of atomic facts.

4 For more see Ray Monk's splendid biography, *Ludwig Wittgenstein: The Duty of Genius* (London: Jonathan Cape, 1990).

5 J. Alberto Coffa, *The Semantic Tradition from Kant to Carnap: To the Vienna Station*, edited by Linda Wessels (Cambridge: Cambridge University Press, 1991), 405 n.4.

3. The logical picture of the facts is the thought.

4. The thought is the significant proposition.[6]

5. Propositions are truth-functions of elementary propositions. (An elementary proposition is a truth-function of itself.)

6. The general form of truth-function is: $[\bar{p},\bar{\xi},N(\bar{\xi})]$

This is the general form of proposition.

These six propositions present us with a variety of *logical atomism*, and they purport to tell a purely *extensional* story about how it is that propositions and thoughts manage to say things about the world—*viz.*, by sharing their logical form with the facts that comprise the world. I shall consider logical atomism and extensionality in §2.3, but let us begin with facts, propositions, and the world.

2.2 FACTS AND PROPOSITIONS

The world, Wittgenstein seems to reason, is not merely the collection of objects that it includes, since those objects might be arranged in many different ways relative to each other, and they might possess properties other than the ones that they do. So the world must be a particular distribution of properties and relations over the objects. That distribution is the totality of "facts" (*Tatsachen*) or *actual* (as opposed to merely possible) "states of affairs" (*Sachlagen*) (TLP §2.014). To imagine the world being different from the way it is is to imagine other possible states of affairs obtaining.

By a fact, however, Wittgenstein does not have in mind primarily the facts that a scientific researcher tries to gather, or the facts that an investigating police officer asks for and which are later disputed in court. Those are all complex combinations of the "atomic facts" (*Sachverhalten*) (TLP §2), which are the most basic metaphysical constituents of the world, and each atomic fact consists in a "configuration of objects" (§2.0272).[7] As one might expect of such a view, the objects configured

6 'Proposition' is Ogden's translation of the German '*Satz*', which can be translated either as 'proposition' or as 'sentence'. I do not think that the distinction is of critical importance here, but we will need to tread cautiously when we consider Wittgenstein's later work.

7 I follow C.K. Ogden's translation. David Pears and Brian McGuinness translate '*Sachlagen*' as 'situations' and '*Sachverhalten*' as 'states of affairs'. See Ludwig Wittgenstein, *Tractatus*

are not the macroscopic—or even microscopic—things that we observe around us, for those things are complex, made up of parts, whereas objects are "simple" (§2.02)—"they cannot be compound" (§2.021). Objects are the "substance of the world" (§2.021), its "fixed form" (§2.023), and they exist "independently of what is the case" (§2.024), for what is the case is the existence of atomic facts, particular *configurations* of objects.[8] Wittgenstein is not saying here that objects can exist *unconfigured*. However the world might have been, objects would have been configured in one way or another. But however they are in fact configured, there are objects, and they could have been configured differently. That's the sense in which their existence is independent of their particular configuration.

The simplicity of objects does not entail that they lack properties. Objects can be of the same or different logical forms (§2.0233)—much as two colours are of the same logical form as each other, but differ in their logical form from geometric shapes—and they have both "external" and "internal qualities" (§2.01231). Their internal qualities dictate what possible states of affairs they may occur in, "so we cannot think of *any* object apart from the possibility of its connexion with other things" (§2.0121). By contrast, the atomic facts have a radical independence from each other (TLP §2.061)—that is part of what makes them atomic: "From the existence or non-existence of an atomic fact we cannot infer the existence or non-existence of another" (§2.062).

The propositions of ordinary language, like the everyday facts we are accustomed to speaking of, are really complex structures, too. And just as complex everyday facts are composed of atomic facts in which objects are configured in one particular way rather than any other possible way, so complex linguistic structures are composed of atomic or "elementary" (TLP §4.21) propositions in which the names of simple objects are configured (§4.22). An atomic proposition thereby provides us with a "logical picture" (§4.03) of a fact. Such propositions express thoughts (§3.1), which are likewise logical pictures of facts (§3), and "the elements of the picture" correspond to the objects that compose the fact that it

Logico-philosophicus, translated by David Pears and Brian McGuinness (London: Routledge and Kegan Paul, 1975). I agree with John O. Nelson ("Is the Pears-McGuinness Translation of the *Tractatus* Really Superior to Ogden's and Ramsey's?" *Philosophical Investigations* 22, no.2 [1999]: 165–75) that the Ogden translation is better insofar as Ogden's 'atomic facts' fulfills directly the need for a term that "satisfies the demand that the method of analysis, as construed in the *Tractatus* imposes, that complexes be resolved into simples" (174). 'States of affairs' clearly does *not* satisfy this demand and is at odds, as Nelson observes, with the dictionary translation of '*Sachlagen*' as 'states of affairs' (173). This is not to say that Ogden's translation is flawless, as we shall see below in §2.5.

8 So what exactly *is* an object? It's hard to say, much as it is difficult for Aristotle to tell us what the substrate underlying all things is.

represents (§2.13). So the objects that compose a fact and the elements that compose a thought (which is a logical picture) also correspond to the names in the elementary proposition that expresses that thought. The meaning of a name in an elementary proposition is the object that it corresponds to. "The name means the object. The object is its meaning" (§3.203).

2.3 ANALYSIS AND EXTENSIONALITY

Atomic propositions are obtained by analyzing the logical form of everyday propositions, according to the model suggested by Russell's Theory of Descriptions. "Russell's merit is to have shown that the apparent logical form of the proposition need not be its real form" (TLP §4.0031). Russell was preoccupied with several questions, inherited from Gottlob Frege, for any theory of meaning that tries to hold that the meaning of a name or description is its bearer. Consider the most easily presented of these questions. If one endorses such a view, as Wittgenstein does in the *Tractatus*, then how can one explain how it is possible for there to be meaningful sentences which contain names and descriptions that do not refer to anything? If the meaning of a name or description is its bearer, then names or descriptions that lack bearers are meaningless, as is any sentence in which such a bearerless name or description occurs.[9]

Russell's way with this problem involved two steps.[10] First, he contended that words which we ordinarily regard as proper names, such as 'Walter Scott', are really disguised definite descriptions—definite, because they purport to pick out exactly one individual; disguised, because they look like simple symbols, even though they really are not. A simple symbol is one that has no meaningful parts, but 'Walter

9 The other questions are, very roughly, "How can identity statements, such as '*Il Divino* is Francesco Canova da Milano' be informative, if the two names are used refer to the same person or thing and thus have the same meaning?" and "How is it possible to believe contradictory things about the same person or object picked out by two different names, if those names have the same meaning because they have the same bearer?" How, for example, can I believe that *Il Divino* was a sixteenth-century Italian lutenist, while also believing that Francesco Canova da Milano was not a sixteenth-century Italian lutenist if the meaning of '*Il Divino*' is the same as the meaning of 'Francesco Canova da Milano'? See Gottlob Frege, "On Sense and Reference" in *Logicism and the Philosophy of Language: Selections from Frege and Russell*, edited by Arthur Sullivan (Peterborough, ON: Broadview Press, 2003), 175–92. For an excellent discussion of Frege and Russell on these points see Alexander Miller, *Philosophy of Language* (Montreal and Kingston: McGill-Queen's University Press, 1998), Chapter 2.

10 See Bertrand Russell, "On Denoting" in Sullivan (2003), 235–47 and "Descriptions" in Sullivan (2003), 279–87.

Scott', Russell argued, really does have meaningful parts (and not just 'Walter' and 'Scott'), because it is really a kind of short-hand for a claim involving a definite description. For example,

(6) There is exactly one person who wrote *Waverly*, and...

is a good Russellian candidate for the meaning of 'Walter Scott', so when one claims that

(7) Walter Scott was Scottish,

one is really claiming that

(8) There is exactly one person who wrote *Waverly*, and that person is Scottish.

So the use of a grammatically proper name always involves an existential claim of some sort.

Secondly, when one uses a proper name that purports to pick out some person, place or thing that does not exist, one is making a *false* existential claim. Thus, if I say that

(9) Santa Claus has eight reindeer,

then what I am really saying is something like

(10) There is exactly one person who is fat, jolly, bearded, lives at the North Pole and brings children gifts at Christmas, and that person has eight reindeer.

What looked like a *meaningless* sentence (9) because it contains a bearerless name, is really a meaningful but *false* sentence (10).

Wittgenstein (and Russell, too) envisioned analysis going somewhat further than it does in the examples above (which themselves contain disguised descriptions, such as '*Waverly*', in Russell's view). Ultimately, a properly analyzed sentence should contain nothing but a "concatenation" (TLP §4.22) of names—that is, genuine or "logically proper" names, not disguised descriptions like 'Russell' and 'Walter Scott'. And, according to Wittgenstein, it should contain no logical quantifiers either.

The key to understanding this latter claim lies in recognizing that ordinary existence claims are to be analyzed as claims about the configuration of simple objects. To say that Santa Claus exists, or that there is beer in the fridge, or that there are weapons of mass destruction in Iraq is to say that the simple objects stand in certain relations with each other and possess certain properties. Similarly, to deny that something exists is to deny that the simple objects are configured in a particular way. So existential quantifiers will disappear from completely analyzed sentences. For related reasons, universal quantifiers will also disappear. Saying of all things, *x*, that they possess some property, *P*, or (*x*)*Px*, is equivalent to saying that nothing, *x*, fails to have the property, *P*, or ~(∃*x*)~*Px*. But claims involving existential quantifiers are to be further analyzed into claims about configurations of simple objects, as we saw above. So even a general assertion like "All dogs are mammals" is to be analyzed as a claim about the relations between and the properties possessed by the simple objects.

If a fully analyzed sentence contains nothing but names, and if the meaning of a name is its bearer, then one cannot meaningfully assert or deny the existence of such a bearer. If I try to say, "*n* exists," where '*n*' is the name of an object, then "*n* exists" is meaningful only if true, so there is no point in saying it. And I cannot even *say* "*n* does not exist," unless this claim is false. Such an analysis will involve no ambiguity, and, moreover, "There is one and only one complete analysis of the proposition" (§3.25). Once we have reached the level of genuine names and their concatenations, which picture possible states of affairs that may or may not obtain, we have reached bottom—the logical atoms from which all meaningful expressions are constructed (hence the term "logical atomism").

The way in which meaningful expressions are constructed from logical atoms is also notable. What Wittgenstein envisions is essentially what textbooks in introductory symbolic logic now teach concerning atomic sentences and their recursive combination by means of truth-functional connectives. Thus if '*P*' is an atomic sentence, then '~*P*' is also a sentence. If '*Q*' is another atomic sentence, then '*P* & *Q*' is a sentence, as are '*P* v *Q*', '~*P* ⊃ *Q*', '(*P* v *Q*) & ~(*P* & *Q*)', and so on. Every meaningful sentence, according to the author of the *Tractatus*, is constructible from such truth-functional combinations of atomic sentences:

> Propositions are truth-functions of elementary propositions.
> (An elementary proposition is a truth-function of itself.) (TLP §5)

Indeed, Wittgenstein is eager to point out that all of these truth-functions can be derived from one basic truth-function:

> The general form of truth-function is: $[\bar{p}, \bar{\xi}, N(\bar{\xi})]$
> This is the general form of proposition. (TLP §6)

"This says," he clarifies, "nothing else than that every proposition is the result of successive applications of the operation *N*'(ξ) to the elementary propositions" (TLP §6.001). The operation that Wittgenstein seems to have in mind is a generalization of an operation discussed by the logician Henry Sheffer, symbolized as '|', which can be read "neither ... nor...."[11] Using this basic logical connective all the other standard connectives—negation (~), conjunction (&), disjunction (v), material implication (⊃)—can be derived. For example, the negation of '*p*', '~*p*', is logically equivalent to '*p* | *p*', and the conjunction of '*p*' and '*q*', '*p* & *q*', can be represented as '(*p* | *p*)|(*q* | *q*)'. And to say that "An elementary proposition is a truth-function of itself" (TLP §5) is in this context to say that '*p*' is logically equivalent to '(*p* | *p*)|(*p* | *p*)'.[12]

If, as TLP §5 claims, all propositions were truth-functions of elementary propositions, then we would be able to substitute for any constituent of a molecular proposition another constituent proposition with the same truth-value, without thereby altering the truth-value of the molecular proposition. Call this the *extensionality thesis*. Thus

> (11) *Il Divino* was an Italian lutenist

can be substituted for

> (12) Francesco Canova da Milano was an Italian lutenist

without affecting the truth-value of

> (13) Francesco Canova da Milano was an Italian lutenist, and he died in 1543.

11 See Henry Sheffer, "A Set of Five Independent Postulates for Boolean Algebras, with Applications to Logical Constants," *Transactions of the American Mathematical Society* 14 (1913), 481–88. Confusingly, many contemporary logicians now use 'p | q' (which they call the "Sheffer stroke") to symbolize "not both p and q," even though this is not how Sheffer himself used it.

12 For a more detailed explanation see Russell's "Introduction" to the *Tractatus* (TLP 13–16).

because (11) and (12) are logically equivalent (*Il Divino was* Francesco Canova da Milano).

However, on the face of it, there are obvious counterexamples to the claim that every meaningful proposition is a truth-function of elementary propositions, since natural languages are full of *non*-truth-functional (or "non-extensional" or "intensional" or "opaque") contexts. Statements about possibility and necessity, statements about beliefs and desires,[13] indirect quotations, and a host of other cases are all, it seems, non-truth-functional.

For example, (11) cannot be automatically substituted for (12) in

> (14) Ludwig believes that Francesco Canova da Milano was an Italian lutenist, and he died in 1543,

because Ludwig may well be ignorant of the identity-statement

> (15) *Il Divino* is Francesco Canova da Milano.[14]

Wittgenstein was well aware of this challenge to his fifth major thesis:

> At first sight it appears as if there were also a different way in which one proposition could occur in another.
>
> Especially in certain propositional forms of psychology, like "A thinks that *p* is the case", or "A thinks *p*", etc.
>
> Here it appears superficially as if the proposition *p* stood to the object A in a kind of relation. (TLP §5.541)

Closer inspection, however, reveals something else:

> But it is clear that "A believes that *p*", "A thinks *p*", "A says *p*", are of the form "'*p*' says *p*": and here we have no co-ordination of a fact and an object, but a co-ordination of facts by means of a co-ordination of their objects. (TLP §5.542)

13 This was another of the Fregean problems that Russell wanted to solve by appeal to his theory of descriptions, but it is not clear that he succeeds.

14 The informativeness of such statements is the third of the Fregean problems that Russell tries to solve by appeal to his theory of descriptions. Again, it is not clear that he succeeds.

'Clear' is not the first word that springs to mind when one considers this proposal,[15] but we might make some headway by considering an example or two. Suppose I am trying to prepare a complicated dessert but find my efforts frustrated. You happen along and helpfully pick up the recipe book. "This says," you offer, "that you should add *lemon* filling, not *melon*." Here you simply read the cookbook and report on what it says on the basis of the words you observe on its pages. We have then a coordination of two facts, the fact that a certain practice is generally observed in the making of certain pies and the fact that the words lie in a certain order on the page. "The propositional sign is a fact" (TLP §3.14). We might similarly imagine observing another person and reporting on what she believes on the basis of words that she utters and signs that she displays or inscribes. Of course, human beings are more complicated than cookbooks, so at times a certain amount of interpretation or translation may have to go on. So when I meet the unfortunately named person, A, and discover that she speaks another language than my own, you, my translator, may inform me that A says that it is snowing or that I am a hideous orangutan (for example). You, as it were, read another person's beliefs in her linguistic behaviour.[16]

This view preserves the extensionality thesis by denying the intuitive premise used above that if *P* and *Q* are descriptions of the same state of affairs, then from the fact that someone believes that *P*, we cannot validly infer that she believes that *Q*. If a person's beliefs are read from her behaviour in the way that instructions are read from a recipe book, then the behaviour that displays the belief that *Il Divino* was an Italian lutenist likewise displays the belief that Francesco Canova da Milano was an Italian lutenist, and *vice versa*. Of course, a person may well manifest other behaviour that displays the belief that *Il Divino* was *not* an Italian lutenist. For example, she may say, "*Il Divino* was *not* an Italian lutenist." But that just goes to show that human psychology is complex and that holding beliefs that contradict each other is something that we are all quite capable of. Or so it might be argued.[17]

15 Then again, Wittgenstein does remark in the Preface that "This book will perhaps only be understood by those who have themselves already thought the thoughts which are expressed in it—or similar thoughts" (TLP 27).

16 For a more sophisticated but related attempt to preserve extensionality see Donald Davidson, "On Saying That" in *Inquiries into Truth and Interpretation* (Oxford: Clarendon Press, 1984), 93–108.

17 For a defence of a similar thesis see Robert M. Martin, *The Meaning of Language* (Cambridge, MA: MIT Press, 1987), Chapters 16, 17.

2.4 LOGICAL PICTURES

We encountered earlier the claim that a proposition is a "logical picture" (TLP §4.03) of a fact, and we have likewise seen that the third major thesis of the *Tractatus* is that "The logical picture of the facts is the thought" (TLP §3). It is important to understand in what way these claims are similar to but different from the claims of defenders of the correspondence-theory of truth because the difference represents Wittgenstein's early attempt to account for the possibility of intentional content.

Proponents of a correspondence-theory of truth hold, unsurprisingly, that a true belief or claim is made true by its correspondence to some relevant portion of the world. In its classical version the correspondence-theory involves a commitment to the view that the world is made up of facts—as Wittgenstein holds in the *Tractatus*—though not necessarily atomic facts, and it is in virtue of corresponding or failing to correspond to some fact or another that a belief or statement gets to be true or false.[18] More recent defences of truth as correspondence have typically avoided commitment to any ontology of articulated metaphysical entities called "facts" and urged instead that we analyze correspondence in terms of relations of reference between words or mental symbols on the one hand and objects and their properties and relations on the other.[19] Often that reference relation is thought to be understandable as some kind of causal or lawlike dependence that obtains between the objects referred to and our thoughts or the use of our words. In its most sophisticated versions, this lawlike relation is thought to be a teleological one—my belief that I am in danger is a belief about my being in danger because it is its proper biological function to make me respond to danger.[20] My early ancestors who lacked such an internal representational state were usually eaten by tigers or swept haplessly into the sea.

Wittgenstein's "picture-theory" of the proposition may look like a variation on the classical correspondence-theory, simply adding a commitment to logical atomism. He does say, after all, that "In order to discover whether the picture is true or false we must compare it with reality" (TLP §2.223). But the view presented in the *Tractatus* differs strikingly from both classical and contemporary

18 Russell seems to have held such a view in "On the Nature of Truth and Falsehood" [1910] in *Philosophical Essays*, rev. ed. (London: George Allen & Unwin, 1966), 147–59, though his position is further complicated by his multiple-relations theory of judgment. See section 2.9 below.

19 See, e.g., Michael Devitt, *Realism and Truth*, 2nd ed. (Princeton: Princeton University Press, 1997), 27–29.

20 See, e.g., Ruth Millikan, *Language, Thought, and Other Biological Categories* (Cambridge, MA: MIT Press, 1984).

correspondence-theories in its insistence that the relation between a true belief or proposition and the facts that make it true is an intrinsic or *internal* relation, rather than an extrinsic or *external* one:[21]

> The gramophone record, the musical thought, the score, the waves of sound, all stand to one another in that pictorial internal relation, which holds between language and the world.
>
> To all of them the logical structure is common.
>
> (Like the two youths, their two horses and their lilies in the story. They are all in a certain sense one.) (TLP §4.014)

For Wittgenstein claims about internal relations seem to be conceptual claims, though these are not sharply delineated from epistemic claims: two relata are internally related if being acquainted with one suffices to identify the other. For example, he justifies his contention that "The proposition is a picture of reality" (TLP §4.021) by saying, "for I know the state of affairs presented by it, if I understand the proposition" (TLP §4.021). Moreover, an internal relation obtains between two *relata* if they possess certain internal properties, and a thing possesses an internal property if it is "unthinkable" that it should not:

> A property is internal if it is unthinkable that its object does not possess it.
>
> (This blue colour and that stand in the internal relation of brighter and darker eo ipso. It is unthinkable that *these* two objects should not stand in this relation.) (TLP §4.123)

It is, thus, in virtue of being internally related to each other—in virtue of sharing a logical form—that my belief that it is snowing or my linguistic claim to the same effect gets to be *about* the fact that it is snowing. It is a logical picture of the fact because it has the same logical form as the fact, though that logical form may well have to be revealed by analysis.[22]

The contrast I am pointing to is most easily brought out by considering the contemporary view that correspondence is to be understood in terms of reference and that reference is, in turn, to be understood in terms of causal relations between words or mental states and their referents. Causal relations are a paradigm

21 There are exceptions, of course. See, for example, David Armstrong, *A World of States of Affairs* (Cambridge: Cambridge University Press, 1997).

22 I discuss the later development of Wittgenstein's conception of an internal relation in "Internal Relations and Analyticity: Wittgenstein and Quine," *Canadian Journal of Philosophy* 26, no.4 (1996): 591–612.

of *external* relations—relations whose relata can be picked out independently of each other. That is why Hume is so eager to tell us that we cannot determine the cause of an event or state of affairs simply by examining the event or state of affairs itself in isolation. "Adam, though his rational faculties be supposed, at the very first, entirely perfect, could not have inferred from the fluidity and transparency of water that it would suffocate him, or from the light and warmth of fire that it would consume him."[23] And so, for causal theorists of reference it is a sceptical possibility that I should be able to identify and use the words of a language while being utterly mistaken about what things in the world those words pick out. For Wittgenstein, by contrast, sceptical worries in general make no sense. "Scepticism is not irrefutable, but palpably senseless, if it would doubt where a question cannot be asked" (TLP §6.51).[24]

2.5 SILENCE

I said that there were seven major propositions that make up the skeletal structure of the *Tractatus*. But, unlike the first six, the seventh gets no elaboration:

> 7. Whereof one cannot speak, thereof one must be silent.

Each of the first six propositions carries sufficient complication to be controversial, but it is proposition 7 that is the really perplexing one—the one that prompts Coffa's joke about no one's really understanding the *Tractatus*. It seems tautologous—or at least convertible into a tautology by the substitution of appropriate synonyms and, hence, analytic. So what is it doing there? Why not "A rose is a rose" instead?

For an answer one naturally turns to the preceding text, where one finds a number of remarks that do not, at first, look like comments on proposition 6:

> My propositions are elucidatory in this way: he who understands me finally recognizes them as senseless, when he has climbed out through them, on them, over them. (He must so to speak throw away the ladder, after he has climbed up on it.)

23 David Hume, *An Enquiry Concerning Human Understanding*, edited by Eric Steinberg (Indianapolis: Hackett Publishing, 1977), Section IV, Part I.

24 Ogden here translates '*unsinnig*' as 'senseless', but 'nonsense' would be more accurate. A similar problem afflicts his translation of TLP §6.54, as we shall see below.

> He must surmount these propositions; then he sees the world rightly. (TLP §6.54)

'Senseless' is the word that C.K. Ogden generally uses to translate '*sinnlos*', which is the word that Wittgenstein uses to describe tautologies and contradictions (TLP §4.461). Such propositions are literally without sense because they are not representations or models of the world, but they still have truth-values. Propositions of logic—tautologies—are the "scaffolding" (§3.42) that makes any representation of the world possible, as we shall see in section 2.6. However, in this instance (and at §6.51, which we encountered above) Ogden uses 'senseless' as the translation for '*unsinnig*', which elsewhere in the *Tractatus* is translated as 'nonsensical'.[25] Is Ogden right here? Are Wittgenstein's propositions merely senseless and not nonsense? If they are merely senseless, then, like tautologies and contradictions, they still have truth-values, but if they are *nonsense*, then they have no truth-values at all. They are not even genuine propositions, but mere "pseudo-propositions" (§§4.1272, 5.535). It is worth observing that Ogden's translation was seen and "carefully revised by the author himself" (TLP 5), as Ogden informs us in a Note at the front of the book. Whatever may have motivated Wittgenstein to write '*unsinnig*', he seems not to have objected to Ogden's milder translation of the term. So maybe we should not either.[26]

Against this argument, however, stands the fact that TLP §7 contrasts with the other propositions of the *Tractatus* in this regard. The book is littered with propositions that are not tautologies (or contradictions), and it seems implausible to suppose that Wittgenstein takes himself to be uttering a long string of tautologies (or contradictions). It is both more consistent with the rest of the text and with the evident fact that most of Wittgenstein's propositions are not tautologies or contradictions to translate '*unsinnig*' as 'nonsensical'. But, if anything, this makes §6.54 even more perplexing, for here we seem to be told that the bulk of what Wittgenstein asserts in the *Tractatus* is, taken literally, nonsense, and this suggests, in keeping with TLP §7, that there is really nothing to be said about the ostensible topics of Wittgenstein's book. Is Wittgenstein's view self-defeating? And what could be the point of writing a book of nonsense? What, moreover, does §6.54 have to do with §6, which tells us what the general form of the truth function is?

25 There are other exceptions. See TLP §4.1272.

26 Then again, Elizabeth Anscombe says that Wittgenstein saw only selected portions of the translation that Ogden consulted him about, not the entire text. See G.E.M. Anscombe *An Introduction to Wittgenstein's Tractatus*, 3rd ed. (London: Hutchison & Co., 1967), 17 n1.

§6.54 is not the only passage that ostensibly concerns proposition 6 but seems to have nothing obvious to do with it. Perhaps we can get a better sense of why such passages occur by examining those with a single digit after the decimal:

6.1 The propositions of logic are tautologies.

6.2 Mathematics is a logical method.
The propositions of mathematics are equations, and therefore pseudo-propositions.

6.3 Logical research means the investigation of *all regularity*. And outside logic all is accident.

6.4 All propositions are of equal value.

6.5 For an answer which cannot be expressed the question too cannot be expressed.
The riddle does not exist.
If a question can be put at all, then it *can* also be answered.

Remark 6.1 expresses, as we saw in Chapter 1, what the logical positivists regarded as Wittgenstein's most important contribution to philosophy, and he elaborates on it by—among other things—challenging Russell's conception of logic as concerned with generality (see, e.g., TLP §§6.1224–6.124). Remark 6.2 gestures at the relationship between logic and mathematics and obliges Wittgenstein to say more. Remark 6.3 comments on the relation between logical necessity and possibility, on the one hand, and the idea of other forms of necessity and possibility (such as causal or natural necessity and possibility), on the other, and so commits Wittgenstein to saying something about causality, scientific laws, and induction. (In particular, he thinks that "There is only *logical* necessity" (TLP §6.37).)

None of this seems out of place. *Most* of the observations that do seem out of place and are ostensibly elucidations of proposition 6 are ones that pertain to remarks 6.4 and 6.5. So perhaps we should take seriously the thought that these odd-sounding remarks belong just where Wittgenstein put them. What remarks do I have in mind? Consider the following elucidations of remark 6.4:

> The sense of the world must lie outside the world. In the world everything is as it is and happens as it does happen. *In* it there is no value—and if there were, it would be of no value.

> If there is value which is of value, it must lie outside all happening and being-so. For all happening and being-so is accidental.
> What makes it non-accidental cannot lie *in* the world, for otherwise this would again be accidental.
> It must lie outside the world.
> Hence also there can be no ethical propositions.
> Propositions cannot express anything higher.
> It is clear that ethics cannot be expressed.
> Ethics is transcendental.
> (Ethics and aesthetics are one.) (TLP §§6.41–6.421)

From here Wittgenstein goes on to add remarks about the will, death, immortality, and God (the metaphysical matters that Kant thought were of concern to everyone, even if we could have no knowledge of them, properly speaking).

Russell and the logical positivists thought that such remarks were best ignored if the fruits of the *Tractatus* were to be harvested and not left to rot where they grew. "What causes hesitation is the fact that, after all, Mr Wittgenstein manages to say a good deal about what cannot be said..." wrote Russell in his Introduction to the *Tractatus*.[27] Their view of the problem still has many adherents, but if we are to understand what Wittgenstein was up to, then I do not think we can just treat these remarks or the paradox suggested by §6.54 as a weed that has inadvertently sprung up in the garden. I shall not attempt to comment on all these remarks, but let me offer a suggestion concerning the occurrence of such topics at this point in the *Tractatus*.

2.6 THE TRANSCENDENTAL

The claim of TLP §6.4 that "All propositions are of equal value" is reminiscent of an earlier remark elucidating the claim of §6.1 that "The propositions of logic are tautologies." At §6.127 Wittgenstein writes, "All propositions of logic are of equal rank; there are not some which are essentially primitive and others deduced from these. Every tautology itself shows that it is a tautology." This is another remark directed at Russell, who held that certain propositions of logic—the axioms—are more fundamental than other propositions of logic and serve as justifying foundations for those others. If the propositions of logic are, one and all, tautologies, then it is not clear what it would be for some of them to be more fundamental than the

27 Bertrand Russell, "Introduction," TLP 23.

others, though some might be more readily recognizable as tautologies. Logical propositions say nothing, and one instance of saying nothing cannot serve as a justification for another instance of saying nothing. One does not prove logical propositions by deriving them from others that are intrinsically more basic: "Proof in logic is only a mechanical expedient to facilitate the recognition of tautology, where it is complicated" (TLP §6.1262). One will be inclined to think otherwise, only if one supposes with Russell that logic concerns the most general things we can say about the world without mentioning anything in particular. However, according to Wittgenstein, "Logic is not a theory but a reflexion of the world. Logic is transcendental" (§6.13). Transcendental! Logic is thus like ethics and aesthetics (§6.421). But what do logic, ethics, and aesthetics have in common?

The philosophical use of the term 'transcendental' is tightly linked to the name 'Immanuel Kant'. When Kant describes something as "transcendental," he typically is describing a concept or a piece of knowledge that employs such a concept. And the distinctive feature of transcendental concepts is that they are *a priori* necessary conditions of the possibility of some other knowledge (B 40).[28] Thus an *a priori* grasp of the category of causality, according to Kant, is a necessary precondition of the possibility of having any experience of unified, enduring objects in space and time (B 232–56). So when Wittgenstein tells us that logic is transcendental, it is reasonable to suppose that he means by this that we have an *a priori* grasp of logic and that such a grasp is a necessary precondition for the possibility of some other knowledge that we have. What knowledge might that be? I suggest that what logic makes possible is nothing short of meaningfulness itself. Without logic we can have no grasp of meanings and can produce no meaningful signs.

Inconveniently for this suggestion, Wittgenstein does not come right out and say so in the *Tractatus*. But he does give some rather broad hints to the same effect. "Logic *precedes* every experience—that something is *so*" (TLP §5.552), he tells us. Without it we could have no determinate grasp of the facts—no chance of distinguishing how things are from how they might have been. And it provides this grasp by providing a "scaffolding" on which a determinate set of facts can be "built":

> 3.4 The proposition determines a place in logical space: the existence of this logical place is guaranteed by the existence of the constituent parts alone, by the existence of the significant proposition.

28 Immanuel Kant, *Critique of Pure Reason*, translated by Norman Kemp Smith (New York: St. Martin's Press, 1965).

3.42 Although a proposition may only determine one place in logical space, the whole logical space must already be given by it.

(Otherwise denial, the logical sum, the logical product, etc., would always introduce new elements—in co-ordination.)

(The logical scaffolding round the picture determines the logical space. The proposition reaches through the whole logical space.)

4.023 ...The proposition constructs a world with the help of a logical scaffolding, and therefore one can actually see in the proposition all the logical features possessed by reality *if* it is true. One can *draw conclusions* from a false proposition.

It is only insofar as a proposition stands in logical relations to other propositions—in "logical space"—that it gets to count as a proposition at all, as something meaningful at all. If I claim that a given object is spherical, for example, my claim is meaningful only insofar as it can be a conclusion drawn from some other claims (for example, that the space the object occupies is bounded by a surface all of whose points are equidistant from its centre) or conclusions can be drawn from it (for example, that the object is not a cube or a tetrahedron or that its circumference is given by the arithmetical product of its diameter and π). Strip away all such entailments, and we are left with nothing meaningful at all, a *mere* noise or mark.

This leaves another question. What is the relation between logic's being transcendental, and hence a necessary precondition of sense, and the claim of §6.41 that "The sense of the world must lie outside the world"? I think that this remark shows that logic is not merely transcendental, but also *transcendent*, occupying a realm of absolute necessity, and ethics also occupy that realm. (As we shall see in Chapter 3, this is a controversial claim.)

But not just logic, ethics, and aesthetics are said to lie outside the world in the *Tractatus*:

> The subject does not belong to the world but it is a limit of the world.
>
> *Where in* the world is a metaphysical subject to be noted?
>
> You say that this case is altogether like that of the eye and the field of sight. But you do *not* really see the eye.
>
> And from nothing *in the field of sight* can it be concluded that it is seen from an eye. (TLP §§5.632–5.633)

"The thinking, presenting subject" (TLP §5.631) does not exist in the world but "is a limit of the world." The subject, it is tempting to say, is itself a transcendental precondition of the possibility of a unified world of experience, a point that Wittgenstein gestures at when he briefly discusses solipsism:

> 5.62 ... In fact what solipsism *means*, is quite correct, only it cannot be *said*, but it shows itself.
>
> That the world is *my* world, shows itself in the fact that the limits of the language (*the* language which I understand) mean the limits of *my* world.
>
> 5.63 I am my world.
>
> 5.64 Here we see that solipsism strictly carried out coincides with pure realism. The I in solipsism shrinks to an extensionless point and there remains the reality co-ordinated with it.

Because my mind does not lie within the world, it cannot be the *only* mind in the world, as the solipsist maintains.[29] But can we conclude that, as a limit of the world, the subject lies *outside* the world? If so, the subject would be something like what Kant calls a "noumenon" (B 569), in contrast to a phenomenon. It would be a non-empirical self, the seat of the will (which is also something of which "we cannot speak" (TLP §6.423)), and the ground of the contingent appearances that make up the empirical subject.[30]

So there is something very Kantian about Wittgenstein's first book. Kant wanted to describe the limits of what we might *know*; Wittgenstein purports to describe the limits of what we can *say* or *think*:

> Philosophy limits the disputable sphere of natural science.
>
> It should limit the thinkable and thereby the unthinkable.
>
> It should limit the unthinkable from within through the thinkable.

---

29 Thanks to Kyle Fraser for suggesting this way of putting the point.

30 Peter Hacker has argued that Wittgenstein's view is heavily influenced by Schopenhauer's, which in turn, is heavily influenced by Kant's. See P.M.S. Hacker, *Insight and Illusion* (Oxford: Clarendon Press, 1972), 62–67. See also Allan Janik and Stephen Toulmin, *Wittgenstein's Vienna* (New York: Simon and Schuster, 1973), Chs. 4–6. The suggestion was earlier made by Anscombe (1967), 11–12.

> It will mean the unspeakable by clearly displaying the speakable.
>
> Everything that can be thought at all can be thought clearly. Everything that can be said can be said clearly. (TLP §§4.113–4.116)

And the transcendental role of logic is central to this enterprise:

> We cannot think anything unlogical, for otherwise we should have to think unlogically.
>
> It used to be said that God could create everything, except what was contrary to the laws of logic. The truth is, we could not *say* of an "unlogical" world how it would look. (TLP §§3.03–3.031)

We wandered down this path because we stumbled on the seemingly oddly-placed assertion that "there can be no ethical propositions" (TLP §6.42). Let us retrace our steps and consider why Wittgenstein takes ethics to be like logic. On the face of it, the claim that "there can be no ethical propositions" (TLP §6.42) bears a resemblance to the claim of the Vienna Circle that ostensible judgments about moral rightness and wrongness lack methods of confirmation or disconfirmation and are, accordingly, meaningless. But the assertion that "Ethics is transcendental" suggests that, like logic, ethics is a necessary condition of the possibility of something in the world.

The connection, I think, is that both logic and ethics are *normative*. This is obvious in the case of ethics, which provides standards by which we judge actions and the agents who perform them as right or wrong, good or bad, virtuous or vicious. It is also true of logic, however. This is not just because logic provides us with standards of good reasoning, but because logic, as the transcendental ground of meaning, provides us with norms without which meaning would be impossible. To grasp a meaning or a concept is to understand what follows from that meaning or concept. As we saw earlier, a proposition must stand in logical relations to other propositions in logical space if it is to be meaningful (that is, if it is even to be a proposition). So from a given proposition it is *correct* (or permissible) to draw certain inferences and incorrect (forbidden) to draw certain others. And from the propositions 'P' and '$P \supset Q$' it is not only correct (permitted) to infer 'Q'; it is logically required or necessary.

Like logic, ethics is characterized by imputations of necessity and possibility. Some actions are required (morally necessary); others are forbidden (morally impossible); still others are permitted (morally possible). But the only kind of necessity, says Wittgenstein, is "*logical* necessity" (§6.37), the sort of necessity that characterizes tautologies, and tautologies say nothing. Should we conclude, then, that ethical propositions are tautologies, that we can say nothing ethical because our attempts to do so result in our uttering nothing but trivial truths?

Although tempting, this would be the wrong conclusion to draw if we take our analogy between logic and ethics seriously. Notice that the normativity of logic is not something that is explicit in logical propositions. Logical propositions are senseless. They are tautologies, and tautologies say nothing. In particular, they do not *tell* us what counts as a valid inference. The normativity of logic is something that we try to express by saying of a particular logical proposition *that it is a tautology*. To say, for example, that '$[P \& (P \supset Q)] \supset Q$' is a tautology is to affirm a rule. It is to say that if something is to count as an intelligible proposition it *must not* contradict '$[P \& (P \supset Q)] \supset Q$'. So it might be better to say, not that *logic* is normative, but that certain propositions *about* logic are normative and that these propositions are analogous to ethical propositions.

What of the other side of the analogy? If logic lies outside the world as the transcendental ground of meaning, what lies outside the world as the transcendental ground of moral value? The answer that Wittgenstein gives in his "Lecture on Ethics" from 1929 is the "absolute good" or "absolute value" (LE 40)[31] (but, I think, we could as easily and accurately say God), and the absolute good must lie outside the world because that is the only way of accounting for the absolute necessity of moral imperatives. "*The* absolutely right road," he tells us , would have to be "the road which *everybody* on seeing it would, *with logical necessity*, have to go, or be ashamed for not going" (LE 40). The logical necessity here applies to the relation between moral conviction and moral motivation. Like Plato, Wittgenstein believes that one cannot apprehend the good without feeling some motivation to pursue it. Other, conflicting motivations might lead one to act for something other than the good, but one's motivation to pursue the good would be manifest in the shame that one would feel at having chosen another course of action. However, Wittgenstein thinks that no merely contingent state of affairs could motivate in this way. Nothing in the world could exercise "the coercive power of an absolute judge" (LE 40). The "absolute good" or "absolute value," therefore, "must lie outside the world" (TLP §6.41). Whatever is transcendental for Wittgenstein is also *transcendent*, lying beyond the contingency of the world in a realm of necessity. What makes an action "non-accidental" or necessary, in the sense of being morally

31 Ludwig Wittgenstein, "Lecture on Ethics" in *Philosophical Occasions: 1912–1951*, edited by James Klagge and Alfred Nordmann (Indianapolis: Hackett Publishing, 1993), 37–44.

required, "cannot lie *in* the world, for otherwise this would again be accidental" (§6.41).[32]

The claim that "there can be no ethical propositions" (TLP §6.42), then, suggests something stronger than that would-be ethical propositions are mere tautologies. In the "Lecture on Ethics" he is quite explicit about it: ethical propositions are "mere nonsense" (LE 43). They are what in the *Tractatus* he calls "pseudo-propositions" (TLP §§4.1272, 5.535, 6.2). And this nonsensicality is not the result of poor formulation that could be repaired by deeper thinking or further experience: "their nonsensicality [is] their very essence" (LE 43), because they try to "*go beyond* the world and that is to say beyond significant language" (LE 43). But if there can be no propositions about ethics for this reason, then it seems that *there can be no propositions about logic either*, because such propositions would also have to go beyond the world. But that is precisely what the *Tractatus* seems to be full of—attempts to describe things that lie beyond the world—and that is why, as Wittgenstein tells us at §6.54, these propositions are nonsense.

2.7 SAYING AND SHOWING

We still have not dealt with the paradox of the *Tractatus*—that someone who understands Wittgenstein recognizes his book to be laden with nonsense. It is beginning to be clear why he says this, but it is still unclear why anyone would write such a book or what it is supposed to reveal about the nature of philosophy. Before we can begin to solve these puzzles we need to assemble some additional pieces.

A couple of the passages we have encountered hint at a distinction between what can be *said* and what can merely be *shown*.

5.62 ... In fact what solipsism *means*, is quite correct, only it cannot be *said*, but it shows itself.

6.127 ... Every tautology itself shows that it is a tautology.

Here are some others:

4.12 Propositions can represent the whole reality, but they cannot represent what they must have in common with reality in order to be able to represent it—the logical form.

32 Accordingly, Wittgenstein rejects all consequentialist theories of moral value. See TLP §6.422.

To be able to represent the logical form, we should have to be able to put ourselves with the propositions outside logic, that is outside the world.

4.121 Propositions cannot represent the logical form: this mirrors itself in the propositions.

That which mirrors itself in language, language cannot represent.

That which expresses *itself* in language, *we* cannot express by language.

The propositions *show* the logical form of reality.

They exhibit it.

4.1212 What *can* be shown *cannot* be said.

Tautologies, remember, say nothing. So if I try to say what the logical form of a given proposition is, then I succeed in saying nothing. For example, suppose that I say that the logical form of

(16) There are no weapons of mass destruction in Iraq

is

(16) There are no weapons of mass destruction in Iraq.

I have succeeded, it seems, in conveying no information whatsoever.

Now it may seem that I could avoid this result by being a little more sophisticated about logical form. After all, Wittgenstein holds that "the apparent logical form of the proposition need not be its real form" (§4.0031). I might say, for example, that the logical form of (16) is really

(17) $\sim(\exists x)(Wx \,\&\, Ix)$,

where 'Wx' symbolizes 'x is a weapon of mass destruction', 'Ix' symbolizes 'x is in Iraq', and '$(\exists x)$' is the existential quantifier (bearing in mind that the complete analysis of this proposition, according to Wittgenstein, is not supposed to contain any quantifiers—see §2.3 above). On the face of it, this seems informative, and it may be useful for certain purposes to break down complex propositions into their truth-functional components in a way that displays how the truth-value of the complex depends on the truth-values of its component parts, but it merely postpones the problem, for (17) is itself a sentence with a logical form, which it shares with whatever fact makes it true. And it seems as though I must already in some sense grasp that logical form before I can understand the assertion that (17) gives the logical form of (16). But if I am told that the logical form of '~(∃*x*)(*Wx* & *Ix*)' is no other than '~(∃*x*)(*Wx* & *Ix*)', it seems that I have again been told nothing.

> The identity of the meaning of two expressions cannot be *asserted.* For in order to be able to assert anything about their meaning, I must know their meaning, and if I know their meaning, I know whether they mean the same or something different. (TLP §6.2322)

More generally, every time I try to determine the logical form of a given proposition, I am referred either to some other proposition—some analysis of the original proposition—whose logical form I cannot informatively express, or to the original proposition itself, which is similarly uninformative.

Nonetheless, the logical form of a proposition, Wittgenstein thinks, is shown by analysis, and it is by grasping a proposition's logical form that I understand it. I can, for example, recognize a tautology *as* a tautology and a contradiction as a contradiction. And when I understand a proposition, I understand what facts would have to obtain in order for it to be true (TLP §4.024). "The proposition *shows* how things stand, *if* it is true. And it *says*, that they do so stand" (§4.022). Logical form is both indispensable for meaning and ineffable. For as we have seen, "Logic is not a theory but a reflexion of the world. Logic is transcendental" (§6.13).

In fact there seem to be two kinds of showing at work in the *Tractatus.*[33] Most of the examples we have just considered are cases in which one thing shows another: "Every tautology itself shows that it is a tautology"; "The propositions *show* the logical form of reality"; logical analysis shows the logical form of the proposition analyzed. However, we have also seen that "In fact what solipsism *means* is quite correct, only it cannot be *said*, but it shows itself" (§5.62). The meaning of solipsism is not shown by anything *else*; it shows *itself.* The same is true of "the inexpressible" or "the mystical": "This *shows* itself" (§6.522).

One might wonder whether there is a deep difference between what is shown by analysis and what shows itself. For my purposes it is important that these two kinds of showing be intimately linked. The connection, I think, is to be found in the fact that those things which show themselves are, like logic (TLP §6.13), transcendental (and transcendent). We have already seen that ethics and aesthetics are inexpressible (§6.421), and this seems to be explained by the fact that they are transcendental. It does not seem a great stretch to say the same of the truth

33 See David G. Stern, *Wittgenstein on Mind and Language* (Oxford: Oxford University Press, 1995), 69–72.

of solipsism: that "The subject does not belong to the world but it is a limit of the world" (§5.632). This "cannot be *said* but it shows itself" (§5.62). Similarly, if "Of the will as the subject of the ethical we cannot speak" (§6.423), then this is because the will as ethical subject is, like ethics, transcendental and can only show itself as a limit of the world, not something *in* the world: "If good or bad willing changes the world, it can only change the limits of the world, not the facts ..." (§6.43).

The inexpressibility of ethics (or of the "mystical") is not a sign that it is unimportant. Indeed, there is reason for thinking that Wittgenstein regarded the ethical to be of supreme importance. In a frequently quoted letter of 1919 to the German publisher, Ludwig Ficker, whom he was trying to interest in the *Tractatus* he wrote,

> [T]he point of the book is ethical. I once wanted to give a few words in the foreword which now actually are not in it, which, however, I'll write to you now because they might be a key for you: I wanted to write that my work consists of two parts: of the one which is here, and of everything which I have *not* written. And precisely this second part is the important one. For the Ethical is delimited from within, as it were, by my book; and I am convinced that, *strictly* speaking, it can ONLY be delimited in this way.[34]

As Allan Janik and Stephen Toulmin have argued, by classifying the ethical as something transcendental, transcendent, and inexpressible, Wittgenstein seems to be trying to *elevate* it—to protect it from a kind of profanation and reduction to nonsense that he thinks would result from trying to put the ethical into words—treating it as though it lacked necessity.[35] "Ethics," Wittgenstein wrote in 1929, "so far as it springs from the desire to say something about the ultimate meaning of life, the absolute good, the absolute valuable, can be no science" (LE 44). That is at least partly why Wittgenstein must write a book of nonsense.

2.8 PHILOSOPHY AS AN ACTIVITY

This long excursion into the labyrinth of the *Tractatus* began as an attempt to appreciate how Wittgenstein's attitude toward philosophy and its relation to natural science differs in his early work from those of his contemporaries, Russell and the Vienna Circle. We may now be in a position to follow our ball of string back to an understanding of these differences.

---

34 Quoted in Ray Monk, *Ludwig Wittgenstein: The Duty of Genius* (London: Jonathan Cape, 1990), 178.

35 Janik and Toulmin (1973), 167–201. See, especially, 198.

In Chapter 1 we saw that Schlick was inspired by the *Tractatus* to hold that "philosophy is that activity through which the meaning of statements is revealed and determined" (TPP 56). Let me quote at length one of the passages from the *Tractatus* that motivated Schlick's position:

> The totality of true propositions is the total natural science (or the totality of the natural sciences).
>
> Philosophy is not one of the natural sciences.
>
> (The word "philosophy" must mean something which stands above or below, but not beside the natural sciences.)
>
> The object of philosophy is the logical clarification of thoughts.
>
> Philosophy is not a theory but an activity.
>
> A philosophical work consists essentially of elucidations.
>
> The result of philosophy is not a number of "philosophical propositions", but to make propositions clear.
>
> Philosophy should make clear and delimit sharply the thoughts which otherwise are, as it were, opaque and blurred. (TLP §§4.11–4.112)

But, although this is a clear source of Schlick's position in "The Turning Point..." (see also TLP §6.53), it would be a mistake to suppose that Wittgenstein's views in the *Tractatus* were of a piece with logical positivism. For one thing, nowhere in the *Tractatus* does Wittgenstein present or endorse a version of the Verification Theory of Meaning, though members of the Vienna Circle later thought they could read such a theory back into that work, and Wittgenstein was peculiarly reluctant to discourage them for a period of several years. (Indeed, for a period of about a year beginning in 1929, Wittgenstein seems actively to have endorsed his own version of the verification theory, though he abandoned it quickly, when he realized that it was in tension with other features of his rapidly changing views.[36])

More seriously, as we have seen, at the heart of Wittgenstein's early work is a paradox about the inexpressible, the mystical, the ground of absolute value, and the logical positivists thought that they could extirpate this strange growth without doing any damage to the roots of Wittgenstein's philosophy. One of the failings of this interpretation of the *Tractatus* is that it overlooks just how significantly Wittgenstein's conception of "elucidation" differs from that of the Vienna Circle. Now that we have encountered the distinction between saying and showing, we

36 See my "Going around the Vienna Circle: Wittgenstein and Verification," *Philosophical Investigations* 28, no.3 (2005): 205–34 and Chapter 3, §3.3 below.

can cast some light on Wittgenstein's paradoxical remark at §6.54, which we began worrying about several sections ago:

> My propositions are elucidatory in this way: he who understands me finally recognizes them as [nonsense], when he has climbed out through them, on them, over them. (He must so to speak throw away the ladder, after he has climbed up on it.)
>
> He must surmount these propositions; then he sees the world rightly. (TLP §6.54)

It seems that if we take Wittgenstein's propositions literally, then we have to regard the whole *Tractatus* as nonsensical by its own lights, so the book begins to look like a self-defeating exercise. But the distinction between saying and showing suggests that perhaps we are not supposed to take Wittgenstein's propositions literally. The fact—if it is a fact—that Wittgenstein cannot *say* the things that he has seemingly been trying to say for 80 pages does not entail, according to the *Tractatus*, that he cannot *show* us something of importance. We might systematically be led by them to notice aspects of the world that had previously escaped us.[37] The text of the book would then be a kind of elaborate performance, which, taken by itself, makes no sense and carries no coherent meaning, but which puts the right kind of reader into a frame of mind in which she can "see the world rightly."

This comes close to what we need to say here, but it is not quite right. This view of the *Tractatus* likens it to things that Donald Davidson has said about metaphors.[38] According to Davidson, there is no special metaphorical or figurative meaning carried by a metaphor, above and beyond the literal meanings of its constituent terms. "This music crept by me on the waters" means nothing more than quite literally that this music crept by me on the waters, which is surely false. But it does manage to evoke in an indirect way various comparisons that I might care to make between this music and a stealthy person or animal. It draws my attention to these similarities without actually *saying* anything about them.[39]

If we take this comparison between the *Tractatus* and Davidsonian metaphors seriously, then there is a problem for Wittgenstein. The problem is that even though a Davidsonian metaphor does not say anything about what it draws my

37 For a suggestion like this see Max Black, *A Companion to Wittgenstein's "Tractatus"* (Ithaca, NY: Cornell University Press, 1964), 381.

38 This suggestion was made to me by Matthew Stephens, though he might not approve of my development of it below.

39 See Donald Davidson, "What Metaphors Mean" in *On Metaphor*, edited by S. Sacks (Chicago: University of Chicago Press, 1978), 29–45.

attention to—what it *shows*, if you like—once I have noticed the similarity, then I *can* readily set about describing it. "This music," I might say, "is similar to a stealthy animal in the sense that it makes a very soft noise and is difficult for the speaker to locate. The speaker hadn't even noticed it was there at first." The mere fact that something *is* shown does not entail that it *cannot* be said, contrary to TLP §4.1212. Frank Ramsey, a friend of Wittgenstein who helped Ogden translate the *Tractatus* and who published an important early review of it, suggested much the same point: "But what we can't say, we can't say, and we can't whistle it either" (1990, 146).[40] (Wittgenstein was actually a virtuosic whistler, so Ramsey's remark is particularly apt.)

I do not think that Ramsey's criticism can be avoided on what I take to be the most plausible interpretation of the paradox, but there are still two reasons to think that the propositions of the *Tractatus* that try to go beyond the world should not be taken to show something that cannot be said.

First, in his "Lecture on Ethics" Wittgenstein considers exactly the point that what a piece of figurative language suggests without saying can be described once it has been suggested. Our attempts to make ethical statements, he contends, at first sound like similes or analogies (LE 42). We say that a chair is a good chair because it serves some prior purpose we have for it, and then we extend the term 'good' by analogy to cover actions or intentions or persons unconditionally or absolutely, not because they serve some prior purpose.

> But a simile must be the simile for *something*. And if I can describe a fact by means of a simile I must also be able to drop the simile and to describe the facts without it. Now in our case as soon as we try to drop the simile and simply to state the facts which stand behind it, we find that there are no such facts. And so, what at first appeared to be a simile now seems to be mere nonsense. (42–43)

If anything is "supernatural," he says, it is ethics (40), and all attempts to describe it fall into nonsense.

Second, the view that takes the propositions of the *Tractatus* to show something that they fail to say does not distinguish adequately between propositions that are senseless and mere pseudo-propositions that are nothing but nonsense.[41]

---

40 Frank P. Ramsey, "General Propositions and Causality," *Philosophical Papers*, edited by D.H. Mellor (Cambridge: Cambridge University Press, 1990), 145–63.

41 For another view of these matters see Andrew Lugg, "Wittgenstein's *Tractatus*: True Thoughts and Nonsensical Propositions," *Philosophical Investigations* 26, no.4 (2003): 332–47. Lugg suggests that the propositions of the *Tractatus* are, indeed, senseless, until one tries to assert something (*Continued*)

It is the former that are said to show things that cannot be said, and that is merely because one of the things that is shown but unsayable is logical form: "Every tautology itself shows that it is a tautology" (TLP §6.127). Of course, all meaningful propositions show us logical form: "The propositions *show* the logical form of reality" (§4.121). But the "propositions" that Wittgenstein dismisses as nonsense at §6.54 are not really propositions at all, but *pseudo-propositions*. They are nonsense because in trying to go beyond the world they violate conditions of meaningfulness, even though they appear on the surface to be meaningful.

Of course, what lies beyond the world *does* show itself, according to Wittgenstein, and it cannot be put into words. Logical form shows itself in facts, thought, and propositions. Moral value shows itself in our actions and in the lives we lead, in the guilt that we feel when we have behaved badly (LE 42). But the present point is simply that the (pseudo-) propositions of the *Tractatus* do not show something that lies beyond the world.

I said earlier that this reading, nonetheless, comes close to capturing what is going on in the *Tractatus*. The difficulty lies not in the suggestion that the book might, in spite of being nonsense, systematically lead the right kind of reader to see "the world rightly" (TLP §6.54) but in thinking that nonsense can show anything. Notice that Wittgenstein does not suggest that an alert reader will understand his *propositions*: "he who understands *me*" (§6.54, my emphasis), he says, will recognize the propositions of the *Tractatus* to be nonsense. What Wittgenstein means by his propositions is not what his propositions mean, because they have no coherent meaning. But in the right kind of context I can mean things by my words that my words do not mean. Speaker's meaning and sentence-meaning are two different things. For example, if I write a letter of recommendation for a student in which I say only that she is very good at meeting deadlines and do not comment on the quality of her work, I manage to convey to my reader something that I have not said—namely, that her work is not of very high quality. All that the *sentence* 'She is very good at meeting deadlines' means is that she is very good at meeting deadlines. But, of course, what *I* mean by praising her ability to meet deadlines without saying anything about her academic performance is that her work is not of very high quality. Similarly, if I wanted my letter to be particularly damning without having actually said anything damning, I might just write a series of nonsense syllables. Exactly, what I mean by doing this may be harder for a reader to discern, but it will at least be apparent that I am not heaping praise on the student. The *Tractatus*, on the suggested reading, is in some ways like the

---

with them, in which case one ends up speaking nonsense (343). This is clever, but Wittgenstein tells us that his propositions, not his assertions of them, are nonsense (TLP §6.54).

second letter of reference, but it differs in two important ways: first, the nonsense that he chooses allegedly has the systematic capacity to direct an attentive reader to what Wittgenstein means in a way that the nonsense letter of reference is not so well-equipped to do; second, what Wittgenstein means is something that cannot in principle be said.

If this way of approaching the *Tractatus* is right, then, as Peter Hacker has observed, at least some kinds of nonsense can be "illuminating" rather than "misleading."[42] Philosophers before the *Tractatus*, Wittgenstein may be taken to suggest, have provided a great deal of misleading nonsense, which tries to go beyond the world and beyond the limits of language and which, moreover, preserves or promotes the illusion that doing so is possible. But the nonsense of the *Tractatus* puts the suitable reader in a position to see that any attempt to go beyond the world is futile, that what lies beyond the world can show itself but cannot be said. And this helps to explain what Wittgenstein tells us at the end of the Preface:

> the *truth* of the thoughts communicated here seems to me unassailable and definitive. I am, therefore, of the opinion that the problems have in essentials been finally solved. And if I am not mistaken in this, then the value of this work secondly consists in the fact that it shows how little has been done when these problems have been solved. (TLP 29)

It shows how little has been done because what philosophers have been trying to do is something that cannot be done—to go beyond the limits of the world.

If this is right, then what Wittgenstein means by "elucidatory" propositions is not what the logical positivists mean, and the task for philosophy envisioned by Wittgenstein—putting an end to philosophy and leading us to see that matters of ultimate importance are transcendent and ineffable—seems profoundly different from the one envisioned by either Schlick or Carnap. Schlick does pay lip-service to the saying-showing distinction, but in his mouth it yields a commitment to epistemological foundationalism and the need for ostensive definitions of our words—definitions in which we point at some object or quality and say, "This is ____." As Schlick sees it, attempts at explaining the meanings of words rely on other words, and if one attempts to explain those other words by appeal to yet more words, then one is in danger of embarking on an infinite regress. If there is to be any real

---

42 Hacker (1972), 18. Lugg rejects this distinction, contending that Wittgenstein "never speaks of nonsense as conveying truths or as being important" (2003, 333). But Wittgenstein does seem to think that the nonsense that results from trying to make ethical claims is worth "respecting deeply" (LE 44).

explanation of meanings, then sooner or later such attempts must come to an end "in actual pointings, in exhibiting what is meant, thus in real acts; only these acts are no longer capable of or in need of, further explanation" (TPP 57). The regress is to be avoided, then, by pointing at something in the world and saying "This is red" or "This is round." One of the key sources of metaphysical confusion, Schlick thinks, is the mistaken belief that "the content of pure quality" can be expressed. "Qualities," Schlick insists, "cannot be 'said'. They can only be shown in experience. But with this showing, cognition has nothing to do" (TPP 57).

The idea that such ostensive definition has nothing to do with cognition, as we shall see in Chapter 4, is one that Wittgenstein takes direct issue with in his later work. But it is unlikely that Schlick's version of the saying/showing distinction can be made to apply to much that Wittgenstein categorizes as unsayable in the *Tractatus*. Perhaps it can be made to map onto the relation between simple names and objects, which is taken in the *Tractatus* to be ineffable:

> 3.26 The name cannot be analysed further by any definition. It is a primitive sign.
>
> 3.262 What does not get expressed in the sign is shown by its application. What the signs conceal, their application declares.
>
> 3.263 The meanings of primitive signs can be explained by elucidations. Elucidations are propositions which contain the primitive signs. They can, therefore, only be understood when the meanings of these signs are already known.

These passages might make us think of ostensive definition. I don't know the meaning of 'red' until I have been presented with samples of red things and told "This is red" of each of them, and the word 'red' has to be used to teach me its meaning. But Wittgenstein never hints that simple names are defined ostensively in the way Schlick thinks of a term like 'red'. Moreover, there is little indication that Schlick would consider an equation of the inexpressible with the mystical, and Carnap would certainly object to elucidation by way of nonsense as suitable perhaps for poetry, but not appropriate for philosophy.

2.9 RUSSELL AND WITTGENSTEIN

It should by now be clear that the difference between Wittgenstein and Russell is not simply the difference between Schlick and Russell. Russell's idea that philosophy is concerned with a body of *a priori* propositions was a non-starter for Wittgenstein: "The result of philosophy is not a number of 'philosophical propositions', but to make propositions clear" (TLP §4.112). This is at least in part because Wittgenstein, as we have already seen, does not regard propositions of logic as the most general of statements that can be made about everything without mentioning anything in particular. "The propositions of logic ... say nothing" (§6.11). But additionally, whereas Russell sees ethics as a perturbing influence on the smooth orbit of scientific philosophy and seeks to keep philosophy on a smooth trajectory, Wittgenstein would likely think that it is ethics that would be sullied by such an encounter. Part of the task of philosophy in the *Tractatus*, it seems, is neither to be an under-labourer for the sciences nor to be their queen, but to protect the value of the world, which must lie beyond the world, from being confused with and diluted by all that is merely contingent and accidental.

Nonetheless, the importance for both Russell and Wittgenstein of their difference concerning logic should not be underestimated. It lies at the heart of Wittgenstein's rejection of Russell's "multiple relation theory of judgment"—a rejection that Russell described as so devastating as to make him doubt whether he was capable of doing anything new and valuable in philosophy—and it is worth mentioning before we turn away from Wittgenstein's early views.

In his 1910 essay "On the Nature of Truth and Falsehood" and again in his popular introductory book *The Problems of Philosophy* Russell advanced the idea that a theory of truth should apply in the first instance to *judgments* and only derivatively to propositions. Propositions, indeed, were to be analyzed in terms of judgments. A judgment, in turn, Russell thought of as a multiple-relation among the judge and the objects of the judgment, including whatever predicates and relations are judged to be possessed by the individuals mentioned in the judgment. As well, because we must be able to distinguish the proposition '*aRb*' from the proposition '*bRa*', every judgment must involve a "sense" or "direction,"[43] which Russell later tries to capture by including in every judgment the logical form of its relational complex. Thus, the judgment that Othello loves Desdemona is to be thought of as relating the judge to both Othello and Desdemona, as relating Othello to

43 Bertrand Russell, *The Problems of Philosophy* (Indianapolis: Hackett Publishing, n.d.), 126; "On the Nature of Truth and Falsehood" in *Philosophical Essays*, rev. ed. (London: George Allen & Unwin, 1966), 158.

Desdemona, and as relating the judge to the *relation* that obtains between Othello and Desdemona.

Russell's motivation for this cumbersome mode of analysis was that if a judgment were merely a two-place relation between the judge on the one hand and some fact on the other, then it would be impossible ever to make a false judgment, for one can be related to a fact only if that fact obtains. Such a binary relation would make it impossible to have a false belief. The problem with Russell's new theory, as Wittgenstein was quick to point out, was that it made the principles of logic dependent on contingent principles of human psychology. Wittgenstein conveyed the criticism to Russell in a letter from June of 1913:

> ... I can now express my objection to your theory of judgement exactly: I believe it is obvious that, from the proposition "A judges that (say) *a* is in a relation R to *b*", if correctly analysed, the proposition "aRb. v. ~aRb" must follow directly *without the use of any other premiss*. This condition is not fulfilled by your theory. (NB 122)[44]

Suppose that I judge that *aRb*. If '*aRb*' is a genuine proposition, then it follows straightaway from the proposition that *aRb* that *aRb v ~aRb* (by something like what we would now call the Rule of Addition). So if propositions are to be reduced to judgments, as Russell hopes, then it should follow straightaway—without any additional premises—from the fact that I *judge* that *aRb* that I also judge that *aRb v ~aRb*. It seems, however, that it is possible for me to judge that *aRb* and fail or *refuse* to judge that *aRb v ~aRb*. Principles of logic are not principles of human psychology, and even if they were, that would be a contingent fact about human beings, not itself a truth of logic—but then the obtaining of a logical truth would seem to depend on some *accidental* fact, a fact about human psychology. Similarly, if propositions of logic are extremely general propositions, as Russell thought, then they need not follow immediately from any contingent proposition, any more than '$E=mc^2$' follows from any arbitrary contingent proposition without additional, contingent premises. By treating propositions of logic as tautologies, one and all, Wittgenstein seems to avoid these problems.[45]

Of course, it could be said that the obtaining of '*aRb v ~aRb*' *does* depend on a contingent fact, namely, the contingent fact that the symbols '*aRb v ~aRb*' mean what they do and not something else. Wittgenstein thought he had a way

44 Ludwig Wittgenstein, *Notebooks 1914–1916*, 2nd ed., edited by G.H. von Wright and G.E.M. Anscombe, translated by G.E.M. Anscombe (Chicago: University of Chicago Press, 1979).

45 I am indebted to David Hyder for this understanding of Wittgenstein's criticism.

around this criticism in the *Tractatus*. Logic is transcendental and transcendent. It lies outside the world as a non-accidental condition of the sense of the world. It is a condition of the very possibility of '*aRb*''s being meaningful, and part of the meaning of '*aRb*' *consists in* the fact that '*aRb v ~aRb*' is a tautology. "That its [a tautology's] constituent parts connected together *in this way* give a tautology characterizes the logic of its constituent parts" (TLP §6.12). But, more to the point, Wittgenstein thinks that logical form can be clearly shown by the choice of an adequate logical symbolism, one that does not rely on the meanings of its symbols (§3.33), but only on their "*logical* grammar" or "logical syntax" (§3.325) to display the logical form of the expressions they comprise: "The sign determines a logical form only together with its logical syntactic application" (§3.327). This, Wittgenstein concedes, does not completely eliminate contingent facts from our expressions of logical truths, for we still choose the symbols, but it is adequate:

> In our notations there is indeed something arbitrary, but *this* is not arbitrary, namely that *if* we have determined anything arbitrarily, then something else *must* be the case. (This results from the *essence* of the notation.)
>
> A particular method of symbolizing may be unimportant, but it is always important that this is a *possible* method of symbolizing. (TLP §§3.342–3.3421)

As I shall argue in the ensuing chapters, it is precisely by its giving up the conviction that what makes for necessity (logical, ethical, or aesthetic) must lie outside the world that Wittgenstein's later philosophical work is characterized.

3

AFTER THE *TRACTATUS*

I remarked in the preceding chapter that it is a disputed question how much continuity is to be found between Wittgenstein's early work and his later work. It is easy enough to understand what might make someone think that there is a significant break with the thinking of the *Tractatus* some time before the *Philosophical Investigations*. In particular, there are passages from the later work in which Wittgenstein seems to tell us that something important has changed in his philosophical views. In the 1945 Preface to the *Investigations* he writes, "[S]ince beginning to occupy myself with philosophy again, sixteen years ago, I have been forced to recognize grave mistakes in what I wrote in that first book" (PI x).[1]

However, in the past two decades or so a wave of scholarship has arisen that poses a serious challenge to the idea that there are "two Wittgensteins," the early and the late. Much of this work rightly eschews the simplistic view that the later Wittgenstein is rejecting wholesale everything he wrote in his earlier work, but its most influential proponents take the assimilation much further. They think that the similarities between the later work and the earlier work vastly outweigh the differences and that the differences are largely differences of detail not of overall approach.

1 Ludwig Wittgenstein, *Philosophical Investigations*, 2nd ed., translated by G.E.M. Anscombe (Oxford: Basil Blackwell, 1968), x.

The *Tractatus*, in the opinion of these "New Wittgensteinians,"[2] as they have become known, does not propound any of the doctrines that I presented in the preceding chapter: logical atomism, the picture theory of the proposition, the saying-showing distinction, the view of normativity as grounded in something lying outside the world. These doctrines, on the contrary, are themselves examples of traditional philosophical temptations that the *Tractatus*, like the later work, is intended to steer us away from.

I shall maintain, against this view, that Wittgenstein held these doctrines in his early work. I shall argue that during the period that runs roughly from 1927 to 1933 Wittgenstein changed his mind about many things he had thought to be "unassailable" (TLP 29)[3] in the *Tractatus*. In particular, he gave up on the doctrine of logical atomism and the accompanying picture-theory of the proposition, in response to the criticisms of Frank Ramsey, but not without passing through a brief, but extraordinary, phase in which, under the influence of Moritz Schlick, he advanced his own version of the Verification Theory of Meaning. Also to fall by the wayside was the ultimately paradoxical doctrine of the *Tractatus* that all value must lie outside the world—that logic (like ethics, aesthetics, the self, and the will) must be something both transcendental and transcendent if it is to serve as a condition of the possibility of meaning and value.[4] This period, as we shall see, is also a rich source of insight concerning Wittgenstein's changing attitude toward the relation between science and philosophy and the appropriate task of the philosopher—an attitude that comes to maturity in the *Philosophical Investigations*.

3.1 CERTAINTY IN A TIME OF DOUBT

> [T]he *truth* of the thoughts communicated here seems to me unassailable and definitive. I am, therefore, of the opinion that the problems have in essentials finally been solved. (TLP 29)

2 The name derives from Alice Crary and Rupert Read, eds., *The New Wittgenstein* (London: Routledge, 2000).

3 Ludwig Wittgenstein, *Tractatus Logico-philosophicus*, translated by C.K. Ogden (London: Routledge & Kegan Paul, 1922), 29.

4 In what follows I shall frequently use the term 'transcendental' in the dual sense that, as we saw in Chapter 2, Wittgenstein gives it in the *Tractatus* to mean both pertaining to grounds of possibility and transcendent—lying beyond the contingency of the world in a realm of unspeakable necessity. As we shall see in Chapter 6, it is eventually necessary to pry these two notions apart to make sense of elements of Wittgenstein's later work.

These words from the Preface to the *Tractatus* were written in Vienna in 1918, shortly before the end of a war that left millions dead and countless others physically and psychologically maimed. They display great confidence and certainty in a time of catastrophic loss and doubt—perhaps a confidence and certainty that Wittgenstein needed. The book itself (*Logische-Philosophische Abhandlung* was its original German title) had been written during the war, much of it during periods when Wittgenstein was on leave from the front, but some of it almost in the fray of battle. By the time of the November 1918 armistice, among the dead was Wittgenstein's eldest brother, Kurt (who committed suicide on the battlefield when troops under his command disobeyed his orders), as well as Wittgenstein's close friend, David Pinsent, to whom the *Tractatus* is dedicated. Wittgenstein's sole surviving brother, Paul, had lost his right arm early in the war after being shot.[5] Wittgenstein himself, who had been decorated more than once for bravery during the war, underwent a religious awakening, reflected in the discussion of ethical propositions and the mystical which appears in the final pages of the *Tractatus*, but he was frequently troubled by suicidal thoughts.

With the war over and the problems of philosophy laid to rest Wittgenstein tried to find peace in other pursuits. He solicited Russell's help in getting the *Tractatus* (as its English translation became known at G.E. Moore's suggestion) published. This proved to be a protracted affair involving numerous rejections that added to his state of depression. He trained to become a rural school teacher—a brief career that came to an ignominious end in 1926 when he resigned amid controversy over his free use of corporal punishment. Thereafter, he spent time as a gardener in a monastery outside Vienna and pursued another short-lived, but more successful, career as an architect, completing the design and overseeing the construction of a house for his sister, Margarete. (It now houses part of the Bulgarian embassy.)

Philosophy seems not to have been much on his mind (after all, what was there left to think about?), except insofar as he pursued the publication of his completed

5 Paul was a renowned concert pianist who subsequently commissioned several of the most significant piano works ever written for the left hand, from such composers as Ravel, Korngold, and Prokofiev. Another brother, Hans, a musical prodigy, who showed promise as a composer, took his own life in 1903, after travelling to America to escape his overbearing father. A fourth, Rudolf, poisoned himself in Berlin in 1904, suffering from deep anxiety about his homosexuality. Wittgenstein's three sisters, Hermine (an accomplished painter), Helene, and Margarete (whose portrait was painted by Gustav Klimt and who was psychoanalysed by Freud, whom she helped escape from the Nazis), avoided such tragedies, but later lived in fear of the Nazis' racial purity laws. For more about Wittgenstein's extraordinary family see Ray Monk, *Ludwig Wittgenstein: The Duty of Genius* (London: Jonathan Cape, 1990) and Alexander Waugh *The House of Wittgenstein: A Family at War* (New York: Doubleday, 2008).

work, but he—or at least his book—was very much on the minds of philosophers after the *Tractatus* appeared, first in a sloppy German edition in 1921 and then in English and German on facing pages in 1922. The mathematician, Hans Hahn—later a member of the Vienna Circle—gave a seminar on the *Tractatus* in 1922 at Vienna University (Monk 213), and the Circle discussed most of the book line by line twice during their weekly meetings of 1926–27.[6]

But in 1927 philosophy seemed to Wittgenstein worth pursuing again. He received a reverential visit from Moritz Schlick,[7] who had written to him well before in 1924, proposing that they meet to talk about the *Tractatus*. The eventual result was a series of philosophical discussions from 1927 to 1932 between Wittgenstein and selected members of the Circle—particularly, Schlick and Friedrich Waismann, but also for a short time Rudolf Carnap, Herbert Feigl and Maria Kasper.[8] Wittgenstein's ideas began a profound transformation.

3.2 THE DEMISE OF LOGICAL ATOMISM

So the "grave mistakes" that Wittgenstein eventually found in the *Tractatus* did not come to his attention all on their own. But it is not his meetings with the Vienna Circle that he later recalls as pivotal for this change. "I was helped to realize these mistakes—to a degree which I myself am hardly able to estimate—by the criticism which my ideas encountered from Frank Ramsey, with whom I discussed them in innumerable conversations during the last two years of his life" (PI viii). Ramsey, fourteen years Wittgenstein's junior and a prodigious thinker in mathematics, economics, and philosophy, suffered from serious liver problems and died in 1930, but not before helping C.K. Ogden translate the *Tractatus* (TLP 5) in 1921, and not before serving in the role of Wittgenstein's PhD supervisor. Wittgenstein

6 For the date see Karl Menger, "Memories of Moritz Schlick" in *Rationality and Science*, edited by Eugene T. Gadol (New York: Springer-Verlag, 1982), 86. In *Wittgenstein's Poker* (London: Faber and Faber, 2001), 119, David Edmonds and John Eidinow report that the book was read twice during this period.

7 According to Schlick's wife, Blanche, he left for the meeting with the "reverential attitude" of a "pilgrim" and "returned in an ecstatic state, saying little, and I felt I should not ask questions." See Brian McGuinness's Preface to Friedrich Waismann, *Wittgenstein and the Vienna Circle*, edited by Brian McGuinness, translated by Joachim Schulte and Brian McGuinness (Oxford: Basil Blackwell, 1979), 14—hereafter WVC.

8 See J. Alberto Coffa, *The Semantic Tradition from Kant to Carnap: To the Vienna Station*, edited by Linda Wessels (Cambridge: Cambridge University Press, 1991), 404f. n.3 and WVC, 15.

submitted the *Tractatus* as his dissertation.[9] "I know you'll never understand it," he told his examining committee: Bertrand Russell and G.E. Moore (Monk 271).

Recall that in the *Tractatus* Wittgenstein had held that the world consisted of *logically independent* atomic facts: "Any one can either be the case or not be the case, and everything else remain the same" (TLP §1.21). In his 1923 review of the *Tractatus*,[10] Ramsey challenged the unassailability of this view, focusing on claims that appear at TLP §§6.375–6.3751:

> 6.375 As there is only a *logical* necessity, so there is only a *logical* impossibility.
>
> 6.3751 For two colours, *e.g.* to be at one place in the visual field, is impossible, logically impossible, for it is excluded by the logical structure of colour.

To say that the logical structure of colour makes it impossible for one point in the visual field to be two colours at the same time is to say that if a given point in the field is blue, then that is because it is not red, and it is not green, and it is not yellow, etc. In that case, either that a given point in the field is blue cannot be an atomic fact—one whose obtaining does not depend on the obtaining or failing to obtain of any other fact—or there must be some kind of necessity other than logical necessity. The latter option seemed incompatible with what the Vienna Circle thought was Wittgenstein's central insight, that the propositions of logic are tautologies, and it is to their tautological form that they owe their necessity, other types of "necessity" lacking any comparably clear explanation. The former option entails either that logical atomism is false (because the fact in question is supposed to be, but fails to be, an atomic fact) or that there must be some further analysis of the proposition about colour that avoids the difficulty. Finding such an analysis, however, seems improbable. It would have to account for a point's being coloured in terms of its possessing or failing to possess some other property. Either the property in question will belong to a spectrum of properties, as colour does, in which case the problem arises all over again, or it will be a brute, isolated, non-spectral property. If the latter, then it is unclear how it could account for the spectral range of the colour-properties that are supposed to supervene on it. It is not even clear that there are such non-spectral properties.

---

9 G.E. Moore, "Wittgenstein's Lectures in 1930–33" in *Philosophical Occasions: 1912–1951*, edited by James Klagge and Alfred Nordmann (Indianapolis: Hackett Publishing, 1993), 46–114, 46.

10 Frank Ramsey, "Critical Notice of L. Wittgenstein's *Tractatus Logico-Philosophicus*," *Mind*, 32, no.128 (1923): 465–78.

Wittgenstein had recognized the importance of this objection by early 1929, since he tried to answer it in the only philosophical journal article that he ever published, "Some Remarks on Logical Form."[11] But by late 1929 he had decided that the problem was insoluble.

> When I was working on my book I ... thought then that every inference depended on the form of a tautology. I hadn't seen then that an inference can also be of the form: A man is 6 ft tall, therefore he isn't 7 ft. This is bound up with my then believing that elementary propositions had to be independent of one another: from the fact that one state of affairs obtained you couldn't infer another did not. But if my present conception of a system of propositions is right, then it's even the rule that from the fact that one state of affairs obtains we can infer that all the others described by the system of propositions do not. (PR 317)[12]

It is by this time no longer an isolated proposition that "reaches up to" reality (TLP §2.1511) "like a scale applied to" it (TLP §2.1512), but a whole "system of propositions." "If I know that the object reaches up to the tenth graduation mark, I also know immediately that it doesn't reach the eleventh, twelfth, etc. The assertions telling me the length of an object form a system, a system of propositions. It's such a whole system which is compared with reality, not a single proposition" (PR 317).

3.3 VERIFICATION FOR A WHILE

In light of Wittgenstein's rejection of logical atomism, it is puzzling that during the very same time period he seems to have embraced a version of the verification theory of meaning—puzzling, because, as we saw in Chapter 1, the insight that a whole system of propositions must, in some sense, be "compared with reality" is precisely the one that Quine later presses into service as a decisive objection against the verification theory of meaning.

It is true that Wittgenstein's version of verificationism differs significantly from the reductionist versions advocated by the Vienna Circle. Most notably, Wittgenstein does not think that the meaning of a theoretical claim is given by

11 "Some Remarks on Logical Form," in *Philosophical Occasions: 1912–1951*, edited by James Klagge and Alfred Nordmann (Indianapolis: Hackett Publishing, 1993), 29–35.

12 Ludwig Wittgenstein, *Philosophical Remarks*, edited by R. Rhees, translated by R. Hargreaves and R. White (Oxford: Basil Blackwell, 1975).

analysing that claim into some set of claims about what observations could be made under various circumstances. Rather, Wittgenstein follows Ramsey in holding that, strictly speaking, scientific hypotheses do not make factual claims.[13] Rather, hypotheses serve as *rules* or *laws* for forming factual claims (PR §228).[14] Thus, the hypothesis that the gravitational force exerted by one body on another is directly proportional to the product of the masses of the two bodies and inversely proportional to the square of the distance that separates them is not, strictly speaking, either true or false. But it does serve as a rule for making claims about particular pairs of bodies that one might encounter.

Why hold such a view? Wittgenstein, under the influence of Schlick, decided during this period to treat his picture theory of the proposition as an account of the empirical verification of a proposition. "In order to discover whether a picture is true or false we must compare it with reality," he had written in the *Tractatus* (§2.223). In the *Tractatus* the point of this assertion was to emphasize that true propositions present pictures of the world as it actually is and that they can do so by sharing a logical form with the facts they represent. But Wittgenstein, the erstwhile verificationist, now interpreted this epistemologically as involving some kind of unmediated encounter with reality. If a proposition is completely analysed, then verifying or falsifying it seems just to be a matter of checking to see whether the objects in the world are organized into facts in the way that the names in the analysed proposition are. Such a direct comparison of simple things might seem to admit of no doubt. So verification is *conclusive* confirmation—confirmation that establishes with objective certainty that such and such is the case. Any proposition that cannot be conclusively tested in this way lacks any truth-value.

This is a wildly implausible view, and logical positivists who were at first tempted by it, like Carnap and Neurath, gave it up very quickly when they realized that general statements could not possibly be conclusively verified in this way because they made claims about a potentially unlimited number of instances. (The illusion that *particular* claims can be conclusively verified was also abandoned by Carnap and Neurath, but not by Schlick.) By contrast, Schlick and Wittgenstein bit hard on the bullet and insisted that only conclusively verifiable statements really counted as statements at all. Anything falling short of this standard needed some other explanation, and theirs was that general statements—scientific hypotheses included—were neither true nor false, but were imperatives of a sort—*rules*.

13 Frank P. Ramsey, "General Propositions and Causality," *Philosophical Papers*, edited by D.H. Mellor (Cambridge: Cambridge University Press, 1990), 145–63.

14 See also Ludwig Wittgenstein, *Philosophical Grammar*, edited by R. Rhees, translated by A.J.P. Kenny (Oxford: Basil Blackwell, 1974), 219—hereafter PG.

Nonetheless, this odd view was a species of verificationism, taking the meaningfulness (or truth-evaluability) of a proposition to depend on its verifiability, and taking its meaning to be its method of verification, which ended up being its truth-conditions as well (because verification was conclusive confirmation). And at the same time as Wittgenstein held this, he saw that the logical analysability of a proposition into elementary propositions, each logically independent of every other one, was problematic. But to say that a proposition, when completely analysed, can be conclusively verified by comparing it one-to-one with the isolated facts that make it true is to endorse the very logical atomism that seemed so problematic.

It is difficult to find any philosophical way of rationalizing Wittgenstein's commitment to these seemingly contradictory theses. In fact, I believe that Wittgenstein's considerable regard for Schlick's "highly cultured personality"[15] must be invoked to explain so glaring an inconsistency.[16] To Wittgenstein's credit, he did not leave the tension unresolved for very long. By 1931 he had given up on verificationism, and, indeed, he later seemed reluctant to acknowledge that he had ever held any such view.

> I used at one time to say that, in order to get clear how a certain sentence is used, it was a good idea to ask oneself the question: 'How would one try to verify such an assertion?' But that's just one way among others of getting clear about the use of a word or sentence. For example, another question which it is often very useful to ask oneself is: 'How is the word learned?' 'How would one set about teaching a child to use the word?'[17]

"Asking whether and how a proposition can be verified is only a particular way of asking 'How d'you mean?' The answer is a contribution to the grammar of the proposition" (PI §353).

15 Paul Engelmann, *Letters from Ludwig Wittgenstein with a Memoir*, translated by L. Furtmüller, edited by Brian McGuinness (Oxford: Basil Blackwell, 1967), 118.

16 See my "Going around the Vienna Circle: Wittgenstein and Verification," *Philosophical Investigations* 28, no.3 (2005): 205–34. Wittgenstein on more than one occasion expressed his admiration for Schlick, and in the absence of any plausible way of reconciling a verification theory with the rejection of logical atomism, I think it is reasonable to appeal to a psychological explanation for Wittgenstein's verificationism in the form of his high regard for Schlick.

17 Quoted in D.A.T. Gasking and A.C. Jackson, "Wittgenstein as a Teacher" in *Ludwig Wittgenstein: The Man and his Philosophy*, edited by K.T. Fann (New York: Dell, 1967), 54.

3.4 WHISTLING IN THE DARK?

There is another important change that Wittgenstein's views undergo in response to his exchanges with the Vienna Circle and Frank Ramsey (among others), but before I discuss it I must consider a criticism that casts doubt on my contention that Wittgenstein gave up on logical atomism and other doctrines of the *Tractatus*. This criticism contends that Wittgenstein did not give up these doctrines because he never really held them in the first place. He could not have held such doctrines, this criticism continues, because, as he tells us at TLP §6.54, the propositions of the *Tractatus* are nonsense, and so there are no doctrines, such as the picture-theory of the proposition to hold.

The interpretation of the closing sections of the *Tractatus* that I have offered is a variation on a standard line of interpretation that has been defended by a number of influential commentators.[18] What is common to these various views is the conviction that Wittgenstein thinks in the *Tractatus* that there are important philosophical truths that cannot be put into words, but which *show* themselves (TLP §6.522), and which, perhaps, we can be led to by the "illuminating nonsense" (Hacker 1972, 18) that makes up the *Tractatus*. According to this kind of reading, as Ramsey worried (see Chapter 2), Wittgenstein was trying to whistle what he could not say.

In the past two decades a rival interpretation of the paradox of the *Tractatus* has found some articulate proponents.[19] The most notable of these "New Wittgensteinians," Cora Diamond and James Conant, insist that the more traditional interpretations of the *Tractatus* fail to take seriously Wittgenstein's claim that his own propositions are nonsense, that they "chicken out" in Diamond's blunt phrase by trying to see Wittgenstein as distinguishing some special kind of philosophical nonsense, which can be shown but not said, from plain, ordinary nonsense, which is just ... nonsense: "To read Wittgenstein himself as not chickening

18 See, e.g., Max Black, *A Companion to Wittgenstein's 'Tractatus'* (Ithaca, NY: Cornell University Press, 1964), 378–86; G.E.M. Anscombe, *An Introduction to Wittgenstein's Tractatus*, 3rd ed. (London: Hutchinson University Library, 1967), 161–173; P.M.S. Hacker, *Insight and Illusion* (Oxford: Clarendon Press, 1972), 17–30. There are, of course, important points of disagreement that distinguish the views of these commentators, but with respect to the criticism at issue, their differences are less important than their similarities.

19 In a recent essay the late Richard Rorty conflates the kind of reading I defend with that of the New Wittgensteinians. For his purposes the more interesting contrast is between interpreters who take Wittgenstein's methodological remarks seriously and those, like him, who emphasize Wittgenstein's affinities with pragmatism. I am inclined to think that there is less to this contrast than meets the eye. See Richard Rorty, "Wittgenstein and the Linguistic Turn" in *Philosophy as Cultural Politics* (Cambridge: Cambridge University Press, 2007), 160–75.

out is to say that it is not, not really, his view that there are features of reality that cannot be put in to words but show themselves."[20] On the contrary, thinks Diamond, when we surmount the final rung of the ladder of TLP §6.54, we see that everything that has preceded, except perhaps the Preface of the book, is nonsense, *including* the saying-showing distinction (1991, 182), and it must all be discarded.

Diamond's language suggests that it is uncharitable to read Wittgenstein as trying to hang on to ineffable truths about logic or ethics or metaphysics—truths that remain truths even though they cannot be put into words, or "things that would be true if they could be said" (Anscombe 162). It is uncharitable because doing so makes Wittgenstein vulnerable to Ramsey's charge that he is trying to whistle what he thinks he cannot say and because doing so represents Wittgenstein as lacking the nerve to accept the full consequences of saying that his own propositions are nonsense.

But if the standard view is in some way *cowardly*—if it errs in supposing that Wittgenstein thought that his nonsense, unlike traditional philosophical nonsense, was in some way illuminating, what does a brave, heroic view of the *Tractatus* have to tell us about the role of all that nonsense? Diamond appeals here to a distinction we encountered in Chapter 2 between understanding Wittgenstein's propositions and understanding Wittgenstein himself. If someone carefully and deliberately talks a great deal of nonsense, we might well wonder why, and the trick we need to accomplish in such a case, thinks Diamond, consists in the "imaginative activity" of trying to "enter into the taking of nonsense for sense" (2000, 157). When I react this way to someone's nonsense, I "let myself feel its attractiveness" (158). What Wittgenstein is trying to do in the *Tractatus*, according to Diamond, is to engage in just this sort of imaginative understanding of a person who is attracted by traditional philosophical propositions. So what readers of the book must do, likewise, is try to understand Wittgenstein, rather than try to understand his nonsense, and doing so, if we are attracted by traditional philosophical propositions, will also result in a kind of self-understanding, which will be manifested in our no longer finding those propositions "attractive" (161).

Diamond's view, like the related views of other New Wittgensteinians, is subtle, sophisticated, elegant, and even beautiful. But for all that, I do not see how it can be right. What exactly is it that I imagine when I try imaginatively to understand

20 Cora Diamond, "Throwing Away the Ladder: How to Read the *Tractatus*" in *The Realistic Spirit: Wittgenstein, Philosophy, and the Mind* (Cambridge, MA: MIT Press, 1991), 179–204 at 181. See, as well, Cora Diamond, "Ethics, Imagination and the Method of Wittgenstein's *Tractatus*" in Crary and Read (eds.), 149–73. See also James Conant, "Must We Show What We Cannot Say?" in *The Senses of Stanley Cavell*, edited by Richard Fleming and Michael Payne (London and Toronto: Associated University Presses, 1989), 242–83, esp. 258–60 and "Elucidation and Nonsense in Frege and Early Wittgenstein" in Crary and Read (eds.), 174–217.

another person whom I take to be spouting nonsense? Diamond's answer is that I imaginatively enter "into the tendency to be attracted by such sentences" (2000, 161). But what does it mean to be attracted by such sentences? I can find them attractive, presumably, only if I think that they say something, that they are not nonsense, but if we stop there and give no further content to what they might be saying, it is difficult to see how I could find them attractive. If they have an attraction for me, it is because I believe that they do say something that I find impossible to express any more clearly than by uttering those sentences, and if I imagine them to have an attraction for me, and if this imagination is to be more than a superficial engagement with a logical possibility, then I must imagine that it is because I believe that they do say something. But if I am to imagine *that* in any way that is not merely superficial, then I must imagine something about *what* they try to say. I must, in short, treat them as sentences that are nonsense, but which are nonetheless *about* something, which is just the puzzling feat that we were supposed to avoid having to attribute to Wittgenstein if we were to avoid "chickening out." We do draw a distinction between understanding what a person says and understanding the person who says it, a distinction that Hacker exploits in his interpretation of the *Tractatus* as purporting to advance illuminating nonsense. But I see no way of understanding the person who speaks nonsense that scrupulously refrains from trying to interpret what she might be trying to say and failing.

Other details of the New Wittgensteinian view might be contested,[21] but, ultimately, what persuades me that this view must be wrong is the great concern that Wittgenstein later shows for the doctrines that he ostensibly did not hold while writing the *Tractatus*. When Ramsey criticizes the logical atomism that he sees in the *Tractatus*, Wittgenstein does not react by saying, "You're missing the point! I never held such a view, and it would be nonsensical to replace it with an improved version that avoids your criticism!" He responds first in "Some Remarks on Logical Form" by trying to find a way around the problem without giving up logical atomism and then in his discussions with Schlick and Waismann by conceding that Ramsey was right: "When I was working on my book *I ... thought then* that every inference depended on the form of a tautology.... This is bound up with *my then believing* that elementary propositions had to be independent of one another: from the fact that one state of affairs obtained you couldn't infer another did not" (PR 317; my emphasis). When Schlick and Waismann presented him with their reading of the *Tractatus*, he responded not by telling them that their view was as much nonsense as the views found in the *Tractatus* but by adopting for a

21 See P.M.S. Hacker, "Was He Trying to Whistle It?" in Crary and Read (eds.), 353–88 for a thorough critique of the Diamond-Conant view.

short period of time his own version of the Verification Theory of Meaning, as we saw above. And, as we saw at the start of this chapter, he begins the *Philosophical Investigations* by telling his readers, "I have been forced to recognize grave mistakes in what I wrote in that first book" (PI x). Notice that they are "grave mistakes," not errors of detail. And he continues: "I was helped to realize these mistakes—to a degree which I myself am hardly able to estimate—by the criticism which my ideas encountered from Frank Ramsey, with whom I discussed them in innumerable conversations during the last two years of his life" (PI viii). What did Ramsey find troubling? We have already seen: logical atomism and the saying-showing distinction. Surely Wittgenstein held these doctrines in the *Tractatus* and later gave them up![22]

3.5 IMPLICIT CONVENTIONS

Logical atomism, the picture theory of the proposition, and the saying-showing distinction were not the only doctrines of the *Tractatus* to disappear. The view of TLP §6.41 that all value must lie outside the world also faces a challenge, but Wittgenstein displays an interesting ambivalence toward it. In his 1929 "Lecture on Ethics," which we encountered in Chapter 2, he still seems firmly committed to the view that the ground of *moral* value must lie outside the world. As a result, when we make ethical pronouncements, we are trying "*to go beyond* the world" (LE 44).[23] If anything is "supernatural" (i.e., both transcendental and transcendent), he says, it is ethics (40), and the result of trying to talk about it is "mere nonsense" (43), even though the impulse to utter such nonsense is one that he "cannot help respecting deeply" (44).

However, if Wittgenstein remained attached to the allegedly transcendental character of ethics in 1929, he did not seem so sanguine about the transcendental character of logic. For early on in the *Philosophical Remarks*, which dates from the same period, we find the following comment:

22 Robert Ackermann in *Wittgenstein's City* (Amherst: University of Massachusetts Press, 1988) tries to reconcile the *Tractatus* with Wittgenstein's later writings by taking a different tack. He seems not to doubt that Wittgenstein accepted logical atomism early on, but he thinks that as late as the *Philosophical Investigations* "The basic ontology of the *Tractatus*... is not reworked" (37). I am not convinced that he really means this, for he also writes that "in the context of the later work, the metaphysical claim in the *Tractatus* that there was a single analysis of all factual assertions into one set of elementary propositions... had to give way" (33). But what exactly is the "basic ontology of the *Tractatus*" if it is not a world composed of the totality of atomic facts?

23 Ludwig Wittgenstein, "Lecture on Ethics" in *Philosophical Occasions: 1912–1951*, edited by James Klagge and Alfred Nordmann (Indianapolis: Hackett Publishing, 1993), 37–44.

> Grammar is a 'theory of logical types'.
>
> I do not call a rule of representation a convention if it can be justified in propositions: propositions describing what is represented and showing that the representation is adequate. Grammatical conventions cannot be justified by describing what is represented. Any such description already presupposes the grammatical rules. That is to say, if anything is to count as nonsense in the grammar which is to be justified, then it cannot at the same time pass for sense in the grammar of the propositions that justify it (etc.). (PR §7)

There is an obvious similarity between the view expressed here and the view of logic in the *Tractatus*. Logical form, remember, was held to be inexpressible in the earlier work. It follows straightaway from this that there could be no question of justifying principles of logic because logic was the transcendental condition that made all meaning and justification possible. Here in the *Remarks* a system of grammatical (logical) rules is likewise said to be unable to provide any justification for itself. But notice now that grammatical rules are said to be *conventions*, not something that transcends and grounds all possible linguistic practice, but something that transcends only a *particular set* of linguistic practices and serves as a kind of ground for them.

This shift from the transcendental to the conventional takes some time for Wittgenstein to assimilate fully. Thus, in his early lectures at Cambridge he at times still seems attached to the Tractarian picture of saying and showing and its accompanying metaphysics of transcendental grounds: "What is essential to the world cannot be *said about* the world; for then it could be otherwise, as any proposition can be negated" (WLC I 34).[24] However, the shift, which goes to the very core of Wittgenstein's later philosophy, does take place. It is made most explicit in his discussions of the foundations of mathematics. Thus by 1933 we find him saying, "[W]hen one says 'You can't count through the whole series of cardinal numbers', one doesn't state a fact about human frailty but about a convention which we have made" (BB 54).[25]

It is easy to give remarks like this the wrong kind of emphasis, and that wrong kind of emphasis can provoke the worry, well expressed by Stanley Cavell, that this reading of Wittgenstein supposes that "he imagines that we have between

24 Ludwig Wittgenstein, *Wittgenstein's Lectures—Cambridge, 1930–1932*, from the notes of John King and Desmond Lee, edited by Desmond Lee (Oxford: Blackwell, 1980)

25 Ludwig Wittgenstein, *The Blue and the Brown Books*, 2nd ed. (Oxford: Blackwell, 1969).

us some kind of contract" (Cavell 41)[26] regarding the grammar of our language. However, to describe Wittgenstein as a "conventionalist" is not to interpret him as saying that the conventions in question are explicit agreements that anyone has made about how to use the word 'infinity' or any other term in mathematics, as Wittgenstein clarifies in a lecture from 1935:

> Suppose we called "2+2=4" the expression of a convention. This is misleading, though the equation might originally have been the result of one. The situation with respect to it is comparable to the situation supposed in the Social Contract theory. We know that there was no actual contract, but it is as if such a contract had been made. Similarly for 2+2=4: it is as if a convention had been made. (WLC II, 156–57)[27]

So that we take expressions like '2+2=4' to express necessary truths is the result of conventions that are implicit in our linguistic practices, not of explicit agreements that we reach at some sort of linguistic bargaining-table.

This is clearly his mature view, as remarks from 1937 indicate: "Now we talk of the 'inexorability' of logic; and think of the laws of logic as inexorable, still more inexorable than the laws of nature," (RFM I §118)[28] but, Wittgenstein goes on to insist, "it is *we* that are inexorable in applying these laws" (RFM I §118). That '[*P* & (*P* ⊃ Q)] ⊃ *Q*' expresses a tautology is determined by our refusal to countenance any deviation from it as constituting a legitimate inference. Its being a tautology is a rule or norm of our language, but not one that we have explicitly agreed to.

But that the inexorability of logic and mathematics should turn on *our* inexorability, rather than on something necessary that lies beyond the world, may seem to threaten us with a new problem. It may seem to trivialize logical or mathematical necessity, turning it into something that we can alter on a whim simply by adopting a new set of conventions. It suggests that there is, as Cavell puts it, a "hook of arbitrariness" (Cavell 51) in Wittgenstein's philosophy. But Wittgenstein makes it clear that we should not conclude from the apparent contingency of our

---

26 Stanley Cavell, "Declining Decline: Wittgenstein as a Philosopher of Culture," in *This New Yet Unapproachable America: Lectures after Emerson and Wittgenstein* (Albuquerque, NM: Living Batch Press, 1989), 29–75.

27 Ludwig Wittgenstein, *Wittgenstein's Lectures, Cambridge, 1932–35*, edited by Alice Ambrose (Amherst, NY: Prometheus Books, 2001).

28 Ludwig Wittgenstein, *Remarks on the Foundations of Mathematics*, 3rd ed., edited by G.H. von Wright, R. Rhees, and G.E.M. Anscombe, translated by G.E.M. Anscombe (Oxford: Blackwell, 1978).

conventions that they are altered easily or arbitrarily.[29] The conventions we have, he thinks, answer to some deep need:

> [I]f you talk about *essence*—, you are merely noting a convention. But here one would like to retort: there is no greater difference than that between a proposition about the depth of the essence and one about—a mere convention. But what if I reply: to the *depth* that we see in the essence there corresponds the *deep* need for the convention. (RFM I §74)

That we have conventions according to which certain truths count as "necessary" is a contingent matter of fact about human beings (and maybe not all human beings). Logic and mathematics are not forced on us by some transcendent power. That we have such practices is possible only because we refuse to countenance deviations from certain norms. But our refusal here is not arbitrary. It is rooted in the kind of universe we inhabit as well as in the kinds of creatures we are and the kinds of cultures we develop—what Wittgenstein later calls our "form of life" (RFM VII §47).[30] To give up on the convention that $2+2=4$ or that '$p \supset p$' is a tautology would be to give up what we know as mathematics and logic, and we could not expect to do that without throwing our lives and various social orders into disarray. But to repeat: that's not to say that we *had* to have either convention. We might never have developed an interest in arithmetic or logic.

The point might be clarified further by remarking that Wittgenstein is not attempting to give a theory of the source or nature of necessity. He is not trying to say, for example, that although it is a necessary truth that $2+2=4$, it might have been merely a *contingent* truth, or it might have been *false*. To say that necessity *consists in* the presence of certain conventions in our practices and then to go on and say that the presence of those practices is not necessary runs the risk of incoherence. It seems to involve appealing to some further, non-conventional notion of necessity in order to ground the judgment that some practices are not necessary.

Just what point *is* Wittgenstein trying to make about necessity with his talk of conventions? The central point, I think, is that propositions that express necessary truths have a special role to play in our linguistic practices. They are what Wittgenstein calls in the *Philosophical Remarks* "norm[s] of representation"

29 This point was made long ago by Barry Stroud, "Wittgenstein and Logical Necessity" in *Wittgenstein: The Philosophical Investigations*, edited by George Pitcher (London: Macmillan, 1966), 476–96.

30 See also PI §§19, 23, 241; PI II §§i, xi; and Ludwig Wittgenstein, *On Certainty*, translated by Denis Paul and G.E.M. Anscombe (New York: Harper Torchbooks, 1972), §358.

(PR §115), rules that govern what is to count as a legitimate move in a game of representation or description.

I think that this will become clearer in Chapter 6, when we turn to Wittgenstein's reflections about norms of representation in *On Certainty*. I shall also have more to say in Chapters 5 and 6 about conventions and our deep need for them. It is further interesting to wonder why Wittgenstein never returns to any extended discussion of ethics in his later work, given the tight connection between ethics and logic and mathematics in his earlier work. If meaning does not rest on some transcendent ground of value, then it seems that neither should moral value. I shall return to this problem in Chapter 7.

3.6 THE SYNOPSIS OF TRIVIALITIES

With the loss of the transcendental comes a loss of the proper task of philosophy, as envisioned by "the author of the *Tractatus Logico-Philosophicus*" (PI §23), as Wittgenstein was later to refer critically to himself—the task of keeping the transcendental safe from being turned into the object of some science and the task of showing what cannot be said by means of "elucidations." However, Wittgenstein's reaction to this relocation of value and normativity within the world—what some might call its *naturalization*—was neither that of the Vienna Circle nor that of Quine. Philosophy was still neither an under-labourer of science nor continuous with the natural sciences. This is made quite clear in his notebooks of the time. Consider part of a draft from 1930 for a Foreword to the *Philosophical Remarks*:

> Our civilization is characterized by the word progress. Progress is its form, it is not one of its properties that it makes progress. *Typically* it constructs. Its *activity* is to construct a more and more complicated structure. And even clarity is only a means to this end & not an end in itself.
>
> For me on the contrary clarity, transparency, is an end in itself.
>
> I am not interested in erecting a building but in having the foundations of possible buildings transparently before me.
>
> So I am aiming at something different than are the scientists & my thoughts move differently than do theirs. (CV 9)[31]

31 Ludwig Wittgenstein, *Culture and Value: A Selection from the Posthumous Remains*, rev. 2nd ed., edited by Georg Henrik von Wright, Heikki Nyman, and Alois Pichler, translated by Peter Winch (Oxford: Blackwell, 1998).

The logical positivists may have considered Wittgenstein one of the "Leading representatives of the scientific world-conception,"[32] but the opinion was clearly not one that he shared. If philosophy is not to be scientific, however, what is it to be?

In 1930, new doctorate in hand, Wittgenstein began lecturing at Cambridge on—what else?—"Philosophy," and those lectures reveal the beginnings of a shift in his conception of philosophy that corresponds to the beginnings of his shift away from the transcendental toward the conventional. The senseless tautologies of the *Tractatus* are no longer so much in evidence, but something similar remains a preoccupation of philosophy—*trivialities*:

> What we find out in philosophy is trivial; it does not teach new facts, only science does that. But the proper synopsis of these trivialities is enormously difficult, and it has immense importance. Philosophy is in fact the synopsis of trivialities. (WLC I 26)

It may seem paradoxical that trivialities should be important—though from the point of view of consistency it looks like an improvement on the conviction that everything of transcendent importance is nonsense. And remember that logic, which produces nothing but tautologies, was in the *Tractatus* the transcendental ground of the possibility of meaning. In what follows, my suggestion will be that the trivialities of interest in philosophy are none other than the contingent conventions that make particular meanings possible in a given language.

3.7 TIDYING UP

The idea of the preceding section that philosophy is concerned with giving a *synopsis* of various trivialities—things that we already know—is of central importance for Wittgenstein. It is one that he returns to frequently, at first comparing the task of giving a synopsis to tidying a room:

> In philosophy we are not laying foundations but tidying up a room, in the process of which we have to touch everything a dozen times.
>
> The only way to do philosophy is to do everything twice. (WLC I 24)

32 Hans Hahn, Otto Neurath, and Rudolf Carnap, "The Scientific Conception of the World: The Vienna Circle," translated by P. Foulkes and M. Neurath, in *Otto Neurath: Empiricism and Sociology*, edited by M. Neurath and R.S. Cohen (Dordrecht: D. Reidel, 1973), 318.

and

> Philosophy tidies a room and so has to handle things many times. The essence of its procedure is that it starts with a mess; we don't mind being hazy so long as the haze gradually clears. (WLC I 42)

The room that I tidy is one that I know, one that I live in perhaps. So it is familiar to me, as are its contents, but until I have tidied it, I am more likely to misplace things, and in the process of trying to find them, I run the risk of being distracted by something else that I have unexpectedly found. Rummaging through a shoebox in search of a photograph that I have misplaced, I discover an old love-letter and forget all about my original quest. The remedy is to try to put things into some sort of surveyable order, and that may mean moving and re-moving the same object several times until I am satisfied that it is where it belongs—old love-letters here, old photographs there.

So the philosopher's job of giving a synopsis of trivialities consists in putting things in order, but what things exactly? Concepts? Certainly when Wittgenstein talks about "having the foundations of possible buildings transparently before me" (CV 9), he seems to have conceptual questions in mind. But this answer would suggest that our concepts themselves are somehow out of order, whereas Wittgenstein thinks that the disorder is not in our concepts but in ourselves:

> Work on philosophy—like work in architecture in many respects—is really more work on oneself. On one's own conception. On how one sees things. (And what one expects of them.) (CV 24; *cf.* BT 300)[33]

It is not so much our concepts that are out of order as our spontaneous description of those concepts and their inter-relations. So much is suggested by the fact that the image of organizing a room reappears in Wittgenstein's later work, with a related purpose but a slightly altered significance.

> If I have learned to carry out a particular activity in a particular room (putting the room in order, say) and am master of this technique, it does not follow that I must be ready to describe the arrangement of the room;

33 *Cf.* Ludwig Wittgenstein, *The Big Typescript TS 213*, edited and translated by C. Grant Luckhardt and Maximilian A.E. Aue (Oxford: Blackwell, 2005). When Wittgenstein was overseeing the construction of the house he had designed for his sister Margarete, his demanding expectations were a continual source of distress to the builders. See Monk 237.

> even if I should at once notice, and could also describe, any alteration in it. (Z §119)[34]

Being familiar with a place does not always entail being able to describe it accurately or clearly, being able to say what lies where. Putting the room in order may help, but only because it helps me to put my *description* of the room in order. If I want to find something, it does not matter whether everything *looks* tidy or not, so long as I know where everything *is*.

It seems, then, that what "we know already" (WLC I 35)[35] when we sit down to practice philosophy is our concepts, but that point itself can be put more clearly. In philosophy we are aiming for a synoptic view or a "perspicuous representation" (PI §122) of our concepts, and because we are animals who *speak*, we must aim at a synoptic view of our uses of words. Insofar as I can use a word or an expression, its use is familiar to me—it is something that I already know, and no new facts are presented when someone describes my use clearly. Indeed, the description of use may seem trivial. When I learn to speak a language I become "master of a technique" (PI §199), but as we saw earlier, I can be "master of this technique" (Z §119), without thereby being able to describe clearly what it is I can do. I do not need to be able to describe clearly the features of a room in order to be able to tidy that room. I do not need to be able to describe clearly the use of a word in order to be able to use that word. My grasp of the conventions governing its use can be largely implicit. However, precisely because my grasp of conventions of use may be implicit, I am vulnerable to a special kind of confusion—philosophical confusion—which can be overcome only by attaining a synoptic view of my linguistic practice. What is that confusion like?

34 Ludwig Wittgenstein, *Zettel*, 2nd ed., edited by G.E.M. Anscombe and G.H. von Wright, translated by G.E.M. Anscombe (Oxford: Basil Blackwell, 1981).

35 "In philosophy we know already all that we want to know; philosophical analysis does not give us any new facts. It is not the results of science which are of interest to philosophy but its methods" (WLC I 35).

3.8 LOST IN THE CITY

The shift from organization to description is reflected in another spatial metaphor that Wittgenstein comes to adopt by the time of the *Philosophical Investigations.* There the task has expanded beyond tidying a room to mapping a geographical area or, at least, getting the lay of the land:

> [T]he very nature of the investigation ... compels us to travel over a wide field of thought criss-cross in every direction. The philosophical remarks in this book are, as it were, a number of sketches of landscapes which were made in the course of these long and involved journeyings. (PI ix)

What matters here is approaching the same points "afresh from different directions" in order to get "a picture of the landscape" (PI ix). That landscape, the landscape of our "conceptual relationships" (CV 90), is the landscape of our language:[36]

> Our language can be seen as an ancient city: a maze of little streets and squares, of old and new houses, and of houses with additions from various periods; and this surrounded by a multitude of new boroughs with straight regular streets and uniform houses. (PI §18)

Why do we need sketches of this landscape (or cityscape)? The answer, still at a metaphorical level, is that we tend to get lost in the city—*that* is philosophical confusion. "Language is a labyrinth of paths. You approach from *one* side and know your way about; you approach the same place from another side and no longer know your way about" (§203). And "A philosophical problem," Wittgenstein tells us, "has the form: 'I don't know my way about'" (§123).

But what exactly does it mean to say that we can get lost in the labyrinth of language? Why and how is that a problem? And how does a synopsis of things that we already know help us to find our way out? In a sense, clear answers to these questions can be given only by looking at particular examples of philosophical problems and Wittgenstein's recommendations for dealing with them—a task

36 Compare "I am showing my pupils sections of an immense landscape, which they cannot possibly find their way around" (CV 64), and "To piece together the landscape of these conceptual relationships out of their individual fragments is too difficult for me. I can make only a very imperfect job of it" (CV 90).

I take up in the remaining chapters of this book. But a simple example of what Wittgenstein has in mind may help for the moment.

In *The Blue Book*, a collection of notes that Wittgenstein dictated to his students in 1933–34 and which foreshadows many of the themes of the *Philosophical Investigations*, Wittgenstein has us consider the imaginary case of a language in which,

> instead of "I found nobody in the room", one said "I found Mr. Nobody in the room". Imagine the philosophical problems which would arise out of such a convention. Some philosophers brought up in this language would probably feel that they didn't like the similarity of the expressions "Mr. Nobody" and "Mr. Smith". (BB 69)

Why worry about such a linguistic convention? Perhaps someone who spoke such a language would be tempted to suppose that there was a *deep* similarity between "Mr. Nobody" and "Mr. Smith"—that the similarity in their grammatical form indicated a deep similarity in their meanings, so that there really must be a Mr. Nobody, just as there is a Mr. Smith. Of course, it would quickly be pointed out that this alleged Mr. Nobody lacked the important attribute of being observable or of occupying a definite spatio-temporal location. "Where exactly in the room was Mr. Nobody?"—"Everywhere. Everywhere. Or, nowhere." But he might be thought to exist in some other way—much as some philosophers and mathematicians have maintained that numbers have real existence, even though they are not observable and seem to lack spatial location.

Here the trouble is that two different uses of language get confused with each other because of a certain superficial similarity. Believers in Mr. Nobody are misled by "certain analogies between the forms of expression in different regions of language" (PI §90). Eagerly exploring the city of language, they wander from one linguistic context to another without realizing it, leaving the busy shopping district for a quiet residential area. Such people would benefit from some "reminders" (PI §127) about where they are going, and the best way for them to avoid getting lost would be to consult a map that might let them "get a synoptic view [*leicht zu übersehen*]" (Z §113) of their location, allowing them to see where they stand now in relation to where they have been.

It should be stressed that this is just one example and that not all cases of philosophical confusion follow precisely this model, and so making confusion manifest will require different techniques in different cases. "There is not *a* philosophical method, though there are indeed methods, like different therapies" (PI §133).

Nonetheless, the situation of the Mr-Nobody-theorists is like our own situation, for we, too, find ourselves falling into confusion when we fail to take a synoptic view of our own language[37]—when we fail to remind ourselves explicitly of what we already know implicitly:

> We keep hearing the remark that philosophy really does not progress, that we are still occupied with the same philosophical problems as were the Greeks. Those who say this however don't understand why it is so. It is because our language has remained the same & keeps seducing us into asking the same questions. As long as there is still a verb 'to be' that looks as though it functions in the same way as 'to eat' and 'to drink', as long as we still have the adjectives 'identical', 'true', 'false', 'possible', as long as we continue to talk of a river of time & an expanse of space, etc., etc., people will keep stumbling over the same cryptic difficulties & staring at something that no explanation seems capable of clearing up. (CV 22; *cf.* BT 312)

> Language sets everyone the same traps; it is an immense network of well kept wrong turnings. And hence we see one person after another walking down the same paths & we know in advance the point at which they will branch off, at which they will walk straight on without noticing the turning, etc., etc. So what I should do is erect signposts at all the junctions where there are wrong turnings, to help people past the danger points. (CV 25; *cf.* BT 312)

3.9 AGAINST EXPLANATION

When we lack a synopsis of trivialities with which we are already acquainted—when we find no "signposts at all the junctions where there are wrong turnings"—we are vulnerable to philosophical puzzlement because, in part, we cannot recognize when we have left one context of application for another, or when we are mistaking superficial similarities for deep affinities—being misled by "a verb 'to be' that looks as if it functions in the same way as 'to eat' and 'to drink'" (CV 22; *cf.* BT 312), for example. But there is a further point here that is of considerable

37 *Whose* language is in question here? European languages for certain are the focus of Wittgenstein's interest. A language that differed quite substantially from English might avoid some of the problems that anglophone philosophers have been obsessed with, but it might be beset by other problems instead.

importance to an understanding of Wittgenstein's mature conception of philosophy and its problems.

When we lack a perspicuous representation of some part of the conceptual terrain that lies before us, we are tempted to draw an analogy with scientific investigation. "Philosophers constantly see the method of science before their eyes, and are irresistibly tempted to ask and answer questions in the way science does" (BB 18). We think that there is something hidden beneath the manifest phenomena, and we adopt the stance that is familiar to us from other contexts in which what is manifest is rendered explicable by what is hidden: we formulate explanatory hypotheses that can be tested against the empirical data in some way. But "This tendency," Wittgenstein warns, "is the real source of metaphysics, and leads the philosopher into complete darkness" (BB 18).

The problem gets started because, as we have seen, I can be "master of [a] technique" (Z §119/RPP II §331), without thereby being able to describe clearly what it is I can do. In particular, I do not need to be able to describe clearly the use of a word in order to be able to use that word. Wittgenstein offers a clear example in *Zettel*:

> One learns the word "think", i.e. its use, under certain circumstances, which, however, one does not learn to describe.
>
> But I can teach a person the use of the word! For a description of those circumstances is not needed for that.
>
> I just teach him the word under particular circumstances. (Z §§114–16)

We can usually recognize when the sorts of circumstances under which we learn to use the word 'think' obtain, but we may be unable to describe them very well. And if we consider the question, "What is thinking?," we find it hard to answer, because our ordinary ability to use 'think' and its cognate terms does not prepare us for such a question. It seems as though there is some mystery here, and so we think of other mysteries: Why do giraffes have such long necks? Why does water freeze when it is cooled? Why don't we fly off the surface of the Earth as it revolves on its axis? "We feel as if we had to *penetrate* phenomena ..." (PI §90). We try to *explain* our mystery by discovering hidden causes. We go in search of some *essence* that is not manifest and open to view. This analogy with natural scientific thinking, however, merely deepens our puzzlement, according to Wittgenstein: we cannot determine what the essence of thought is, for we have mistaken the nature of the investigation that we need to carry out. "[O]ur investigation... is directed not towards phenomena, but, as one might say, towards the '*possibilities*' of phenomena" (PI §90), he says, replaying a theme from section 3.7 above, and it is "therefore a grammatical one" (PI §90). That is, it is an attempt to make explicit to us what we already know—the rules and conventions that govern our linguistic practices. Accordingly, "The concept of a perspicuous representation [*übersichtliche Darstellung*]," Wittgenstein observes, "is of fundamental significance for us" (PI §122).

3.10 ILLUSION, WEAKNESS, ILLNESS, THERAPY

Let me summarize what we have managed to tease out of Wittgenstein so far. In order to deal with philosophical problems we need to command a clear overview of how our words are used, and we accomplish this by rearranging the ordinary expressions of our language, which have been put in a state of disarray by philosophical questions. This provides us with a synoptic view of our language, which is what is supposed to free us from philosophical puzzlement. Such an investigation can be called a "grammatical" one (PI §90), because we need to examine our customary forms of expression, the conventions that govern our use of words, which are familiar to us but which we grasp implicitly without necessarily being skilled in describing them. And it plainly differs in its character from a scientific investigation, since science tries to uncover the hidden essence that underlies the phenomenon and connects it with other phenomena of the same kind. In philosophy "nothing is hidden" (PG 104; PI §435).

We also encountered earlier the contention that "Work on philosophy... is really more work on oneself" (CV 24; *cf.* BT 300), and this is a theme that repays further examination. If philosophical work is work on oneself, "On one's own conception. On how one sees things. (And what one expects of them.)" (CV 24; *cf.* BT 300), that is because we are *vulnerable* to certain kinds of "misunderstanding" (PI §93) and "illusions" (PI §96). Those misunderstandings may be produced by systematically misleading features of our language, but if it were not for some inadequacy in *us*, those features could not *be* misleading for us. At times in his early lectures he compares this inadequacy to immaturity:

> We start with a vague mental uneasiness, like that of a child asking "Why?". The child's question is not that of a mature person; it expresses puzzlement rather than a request for precise information. So philosophers ask "Why?" and "What?" without knowing clearly what their questions are. They are expressing a feeling of mental uneasiness. (WLC I, 22; see BB 25)

And in his notebooks from 1931 he writes:

> Philosophers are often like little children who first scribble some marks on a piece of paper at random and now ask the grown-up "what's that?"—It happened like this: The grown-up had often drawn something for the child & said: "this is a man", "this is a house" etc. And now the child makes some marks too and asks: and what's this then?" (CV 24; *cf.* BT 315)

The problem with the child's question here, I take it, is that it confuses the conventional nature of representation with the intrinsic properties of the thing used to represent, as though any line or mark is automatically a representation of something. The child is misled by a superficial analogy and falls into confusion. By extension, we might guess that it is the philosopher's habit to mistake uses of language that are contingent matters of convention, for timeless properties that inhere in the world itself—or, indeed, which lie beyond the world as grounds of possibility for things in the world.

The sort of weakness that Wittgenstein has in mind here is a kind of weakness of will, an inability to resist the urge to use a certain kind of expression to draw certain kinds of analogies when giving a spontaneous description of linguistic practice. (Remember Mr. Nobody.) Here is a remark from 1931:

> What makes the object hard to understand—if it's significant, important—is not that you have to be instructed in abstruse matters in order to understand it, but the antithesis between understanding the object & what most people want to see. Because of this precisely what is most obvious may be what is most difficult to understand. It is not a difficulty for the intellect but one for the will that has to be overcome. (CV 25; *cf.* BT 300)

If philosophical problems are the result of a kind of flaw or weakness or vulnerability to temptation, this might seem to suggest that such problems are to be dealt with, not by *answering* the questions that they raise, but by *ridding* ourselves of the temptation to ask such questions. And this is just the sort of thing that is supposed to happen when we come up with a perspicuous representation: "For the clarity that we are aiming at is indeed *complete* clarity. But this simply means that the philosophical problems should *completely* disappear" (PI §133). "My aim," he writes, is "to teach you to pass from a piece of disguised nonsense to something that is patent nonsense" (PI §464). The task of the philosopher is not to *solve* problems but to *dissolve* them—to make them disappear and cease to bother us. Philosophy should aim at being *therapeutic*. "The philosopher's treatment of a question is like the treatment of an illness" (PI §255), he tells us. "There is not *a* philosophical method, though there are indeed methods, like different therapies" (PI §133).

So we have a new metaphor, one that largely supplants the metaphor of immaturity in Wittgenstein's later writings. At times the sort of illness in question seems to be analogous to something physiological, like scurvy or arterial sclerosis, which may be caused by eating poorly: "A main cause of philosophical disease—a one-sided diet: one nourishes one's thinking with only one kind of example" (PI §593). But the more suggestive comparison, of course, is to various psychological disorders—ones, at any rate, that do not (at least yet) have any clear physiological explanation. That weakness of the will that characterizes philosophical puzzlement involves a kind of compulsive behaviour on our part, which stands in need of therapy: "What we 'are tempted to say' ... is, of course, not philosophy; but it is its raw material. Thus, for example, what a mathematician is inclined to say about the objectivity and reality of mathematical facts, is not a philosophy of mathematics, but something for philosophical *treatment*" (PI §254).

Rush Rhees reports that around the time of World War II Wittgenstein often referred to himself as a "disciple of Freud."[38] The appropriate point of comparison here is not with Freud's theoretical apparatus—the Oedipus complex and the unconscious mind and so on—but with Freud's therapeutic technique, and one way we could understand that technique is as providing the patient with a liberating redescription of herself. Important here is the fact that it is not enough for the psychoanalyst to just *give* the patient a new description; rather, the description must be one that the patient comes gradually to see as making sense of her own behaviour. The patient has to acknowledge the re-description as "correct" in some way.

Similar considerations must hold for Wittgenstein's technique. The reader or the student of Wittgenstein must come to acknowledge a certain picture of her thinking as a correct one, and must not simply be cowed into accepting it by the authority of the author. "For only if he acknowledges it as such, *is* it the correct expression" (BT 303).[39] Ultimately it is up to the individual thinker to resolve her own philosophical "complexes," and an incomplete therapeutic analysis is no better than no analysis alone. What is the standard of completeness here? "The real discovery is the one that makes me capable of stopping doing philosophy when I want to.—The one that gives philosophy peace, so that it is no longer tormented by questions which bring *itself* into question" (PI §133).

38 Ludwig Wittgenstein, *Lectures and Conversations on Aesthetics, Psychology and Religious Belief*, edited by Cyril Barrett (Berkeley: University of California Press, 1967), 41.

39 Compare: "I must be nothing more than the mirror in which my reader sees his own thinking with all its deformities & with this assistance can set it in order" (CV 25).

3.11 FAREWELL TO PHILOSOPHY?

Just what does Wittgenstein have in mind when he writes of "stopping doing philosophy when I want to"? The therapeutic and descriptive spirit of Wittgenstein's meta-philosophy has provoked considerable hostility amongst critics of varying stripes. Some have thought that Wittgenstein is recommending that we just give up philosophy and concern ourselves with other pursuits.[40] Others have complained that Wittgenstein is naively privileging "ordinary language," as though it were somehow immune to philosophical confusion,[41] or as though philosophical language itself were not in an important sense "ordinary." Still others have dismissed Wittgenstein's injunction to refrain from giving explanations in philosophy as a species of "quietism" or, worse, as reflecting an ill-considered pessimism about philosophical problems, treating them as though they were mysteries that are too hard for us to sort out.[42] Moreover, it seems to such critics that Wittgenstein regularly violates his own strictures against giving explanations.[43] Wittgenstein's "quietism" and descriptivism have also been interpreted by some as an inherently conservative attempt to discourage critique of linguistic expressions that play the ideological role of misrepresenting the oppressive advantage of the powerful as though it were somehow necessary, inevitable, or just.[44]

Although these criticisms are all understandable in light of various bits of textual evidence and deserve reasoned responses, I believe that none of them stands up to closer scrutiny of Wittgenstein's remarks on philosophical method. However, that case is better made, I think, after an examination of how Wittgenstein's method is put into practice. It is to that task that I shall turn next, saving my responses until Chapter 7.

---

40 See, e.g., Jürgen Habermas, "Philosophy as Stand-in and Interpreter," translated by C. Lenhardt in *After Philosophy: End or Transformation?* edited by Kenneth Baynes, James Bohman, and Thomas McCarthy (Cambridge, MA: MIT Press, 1987), 296–315 and Bertrand Russell, *My Philosophical Development* (London: Unwin, 1959), 214, 216–17.

41 See, e.g., Terry Eagleton, "Wittgenstein's Friends," *New Left Review* I, no.135 (September-October 1982): 64–90, especially 72–73, and Russell (1959), 214.

42 See, e.g., Crispin Wright, *Truth and Objectivity* (Cambridge, MA: Harvard University Press, 1992), 202–30.

43 See, e.g., Ernest Gellner, *Words and Things: A Critical Account of Linguistic Philosophy and a Study in Ideology* (London: Victor Gollancz, 1959), Chapter III.

44 See, e.g., Herbert Marcuse, *One-Dimensional Man* (Boston: Beacon Press, 1964), 170–78, and, more subtle by far, Eagleton, "Wittgenstein's Friends." Wittgenstein has also been enthusiastically embraced by some conservatives. See, e.g., J.C. Nyíri, "Wittgenstein's Later Work in Relation to Conservatism" in *Wittgenstein and His Times*, edited by Brian McGuinness (Oxford: Blackwell, 1982), 44–68.

4

LANGUAGE WITHOUT ESSENCE

Wittgenstein's description of his philosophical method in the Preface to the *Philosophical Investigations* could also serve as a description of his literary style:

> The same or almost the same points were always being approached afresh from different directions, and new sketches made. Very many of these were badly drawn or uncharacteristic, marked by all the defects of a weak draughtsman. And when they were rejected a number of tolerable ones were left, which now had to be arranged and sometimes cut down, so that if you looked at them you could get a picture of the landscape. Thus this book is really only an album. (PI ix)[1]

There is less metaphor in these remarks than there may at first seem, for Wittgenstein's preferred method of composition was to write down individual remarks, have them typed up, and then with a pair of scissors cut the pages into strips, each containing a single remark. The various pieces would then be arranged into different orders until he was pleased with the result, after which the whole

1 Ludwig Wittgenstein, *Philosophical Investigations*, 2nd ed., translated by G.E.M. Anscombe (Oxford: Basil Blackwell, 1968), viii.

collection would have to be re-typed in the new, preferred order.[2] This procedure, he says, "was connected with the very nature of the investigation. For this compels us to travel over a wide field of thought criss-cross in every direction" (PI viii).

Wittgenstein's attempts to view the terrain from different angles are also represented in his practice of not speaking with a unified voice. He does not present his views in the form of a philosophical essay. He does not advance a thesis, present arguments in its favour, and then respond to likely objections. Sometimes he seems to speak plainly in his own voice, as when he introduces the idea of "language-games" (PI §7). At other times he seems to stage debates, expressing what he is "tempted to say"—things that constitute the "raw material" (PI §254) of philosophy—and then responding critically to the consequences of yielding to such temptation. It can be tempting to identify Wittgenstein's views with those of one of the characters in these debates. But work in philosophy is work on oneself, as we saw in Chapter 3, and each exchange is better thought of as presenting us with another sketch for the album, as part of another attempt to make explicit where our philosophical temptations lead us, where the "wrong turnings" (CV 25; *cf.* BT 312)[3] of thought lie in relation to the rest of the landscape of our language. (I return to these considerations at the end of this chapter.)

The *Philosophical Investigations* falls into two parts, the first of which, according to the editors, was completed by 1945 and the second of which comprises material from 1946 to 1949. Many of the "sketches" in this album, however, date from much earlier, some of them having made an appearance in Wittgenstein's transitional *Philosophical Grammar*. (Indeed, much of what Wittgenstein wrote during World War II—nearly half of which he spent working as a hospital porter and laboratory assistant, instead of teaching—was on the philosophy of mathematics, which, in the end, gets very little attention in the *Investigations.*) Most of my discussion in this chapter and the next focuses on remarks from Part I, with occasional reference to material from Part II where I think it casts light on key passages in Part I. I do not aim to provide a comprehensive reading of all that is said in Part I. Rather, my intention is to try to illustrate the application of the methodological remarks that

2 After Wittgenstein's death from prostate cancer in 1951, his literary executors discovered a box containing numerous such strips of remarks that had not been placed in any particular order. They arranged them in a plausible order and published the resulting text as *Zettel*. See the Editors' Preface to Ludwig Wittgenstein, *Zettel*, 2nd ed., edited by G.E.M. Anscombe and G.H. von Wright, translated by G.E.M. Anscombe (Oxford: Basil Blackwell, 1981), iii-iv.

3 Ludwig Wittgenstein, *Culture and Value: A Selection from the Posthumous Remains*, rev. 2nd ed., edited by Georg Henrik von Wright, Heikki Nyman, and Alois Pichler, translated by Peter Winch (Oxford: Blackwell, 1998); Ludwig Wittgenstein, *The Big Typescript TS 213*, edited and translated by C. Grant Luckhardt and Maximilian A.E. Aue (Oxford: Blackwell, 2005).

we encountered in Chapter 3 to a number of important, inter-related problems that Wittgenstein takes up in Part I—in particular, naming, family resemblances, rule-following, and sensation language. Each of these is importantly connected with Wittgenstein's rejection of the idea that language has a hidden essence that can or should be probed by an inquiry that models itself on natural science. Each of these, therefore, is importantly connected with Wittgenstein's contention that the task of philosophy consists in reminding ourselves of what we already know—of making explicit the implicit conventions that constitute the meanings of our words. I begin, however, with some further methodological remarks.

4.1 LANGUAGE-GAMES

I claimed in the preceding chapter that Wittgenstein's new philosophical goal, beginning in the early 1930s, is to help us attain a synoptic overview of those parts of our language that lead us into philosophical puzzlement. In the *Investigations* Wittgenstein proposes that this difficult task may be rendered more manageable by first considering simpler applications of language which he refers to as "language-games" (PI §7):

> It disperses the fog to study the phenomena of language in primitive kinds of application in which one can command a clear view of the aim and functioning of words. (PI §5)

In such "primitive" cases, we are released from the worry that we shall, for example, be misled "by certain analogies between the forms of expression in different regions of language" (PI §90) because we attend to a clearly delineated context in which the conventions governing the uses of words are made explicit to us. We encounter such a language-game in the opening section of the *Investigations*:

> I send someone shopping. I give him a slip marked "five red apples". He takes the slip to the shopkeeper, who opens the drawer marked "apples"; then he looks up the word "red" in a table and finds a colour sample opposite it; then he says the series of cardinal numbers—I assume that he knows them by heart—up to the word "five" and for each number he takes an apple of the same colour as the sample out of the drawer. (PI §1)

This transaction may seem artificial, precisely because the motions that the customer and the shopkeeper go through are laid out in explicit detail—counting out loud, consulting a table of colour-samples, and so on—things we normally do "in our heads." Their behaviour is like that of someone who has not yet internalized certain operations that we take for granted. It seems *childish*. But that fact highlights another aspect of language-games that Wittgenstein stresses: "A child uses such primitive forms of language when it learns to talk" (PI §5). It is just by having children engage in such games that we teach them to speak, a feature that is brought out vividly in the builders' language-game of §2:

> The language is meant to serve for communication between a builder A and an assistant B. A is building with building-stones: there are blocks, pillars, slabs and beams. B has to pass the stones, and that in the order in which A needs them. For this purpose they use a language consisting of the words "block", "pillar", "slab", "beam". A calls them out;—B brings the stone which he has learnt to bring at such-and-such a call.—Conceive this as a complete primitive language. (PI §2)

It takes little effort to imagine playing a game like this with a small child, using a set of building blocks.[4] I call for a slab, and the child brings me one. "Good!" I say. I call again, and she brings me a pillar, instead. "No," I say, "slab," and I point to a slab, repeating the word. I may go on to prompt her to repeat the words after I say them, pointing each time to an object of the appropriate kind (PI §7).[5]

"Here," as Wittgenstein proceeds to point out, "the teaching of language is not explanation, but training" (PI §5). I do not attempt to give distinctive descriptions of slabs and pillars that would allow an adult speaker to tell the one from the other if she somehow did not already know. This would be useless. Instead, I try to train the child to behave in a way that counts as an appropriate response to my request, and once she can do this, I count her as having mastered a particular, simple technique. Insofar as I look for her to make an *appropriate* response, this activity is a normative one, and insofar as she masters the technique, she acquires an implicit grasp of the norms for this language-game. But I do not trouble with explaining to her what kind of word 'slab' is, or how I am using it. In training her to respond in a certain way under certain circumstances, I acquaint her with one of the many tasks that language can be used to perform. I teach her practical employments for these words, not dictionary definitions of them, and not descriptions of the

4 Or imagine it performed as a sketch by puppets on *Sesame Street*.

5 I have cheated a bit by adding the words 'good' and 'no' to the example, but we could as easily imagine an incorrect response to my order being corrected by my simply repeating, "Slab," until the child gets it right.

circumstances of the language-game. Thus, Wittgenstein remarks, "I shall also call the whole, consisting of language and the actions into which it is woven, the 'language-game'" (PI §7). And later: "Here the term 'language-*game*' is meant to bring into prominence the fact that the *speaking* of language is part of an activity, or of a form of life" (PI §23).

It is, of course, the mastery of a linguistic technique "under certain circumstances, which, however, one does not learn to describe" (Z §114), that Wittgenstein identifies as a significant factor in the production of philosophical confusion. A description of a language-game seeks to avoid or alleviate such confusion by making the circumstances and norms explicit. In doing so, it also reveals how linguistic practices are woven into ways of acting.

But what kind of investigation is this?[6] Is it an empirical one? Is it some form of reflection on our intuitions about child learning-psychology? If it is the former, why does it not just reduce to child-psychology, and should that not be left to child-psychologists? If it is the latter, then why should we regard the results of the investigation as reliable? What is to prevent my intuitions about these cases from differing from yours, and how could we ever determine which of us is right?

In part, I think that Wittgenstein is asking us to reflect on our own experience with teaching others to speak or to employ certain concepts. If we do that, then we will notice that various sorts of language-games do have a role to play in language-instruction (and not just in the case of children—anyone who has studied a second language will be familiar with performing various drills and exercises). To this extent, there is an empirical element involved in the method of language-games.

However, Wittgenstein goes on to emphasize that he is not doing natural science, nor even natural history:[7]

> If the formation of concepts can be explained by facts of nature, should we not be interested, not in grammar, but rather in that in nature which is the basis of grammar?—Our interest certainly includes the correspondence between concepts and very general facts of nature. (Such facts as mostly do

---

6 Thanks to Sheldon Wein and Letitia Meynell for pressing me to be clearer about this.

7 Wittgenstein displays some ambivalence about this second point. For example at PI §415 he says, "What we are supplying are really remarks on the natural history of human beings; we are not contributing curiosities however, but observations which no one has doubted, but which have escaped remark only because they are always before our eyes" (PI §415). Similar remarks appear elsewhere in his writings. Perhaps we can reconcile these claims if we suppose that to the extent that he succeeds in uncovering our actual grammatical norms Wittgenstein takes himself to be doing natural history, but that the invention of language-games that serve as objects of comparison (see below) is not itself natural history.

> not strike us because of their generality.) But our interest does not fall back upon these possible causes of the formation of concepts; we are not doing natural science; nor yet natural history—since we can also invent fictitious natural history for our purposes. (PI II §xii)

The "very general facts of nature" that Wittgenstein mentions here came to our attention in Chapter 3 when we considered why Wittgenstein's tacit conventionalism does not entail that our norms are arbitrary, and they will be important again later in this chapter. But acknowledging that such facts place limitations on the kinds of norms that seem plausible to us does not amount to doing natural science. And we don't need to do natural history in the sense of investigating the actual origins of our concepts in order to get a clearer picture of what kinds of norms are actually at work in our linguistic practices. It is useful enough to be able to tell a story about how those concepts and practices—or ones very like them—could have come about. Language-games appear to be precisely such fictitious natural history in Wittgenstein's estimation:

> The language-games are ... set up as *objects of comparison* which are meant to throw light on the facts of our language by way not only of similarities, but also of dissimilarities. (PI §130)

In many respects our actual uses of words are far more complicated than simple language-games (although, as his discussion develops, it seems that Wittgenstein begins to refer to more and more complicated, *actual* linguistic practices as language-games), and it is important to bear such differences in mind, but to the extent that language-games seem familiar—to the extent that they remind us of our own practices—they help us to make explicit the implicit norms at work in our linguistic activities, and they remind us that those activities are often bound up with practical, non-linguistic activities. Moreover, the particular examples of language-games that Wittgenstein presents help us to recognize the *contingency* of many of our practices. They allow us to see those practices as rooted not in something that lies beyond the world in a realm of unspeakable necessity, but in something that lies in the world: our practical activity (which, in turn, is bounded in some ways by those "very general facts of nature" mentioned above).

4.2 LEARNING NAMES

Many of the first one hundred or so remarks of the *Investigations* read like a sustained assault on the doctrines of the *Tractatus*, culminating in a rejection of the twin ideas that logic is "something sublime" (PI §89) and that when it comes to language and thought "*The essence is hidden from us*" (PI §92). But if these are the grand theses to be rejected by a therapeutic philosophy, numerous corollaries must also fall by the wayside. One of these is the initially odd-sounding contention that all words are names. Quoting Augustine, Wittgenstein identifies the target of his criticism in the first section of the *Investigations*:

> These words [of Augustine], it seems to me, give us a particular picture of the essence of human language. It is this: the individual words in language name objects—sentences are combinations of such names.—In this picture of language we find the roots of the following idea: Every word has a meaning. This meaning is correlated with the word. It is the object for which the word stands. (PI §1)

Whether Augustine actually held such a view is unimportant to Wittgenstein's point,[8] for Wittgenstein himself held this view, or something very like it, in the *Tractatus*. Recall that in the early work a complete analysis of a proposition is supposed to culminate in a concatenation of logically proper names (TLP §4.22),[9] each of which is correlated with a simple object that is its meaning (TLP §3.203). And the configuration of names mirrors the configuration of objects in the state of affairs it presents (TLP §3.21).

What would it be like for language to be as Wittgenstein envisioned it in the *Tractatus*? The language-game of the builders, he suggests, is such a language (PI §2), for it contains nothing but names. However, the similarity is weaker than Wittgenstein initially suggests, for it is the essence of language and thought in the *Tractatus* to represent the states of affairs that—if they obtain, if they are facts—make up the world. And this representation is achieved by a correlation of simple names with primitive objects and a sharing of logical form between concatenations of each. No such representation of facts seems to be at work in the builders' language, whose primary purposes are practical, and whose meanings (to use a

8 Some critics have leapt to Augustine's defence. See, e.g., Patrick Beardsley, "Augustine and Wittgenstein on Language," *Philosophy* 58 (1983): 229–36.

9 Ludwig Wittgenstein, *Tractatus Logico-philosophicus*, translated by C.K. Ogden (London: Routledge & Kegan Paul, 1922).

word that Wittgenstein would warn us about) are bound up with those purposes and practices.

This introduces a theme of considerable importance: that naming is not just a simple relation between a word and an object (or a group of objects, since we are beginning with common names like 'slab' and 'pillar'), but a relation that can be identified—indeed, can obtain—only against a complex background of practical purposes and activities. It is not long before Wittgenstein comes to the point himself:

> Of course, one can reduce the description of the use of the word "slab" to the statement that this word signifies this object. This will be done when, for example, it is merely a matter of removing the mistaken idea that the word "slab" refers to the shape of building-stone that we in fact call a "block"—but the kind of '*referring*' this is, that is to say the use of these words for the rest, is already known. (PI §10)

Sure enough, 'slab' refers to slabs (objects of *this* kind, not *that*), but this is informative only in the context in which it is already clear what kind of word 'slab' is and what kinds of object we are interested in distinguishing—what their practical use is, for example. "When we say: 'Every word in language signifies something' we have so far said *nothing whatever*; unless we have explained exactly *what* distinction we wish to make" (PI §13).

The sorts of distinctions that Wittgenstein has in mind here include, of course, the distinction between the functions of slabs and pillars, but philosophical difficulties arise from more profound confusions, which threaten to make a showing when we consider extending the language-game of the builders with new vocabulary. Suppose we add the letters of the alphabet to serve as numerals, the words 'this' and 'there' to be used when pointing, and a set of colour samples:

> A gives an order like: "d—slab—there". At the same time he shews the assistant a colour sample, and when he says "there" he points to a place on the building site. From the stock of slabs B takes one for each letter of the alphabet up to "d", of the same colour as the sample, and brings them to the place indicated by A.—On other occasions A gives the order "this—there". At "this" he points to a building stone. And so on. (PI §8)

When we think of numerals in our language as names for numbers—and they do play this grammatical role—we are tempted to think that they must be the names of objects, just as 'slab' and 'pillar' are in this simpler language-game. But the letters used for numbers in this language-game function primarily as adjectives, and so modify the nature of the commands or requests that the builders give to each other, *just as* the display of a colour sample does, which is not plausibly thought of as the name of anything.

There is, to be sure, a further similarity between 'slab' etc. and 'a', 'b', 'c', etc. That is that "ostensive teaching" (PI §6) has a role to play in a child's learning of these terms:

> When a child learns this language, it has to learn the series of 'numerals' a, b, c,... by heart. And it has to learn their use.—Will this training include ostensive teaching of the words?—Well, people will, for example, point to slabs and count: "a, b, c slabs".—Something more like the ostensive teaching of the words "block", "pillar", etc. would be the ostensive teaching of numerals that serve not to count but to refer to groups of objects that can be taken in at a glance. Children do learn the use of the first five or six cardinal numerals in this way. (PI §9)

Cognitive scientists refer to this ability of children to recognize numerical differences in small groups of objects as "subitizing," and some argue that the capacity is innate rather than learned.[10] Whichever is the case (assuming that there is even a defensible distinction between them), this role for ostension is of no comfort to the would-be Platonist, who thinks of numbers as transcendent "abstract objects," since what is pointed to here is not any such "object," but groups of sensible, concrete objects—blocks and slabs and the like—and the use of the letter-numerals, contrasted with the use of 'block' and the rest, shows that they are not the names of such groups of objects.

So it is true, Wittgenstein allows, "that naming something is like attaching a label to a thing" (PI §15), but until we know how the label is to be *used*, we have no real grasp of what it means. Consider, for example, how different it would be to attach the labels 'apple', 'red', and 'square' to, respectively, a red apple, a square of red cloth, and another square of red cloth. If we are inclined to think that all words are names because all words signify something, then this is the result of being impressed by a superficial similarity and forgetting or overlooking "that what makes these labels important is their use" (BB 69).[11] Attaching a label to a thing, as Wittgenstein later remarks, "is preparatory to the use of a word. But *what*

10 See, for example, George Lakoff and Rafael Núñez, *Where Mathematics Comes From: How the Embodied Mind Brings Mathematics into Being* (New York: Basic Books, 2000), 19–21.

11 Ludwig Wittgenstein, *The Blue and the Brown Books*, 2nd ed. (Oxford: Blackwell, 1969).

is it a preparation *for*?" (PI §26). That is the question that we need to focus on if we are to avoid conflating different conventions that are implicit in our linguistic practice, and it is that question that is effectively answered for the terms in the builders' language.

Of course, when *we* describe that language-game, we shall undoubtedly want to say at times that 'a' is the name of a number. There is nothing wrong with this, says Wittgenstein,

> when for example this removes the mistaken idea that "a", "b", "c", play the part actually played in language by "block", "slab", "pillar". And one can also say that "c" means this number and not that one; when for example this serves to explain that the letters are to be used in the order a, b, c, d, etc. and not in the order a, b, d, c.
>
> But assimilating the descriptions of the uses of words in this way cannot make the uses themselves any more like one another. For, as we see, they are absolutely unlike. (PI §10)

For example, nothing in the use of the letter-numerals in the builders' language-game licenses the conclusion that those numerals are the names of *objects*—the number 2 or the number 3. (As we shall see, this attempt to short-circuit the sort of debate that leads to Platonism in mathematics is extended in Wittgenstein's discussion of family-resemblances.)

I noted above that in the two versions of the builders' language-game teaching consists in *training*. Children learn the names of slabs and blocks by learning how to employ them in the course of practical activity, and this involves ostensive teaching. I point to a slab and say "slab" and have the child repeat "slab." But this ostensive teaching, it is worth emphasizing, does not amount to giving an "ostensive definition" (PI §6) of a term any more than the builders' game involves verbal explanations or definitions of terms. One gives an ostensive definition of a term when one points to a thing and says, "That is a slab" (for example), or "That is called a 'slab.'" Doing so, Wittgenstein insists, is a further language-game all on its own, together with "asking something's name" (PI §27). This is so because the ability to ask a thing's name or to appreciate the point of an ostensive definition *presupposes* the kind of training that is involved in learning the builders' language-game. "When one shews someone the king in chess and says: 'This is the king', this does not tell him the use of the piece—unless he already knows the rules of the game up to this last point: the shape of the king" (PI §31). Merely pointing at a slab and saying "slab" does not by itself explain or otherwise convey anything about the use of the word 'slab'. I could as easily be pointing to the colour of the slab or to the number of objects present in a group: "an ostensive definition can be variously interpreted in *every* case" (PI §28). What serves to disambiguate my pointing, to rule out the various other interpretations of my ostensive definition, is "the circumstances—...what happened before and after the pointing" (PI §35),[12] and those are the sorts of circumstances that a child becomes familiar with in the course of her earlier linguistic training—in the course, that is, of certain kinds of practical activity.

4.3 ANALYSIS AND BEARERLESS NAMES

This practical focus on the teaching and use of language also has consequences for the doctrine of analysis advanced in the *Tractatus*. That doctrine said that the meaning and logical form of sentences of natural language could be reached (*shown*, but not *said*) by breaking them down into elementary sentences consisting of simple names. Meaning, in short, was something hidden and standing in need of recovery or discovery by reaching the "one and only one complete analysis of the proposition" (TLP §3.25). In the *Investigations* Wittgenstein thinks that this doctrine projects a kind of bogus rigour onto our standards of clarity and understanding. He parodies it by attending to another simple linguistic exchange:

> Suppose that, instead of saying "Bring me the broom", you said "Bring me the broomstick and the brush which is fitted on to it."!—Isn't the answer: "Do you want the broom? Why do you put it so oddly?"—Is he going to understand the further analysed sentence better?—This sentence, one might say, achieves the same as the ordinary one, but in a more roundabout way. (PI §60)

At least part of the point here is that the "real" meaning of the expression uttered need not be something hidden from view. When I ask someone to bring me the broom, I say exactly what I mean. If confusion arises, then I may have to rephrase my request, but there is no automatic reason why that reformulation must break the original expression down into simpler parts. I may instead simply substitute one expression for another until I achieve the desired result. We could

12 The fact that ostension can be disambiguated in Wittgenstein's account shows that his point is very different from the one intended by Quine's notorious thesis of the inscrutability of reference, according to which the totality of a speaker's observable behaviour is insufficient to decide between rival hypotheses regarding the reference of her terms. See W.V. Quine, *Ontological Relativity and Other Essays* (New York: Columbia University Press, 1969), 26–68.

call that successful formulation an "analysis" (PI §90), if we wanted to, but there is no reason why it must be unique, for some other substituted expression might have done just as well. "The meaning of a word is what is explained by the explanation of the meaning" (PI §560), as Wittgenstein later says. That is, when I remove your confusion about what I have said by substituting some other expression, I have explained the meaning of what I said, and I have done so without recourse to elementary propositions.

Of course, there may be situations in which it is useful to break complex expressions into simpler ones—for example, when trying to reconstruct the logic of a philosophical argument. But 'simpler' here means 'clearer' or 'easier to understand' given the backgrounds of one's readers or audience, not 'intrinsically simpler because correspondent to the fundamental constituents of reality'. An audience of logicians may find a formal symbolization of an argument easier to understand, but an audience of literary theorists may find it opaque. Simplicity, Wittgenstein takes pains to point out, is not a property that can be assigned to a thing independently of a specific context and a specific set of interests that motivate questions about simplicity and complexity:

> We use the word "composite" (and therefore the word "simple") in an enormous number of different and differently related ways. (Is the colour of a square on a chessboard simple, or does it consist of pure white and pure yellow? And is white simple, or does it consist of the colours of the rainbow?—Is the length of 2 cm simple, or does it consist of two parts, each 1 cm long? But why not of one bit 3 cm long, and one bit 1 cm long measured in the opposite direction?) (PI §47)

Elementary names in the *Tractatus* were supposed to be absolutely simple, like the fundamental objects that they were supposed to name and which were supposed to be their meanings. Here, unexpectedly, we run into TLP §6.41 again—the doctrine that "The sense of the world must lie outside the world" in something "non-accidental." It is not just logic, but the simple objects themselves that must exist if there is to be any meaning at all and, indeed, any world at all—any contingent totality of possible states of affairs. Objects are the "substance of the world," and it is because of this that they must be simple (TLP §2.021), because for an object to be complex is for two simpler objects to stand in some *contingent* relation to each other.

But just as the transcendental and transcendent nature of logic led us into the paradox of not being able to say anything about logical form, the absolute simplicity of objects and their (transcendental) necessity leads us into another paradox, the paradox of bearerless names, which we encountered in Chapter 2. That problem, as we saw, was one familiar to Frege and Russell. If the meaning of a name is its bearer, then if the bearer ceases to exist—or worse, never existed at all—then the name must be meaningless. Yet we seem to be able to speak meaningfully of characters in fiction who do not exist and of the objects of failed scientific hypotheses (e.g., phlogiston, the planet Vulcan) that do not exist either. If the meaning of 'Vulcan' were the object Vulcan, then I could not even meaningfully deny the existence of Vulcan because I would have to say something like, "Vulcan does not exist." But if Vulcan does not exist, then 'Vulcan' is meaningless, and so is 'Vulcan does not exist'. The only way I can meaningfully deny the existence of Vulcan is if Vulcan exists, and then my denial is false. So it seems as though Vulcan *has* to exist—paradox! (Likewise, if it is true that God does not exist, then that should not prevent us from meaningfully saying, "God does not exist.")

Frege tried to solve this problem by arguing that in addition to their reference, names (and uniquely referring descriptions) also possessed a further semantic property called a "sense," so that lacking the one, they could still be meaningful by retaining the other. However, Frege thought that reference was still required if the sentences in which a name occurred were to be true or false,[13] so we are still left with the problem of how it can be true to assert that Vulcan does not exist. Wittgenstein, inspired by Russell's theory of descriptions, which we met in Chapter 2, took a different tack, which he describes in the *Investigations*:

> [I]f "Excalibur" is the name of an object, this object no longer exists when Excalibur is broken in pieces; and as no object would then correspond to the name it would have no meaning. But then the sentence "Excalibur has a sharp blade" would contain a word that had no meaning, and hence the sentence would be nonsense. But it does make sense; so there must always be something corresponding to the words of which it consists. So the word "Excalibur" must disappear when the sense is analysed and its place be taken by words which name simples. It will be reasonable to call these words the real names. (PI §39)

The real names, in turn, correspond to the simple objects. But, obviously, the very same paradox arises in connection with the simple objects. Their existence cannot

13 Gottlob Frege, "On Sense and Reference" in *Logicism and the Philosophy of Language: Selections from Frege and Russell*, edited by Arthur Sullivan (Peterborough, ON: Broadview Press, 2003), 175–92.

be denied unless they exist, and then the denial is false. So they *have* to exist. This, however, is exactly the result that Wittgenstein wanted.

Taken as a proof of the existence of simple objects, this may seem like sophistry, but how does one avoid it? Russell did not make recourse to objects, but he did want absolute simples of a sort in the form of his own (allegedly) raw, unconceptualized sense-data, and he thought that the real names were demonstrative pronouns like 'this' and 'that'. When I mentally point to something and say "this," Russell thought, I cannot fail. I always manage to pick out something, even if I am confused about exactly what I pick out.[14]

Remember that 'this' is one of the words that gets added to the builders' language-game at PI §8, and the description of that language-game tells us that 'this' is not used in the same way as names like 'block' and 'slab', nor in the same way as the letters used as numerals: "—On other occasions A gives the order 'this—there'. At 'this' he points to a building stone" (PI §8). 'This', Wittgenstein wants to insist, does not function as a name at all: "we call very different things 'names'; the word 'name' is used to characterize many different kinds of use of a word, related to one another in many different ways;—but the kind of use that 'this' has is not among them" (PI §38). We may well use 'this' to help give an ostensive definition of a name ("This is called Excalibur"), and perhaps this use is what tempts Russell to think of 'this' as a name, but we do not give ostensive definitions of 'this' itself, as we would if it functioned as a name (PI §38).

4.4 PROPER NAMES

So we are returned to our earlier question: how do we avoid the conclusion that simple objects must exist if we are to deal with the paradox of bearerless names in unanalyzed natural language? Wittgenstein has two replies.

First, "the word 'meaning' is being used illicitly if it is used to signify the thing that 'corresponds' to the word. That is to confound the meaning of a name with the *bearer* of the name" (PI §40). To say this, of course, is to reject the picture of naming that gives rise to the problem, and it seems natural to ask what alternative picture of naming Wittgenstein would offer in its place. Some have thought that Wittgenstein means to endorse a version of "cluster descriptivism," according to which what we ordinarily take to be proper names of natural language are

14 Bertrand Russell, "Descriptions" in Sullivan (2003), 279–87 at 286. See also Russell's "The Philosophy of Logical Atomism," Lecture II in *The Collected Papers of Bertrand Russell*, Vol. 8, edited by John G. Slater (London: George Allen & Unwin, 1983), 179.

really either shorthand expressions for disjunctive clusters of uniquely identifying descriptions or terms whose reference is determined by some such cluster. Both views can be seen as natural descendants of Russell's theory of descriptions, and, given Wittgenstein's early admiration for that theory, it is not so implausible to suppose that he might be attracted to some revised version of it (though, presumably, shorn of the further claim that in addition to clusters of descriptions, there are also "real" names). Indeed, later in the *Investigations* he offers an example that seems to clinch the case for this reading:

> If one says "Moses did not exist", this may mean various things. It may mean: the Israelites did not have a *single* leader when they withdrew from Egypt—or: their leader was not called Moses—or: there cannot have been anyone who accomplished all that the Bible relates of Moses—or: etc. etc.—We may say, following Russell: the name "Moses" can be defined by means of various descriptions. For example, as "the man who led the Israelites through the wilderness", "the man who lived at that time and place and was then called 'Moses'", "the man who as a child was taken out of the Nile by Pharaoh's daughter" and so on. And according as we assume one definition or another the proposition "Moses did not exist" acquires a different sense, and so does every other proposition about Moses. (PI §79)

The "cluster" descriptivism that I mentioned above suggests that we just disjoin all these descriptions of Moses and take the logical sum of them to be the meaning of 'Moses' (or, at least, to determine the reference of 'Moses'), possibly weighting some of the descriptions as more important than others.[15] Wittgenstein may seem to endorse the cluster view when he goes on to ask, "Is it not the case that I have, so to speak, a whole series of props in readiness, and am ready to lean on one if another should be taken from under me and vice versa?" (PI §79).

Saul Kripke has persuaded many philosophers that such a view must be false. If it were correct, then the claim that Moses was the man who led the Israelites through the wilderness (or at least one of the other disjunctive claims about Moses that makes up the cluster), if true at all, would have to be analytic, because it is just part of the meaning of 'Moses' that he was the man who led the Israelites through the wilderness. This consequence, however, seems implausible. Surely it is a contingent, synthetic fact about Moses, if it is true at all, that he led the Israelites. He might, after all, never have been retrieved from his basket in the Nile by the pharaoh's daughter, but floated downstream and drowned in the Mediterranean.

15 See John Searle, "Proper Names," *Mind* 67 (1958): 166–73.

The fact that we can speak intelligibly in this way about other possibilities for Moses shows that proper names must be "rigid designators"—devices that allow us to pick out one and the same individual as she, he, or it might have been, had some other possible state of affairs been actual.[16]

A philosophical point is worth making before considering the plausibility of interpreting Wittgenstein as holding a version of the cluster theory. It seems plain that we *can* use proper names in *either* the way that Kripke insists *or* in something like the way that the cluster theory predicts. If I say, "Moses did not exist," I may, indeed, mean that there was no single leader whom the Israelites followed out of Egypt. (Just ask me, and I'll tell you.)[17] It is not an impossible use of language. But I may, likewise, use 'Moses' as a rigid designator. So we are not faced with an all-or-nothing choice here.

This philosophical point is one that, I think, can be readily extracted from Wittgenstein. First, a closer examination of the example of Moses shows that Wittgenstein does not mean to reduce the role of a proper name to that of a disjunctive cluster of definite descriptions. His point, rather, is to emphasize the "many different kinds of use of a word, related to one another in many different ways" (PI §38) that are characterized by the word 'name'. "I use the name," he goes on to say, "without any *fixed* meaning. (But that detracts as little from its usefulness, as it detracts from that of a table that it stands on four legs instead of three and so sometimes wobbles.)" (PI §79). This observation is perfectly compatible with Kripke's contention that any particular definite description is inessential to the meaning or to the fixing of the reference of a proper name. As Kripke acknowledges (1980, 96), the reference of a proper name may well be fixed by employing a definite description. "Who was Moses?" I ask. "He was the man who led the Israelites out of Egypt," you respond. That description fixes the reference of 'Moses', but it could be used to do that, Kripke insists, even if it were false, unbeknownst to contemporary speakers. All the definite descriptions popularly associated with Moses might be false without undermining the reference of 'Moses' to Moses. But that detracts as little from its usefulness, as it detracts from that of a table that it stands on four legs instead of three and so sometimes wobbles.

16 See Saul Kripke, *Naming and Necessity* (Cambridge, MA: Harvard University Press, 1980).

17 Kripke would regard this as a conflation of speaker's meaning and semantic meaning—of pragmatics and semantics, but I think that Wittgenstein's view entails that no sharp distinction can be maintained between the two (which is not to say that there is no distinction at all).

4.5 MEANING AND USE

Secondly, when Wittgenstein offers his alternative to the claim that the meaning of a name is its bearer, he makes explicit what has been hinted at in his examples of various language-games—that word-meaning is explained by *use*:

> For a *large* class of cases—though not for all—in which we employ the word "meaning" it can be [explained][18] thus: the meaning of a word is its use in the language.
>
> And the *meaning* of a name is sometimes explained by pointing to its *bearer*. (PI §43)

Pointing to the bearer of a name helps to explain how that name is to be applied, but only in conjunction with a great deal of other learning. Remember: "the ostensive definition explains the use—the meaning—of the word when the overall role of the word in language is clear" (PI §30). Merely pointing does not distinguish the individual named from its shape, its colour, its number, etc., and, as we have seen, names for these multifarious things function in multifarious ways: "we call very different things 'names'; the word 'name' is used to characterize many different kinds of use of a word, related to one another in many different ways" (PI §38).

The difference between a common name and a proper name, which has crept into our considerations, involves yet further teaching to grasp. "Think in this connexion how singular is the use of a person's name to *call* him!" (PI §27). That we do use proper names as rigid designators in imagining what alternative possibilities might have befallen someone is a reminder that Wittgenstein should be happy to acknowledge as a contribution to making our linguistic conventions explicit.

It may seem as though the importance of use for meaning was already recognized in the *Tractatus*. Wittgenstein does say, after all, that "What does not get expressed in the sign is shown by its application. What the signs conceal, their application declares" (TLP §3.262). However, the application that Wittgenstein has in mind there is exhausted by an account of the logical relations between a given sentence and other sentences—by an account of its inferential role. Remember the importance of a proposition's situation in logical space for its meaning: "The logical scaffolding round the picture determines the logical space. The proposition reaches through the whole logical space" (TLP §3.42). By contrast, it is not only a proposition's relation to other propositions that matters in the *Investigations*, but also its relation to practical activities, to gestures and facial expressions, to

18 Anscombe here has 'defined', but the German '*erklären*' is better translated as 'explained'.

various props and samples that are also used in the activity (more on these below). And notice also that it is the meaning of a *word*, not of a sentence or proposition,[19] that is said to be explained by its use (PI §43).

4.6 FROM NECESSARY OBJECTS TO CONTINGENT CONVENTIONS

We were led innocently down this narrow, winding path by the observation that in order for meaning to be possible, absolutely simple objects must exist, because their non-existence can be meaningfully asserted only if it is falsely asserted. One reply, which we have just examined, said that the meaning of a name is not its bearer, but is explained by its use. Wittgenstein's second reply responds directly to the Tractarian view (TLP §6.41) that all value, including semantic value—i.e., meaning—presupposes something necessary that transcends the world. And his response is the one that I emphasized in Chapter 3: what looked as though it was grounded in something beyond the world is really the result of a contingent convention that is implicit in our linguistic practices. Here is how he formulates it:

> One would ... like to say: existence cannot be attributed to an element, for if it did not *exist*, one could not even name it and so one could say nothing at all of it.—But let us consider an analogous case. There is *one* thing of which one can say neither that it is one metre long, nor that it is not one metre long, and that is the standard metre in Paris.—But this is, of course, not to ascribe any extraordinary property to it, but only to mark its peculiar role in the language-game of measuring with a metre-rule. (PI §50)

Critics of this passage have thought that Wittgenstein is making an elementary blunder on grounds that 'The standard metre is a metre long' is clearly an *a priori* truth (Kripke 1980, 54) in virtue of being tautologous. But this is to miss the point. As early as 1915 in his preparatory notebooks for the *Tractatus* Wittgenstein expresses discomfort with the idea that tautologies should be thought of as having truth-values: "One cannot say of a tautology that it is true, for it is *made* so

19 For Wittgenstein a proposition is, roughly, a (declarative) sentence *in use*, not an "abstract object" that counts as the meaning of a sentence (as it was, with a few refinements, for Frege). As Wittgenstein's talk of giving ostensive definitions of numbers (PI §28) might hint, and as his discussion of family resemblances will confirm, Wittgenstein thinks that talk of "abstract objects" is largely otiose, a product of getting our language-games confused.

as to be *true*."[20] Tautologies are not pictures of reality, and, therefore, they are not assessable according to whether they present a picture of a fact or merely of some possible, but non-actual state of affairs. A later comment from 1939–40 is less categorical. He describes the tautology '$p \supset p$' as "a degenerate proposition which is on the side of truth" (RFM III §33).[21] Whether one thinks that tautologies are true or not, Wittgenstein is adamant that they play a role in our linguistic practices very different from the ones played by empirical propositions. That a given proposition expresses a tautology is the result of a contingent convention.

The same is true of 'The standard metre is a metre long'. It makes explicit a convention according to which the standard metre plays the role of that sample or paradigm against which the lengths of other things are measured and other length-measuring devices are calibrated. Since the standard metre cannot be used to calibrate *itself*, it cannot be measured in the system of metric measurement which takes it as the standard. "In this language-game it is not something that is represented, but is a means of representation" (PI §50). But, of course, that system of measurement is just one contingent set of conventions, so there is nothing preventing the standard metre from being measured in some other system—imperial units, for example, or subsequent, revised versions of the metric system in which the standard metre in Paris is replaced by a more stable physical standard. Nor is there anything preventing us from treating our favourite metre stick as a standard and using it to measure the "standard" metre, but it is important to see that in doing so we have changed standards.

Now, consider the analogous move in the case of names for simples. Wittgenstein has us consider another language-game (PI §48) in which we are to describe combinations of red, green, white, and black squares by use of the words 'R', 'G', 'W', and 'B'. A series of these words is a sentence describing the arrangement of squares in an order that proceeds from left to right, and from top to bottom. The coloured squares are simples, and the words are elementary names, modelled on the picture-theory of the *Tractatus*. Just as the standard metre is a means of representation, so too is a simple coloured square in this game:

> —And just this goes for an element in language-game (48) when we name it by uttering the word "R": this gives the object a role in our language-game; it is now a *means* of representation. And to say "If it did not *exist*, it could

20 Ludwig Wittgenstein, *Notebooks 1914–1916*, 2nd ed., edited by G.H. von Wright and G.E.M. Anscombe, translated by G.E.M. Anscombe (Chicago: University of Chicago Press, 1979), 55.

21 Ludwig Wittgenstein, *Remarks on the Foundations of Mathematics*, 3rd ed., edited by G.H. von Wright, R. Rhees, and G.E.M. Anscombe, translated by G.E.M. Anscombe (Oxford: Blackwell, 1978).

> have no name" is to say as much and as little as: if this thing did not exist, we could not use it in our language-game.—What looks as if it *had* to exist, is part of the language. It is a paradigm in our language-game; something with which comparison is made. And this may be an important observation; but it is none the less an observation concerning our language-game—our method of representation. (PI §50)

The apparent necessity that there be simple objects is an artifact of a certain contingent convention of representation. Likewise, the apparent necessity that the distance between two marks on a certain piece of metal in Paris (the standard metre) be exactly one metre long is an artifact of the role that this marked piece of metal plays in a very contingent linguistic practice—not the effect of something that lies outside the world as a transcendent, transcendental condition of metric measurement.

The idea that an *object*, functioning as a sample or paradigm—"something with which comparison is made" (PI §50)—might actually be "part of the language" (PI §50) is one that returns us yet again to the language-game of the builders, for remember that at PI §8 not only are new words added to this game, but also "a number of colour samples" (PI §8), and these samples play the role of modifying the commands given by a builder to an assistant. I hold up a colour-sample and say "d—slab—there." Someone trained in this language-game will respond by finding four slabs of the same colour as the sample I hold up and putting them there where I point. From the perspective of the *Tractatus*—and, indeed, from the perspective of most contemporary philosophy of language—such samples are just practical features of context, not linguistic tools themselves. But from the point of view of the *Investigations* this Tractarian perspective leaves out a central feature of the practical activities with which our uses of words are intertwined:

> What about the colour samples that A shews to B: are they part of the *language*? Well, it is as you please. They do not belong among the words; yet when I say to someone: "Pronounce the word 'the'", you will count the second "the" as part of the sentence. Yet it has a role just like that of a colour-sample in language-game (8); that is, it is a sample of what the other is meant to say.
>
> It is most natural, and causes least confusion, to reckon the samples among the instruments of the language. (PI §16)

The same might be said for certain gestures. When I say "d—slab—there," I must also point to the location I want the four slabs to be placed.

There may well be practical reasons for isolating words from other instruments of language. A linguist who is trying to capture the syntactic properties of English, for example, will find her task needlessly complicated if she tries to assign such properties to ostensions or displays of colour-samples. The legitimacy of this exclusion for a particular purpose, however, may tempt us to think that we have identified something about the timeless essence of language: that language *essentially* consists of a lexicon of words that can be combined according to a finite set of recursive rules, for example. And then we want to say that language and things in the world are set apart from each other—the representations on one side, the things or facts represented on the other. And this, in turn, threatens us with a mystery about how the representations get to be *about* the facts or things—a mystery that Wittgenstein purported to solve in the *Tractatus* by suggesting that facts, thoughts, and propositions share a logical form. To say this, however, is merely to put another name to the mystery. The Wittgenstein of the *Investigations* counsels us to avoid the mystery altogether: "Like everything metaphysical the harmony between thought and reality is to be found in the grammar of the language" (PG 162[22]/Z §55).

4.7 THE MULTIPLICITY OF LANGUAGE-GAMES

The "mystery" of how language and thought make contact with the world is a product of looking for the essence of language, of ignoring what Wittgenstein calls the "multiplicity of language-games" (PI §23). This multiplicity is a feature of language that we need to remind ourselves of, because the possibility of, for example, drawing superficial comparisons between the names of physical objects and the names of colours or the names of numbers—the presence of "certain analogies between the forms of expression in different regions of language" (PI §90)—can lead us into confusion. These superficial analogies feed our—i.e., philosophers'—"craving for generality," which is in part the product of "our preoccupation with the method of science" (BB 17).

This multiplicity applies to the "many different kinds of use of a word, related to one another in many different ways" (PI §38) that we group together under the

22 Ludwig Wittgenstein, *Philosophical Grammar*, edited by R. Rhees, translated by A.J.P. Kenny (Oxford: Basil Blackwell, 1974).

category 'name', but there are, of course, many other kinds of words and many other uses for them, such as ...

> Giving orders, and obeying them—
> Describing the appearance of an object, or giving its measurements—
> Constructing an object from a description (a drawing)—
> Reporting an event—
> Speculating about an event—
> Forming and testing a hypothesis—
> Presenting the results of an experiment in tables and diagrams—
> Making up a story; and reading it—
> Play-acting—
> Singing catches—
> Guessing riddles—
> Making a joke; telling it—
> Solving a problem in practical arithmetic—
> Translating from one language into another—
> Asking, thanking, cursing, greeting, praying. (PI §23)

The Tractarian idea that there is something interesting to be said about the general form of the proposition and that this captures what is essential to language strikes the Wittgenstein of the *Investigations* as a non-starter. But, precisely because philosophers have a craving for generality, this is bound to seem unsatisfying, and the objection will be that Wittgenstein is side-stepping the question of what all the multiple language-games have in common: "So you let yourself off the very part of the investigation that once gave you yourself most headache, the part about the *general form of propositions* and of language" (PI §65).

Wittgenstein acknowledges the temptation to say this, but he diagnoses that temptation as a symptom of philosophical disorder rather than as an indication that there really is something missing from the piecemeal approach of language-games. Grouping various phenomena together under the rubric 'language' does not require that those phenomena share anything interesting enough to be called an essence:

> —Instead of producing something common to all that we call language, I am saying that these phenomena have no one thing in common which makes us use the same word for all,—but that they are *related* to one another in many different ways. And it is because of this relationship, or these relationships, that we call them all "language". (PI §65)

The multiplicity of language-games is, indeed, analogous to the multiplicity of games. There need not be anything common to all "board-games, card-games, ball-games, Olympic games, and so on" (PI §66) in order for us to classify them all as games.

> —Don't say: "There *must* be something common, or they would not be called 'games'"—but *look and see* whether there is anything common to all.—For if you look at them you will not see something that is common to *all*, but similarities, relationships, and a whole series of them at that. To repeat: don't think, but look! (PI §66)

The injunction to "*look and see*" may seem naive, and it is tempting to say that what we are really being asked by Wittgenstein to do is formulate hypotheses that regiment the available data. But our examination of Wittgenstein's metaphilosophy in Chapter 3 should make us consider that the business of looking and seeing is by no means simple and unclouded. A great many factors may prevent one from seeing clearly, and a great many factors may give one an incentive not to look very carefully. Work in philosophy is work on oneself, remember.

So when Wittgenstein exhorts us to look and not think, he is urging us to try to command a clear view of our language, to remind ourselves of things that we already know but may have forgotten in the grip of our craving for generality. We are not in the position of radical interpreters of our own language, struggling to make some hypothesis or another fit the data of our many applications of the word 'game'. We are speakers of the language who have been trained in its use, which is to say that we have acquired an implicit grasp of the conventions governing this and related terms. No one told us what a game was. No one gave us an explicit definition, and none was needed. It was enough that we were presented with examples of games and trained how to apply the term 'game' to them. There need be no single property shared in common by all games, nor any single way in which all games resemble each other, in order for us to be justified in calling them all "games." When we attend to the many different kinds of activities that we classify as games, we need discover no non-trivial set of core-characteristics, no set of features whose presence is individually necessary and jointly sufficient to make any given activity a game. On the contrary, "we see a complicated network of similarities overlapping and criss-crossing: sometimes overall similarities, sometimes similarities of detail" (PI §66):

> —Look for example at board-games, with their multifarious relationships. Now pass to card-games; here you find many correspondences with the

> first group, but many common features drop out, and others appear. When we pass next to ball-games, much that is common is retained, but much is lost.—Are they all 'amusing'? Compare chess with noughts and crosses. Or is there always winning and losing, or competition between players? Think of patience. In ball games there is winning and losing; but when a child throws his ball at the wall and catches it again, this feature has disappeared. (PI §66)

These similarities Wittgenstein describes as "family resemblances" (PI §67) because they are analogous to the ways in which members of a family may bear a likeness to each other without there being any one observable characteristic possessed by all members of the same family.

But is it really true? Are there *no* properties at all that all games share in common? Suppose that there is some such property.[23] It is important to see that for Wittgenstein's purposes this fact does not matter at all, for he is making a point about our learning and application of the concept "game," and we do not learn this concept from a verbal definition that lays out for us some unifying property. What we learn when we learn the concept is how to apply it correctly—which, in turn, consists in large measure in being able to apply the *word* 'game' correctly. So correct application of the concept does not consist in tracking some set of necessary and sufficient conditions for game-hood, even if someone is clever enough to show that there is such a set.

Furthermore, Wittgenstein's account should alert us to the fact that our concepts are not static and fixed. They change over time. We speakers of English did not begin with a whole field of possible human activities laid out before us and then select the word 'game' as a name for a discrete subset of those activities. Rather, our ancestors began with some word that is the ancestor of the word 'game' and applied it, we may suppose, to a tiny handful of activities. (Such armchair archaeology has its dangers, but I think I am digging in safe ground here.) Then, Wittgenstein's story suggests, our ancestors *extended* the application of the term 'game' (or its ancestor) to include new instances that were not foreseen in the initial usage of the term—new games that no one had thought of playing before, for example. In doing so, they judged that these new instances were in some way similar to older instances, but the dimension of similarity was not held fixed. As a result, over time a great many different kinds of activities all came to be called

---

23 For example, Bernard Suits argues in *The Grasshopper: Games, Life and Utopia* (Peterborough, ON: Broadview Press, 2005) that every game "is a voluntary attempt to overcome unnecessary obstacles" (41)—though put so baldly this definition seems to classify the development of any skill as a game.

by the same general term, and within the category of "game" we can find activities that seem radically different from one another—playing solitaire and hurling a javelin—but which can be linked in a more circuitous way by a chain of similarities. And we can anticipate that our current concept may change in the future, as we extend it to include new instances that we find similar in new ways. "We do not know the boundaries because none have been drawn" (PI §69).

That is not to say that we cannot "draw a boundary—for a special purpose" (PI §69). Mathematical game-theory, for example, does just that. An anthropologist interested in the social cohesion promoted by certain games may choose to ignore games that have only one player. But the special purposes served by imposing such boundaries are not the workaday purposes for which we often employ the concept "game," and in the absence of such special purposes the lack of a sharp boundary for the concept is seldom any cause for worry:

> One might say that the concept 'game' is a concept with blurred edges.—"But is a blurred concept a concept at all?"—Is an indistinct photograph a picture of a person at all? Is it even always an advantage to replace an indistinct picture by a sharp one? Isn't the indistinct one often exactly what we need? (PI §71)

The bogus rigour that guided the insistence that one has not really made the meaning of a sentence clear unless one has found its unique, correct analysis returns in the interlocutor's question, "But is a blurred concept a concept at all?"

> Frege compares a concept to an area and says that an area with vague boundaries cannot be called an area at all. This presumably means that we cannot do anything with it.—But is it senseless to say: "Stand roughly there"? (PI §71)

The answer to this rhetorical question, of course, is, "No!" Blurred concepts work very nicely for many purposes, and if on some occasion they lead to misunderstanding, then that misunderstanding is removed by whatever clarifications or refinements of the concept are needed *on that occasion*.

4.8 THE PROBLEM OF UNIVERSALS

If Wittgenstein's discussion of family-resemblances arises in the course of explaining his use of language-games as a way of simultaneously attaining a clear view of linguistic conventions and undermining the thought that language has a hidden essence, it also seems that both family-resemblances and language-games have consequences for a very old philosophical problem, the so-called problem of universals—also known as the problem of the one and (or over) the many: How is it possible that many distinct particular things can, nonetheless, in some sense, be *one*? How, for example, can Socrates, Virginia Woolf, and Wittgenstein, as different as they are, all be human beings? How can old fire-engines, British phone-booths, and oxygenated blood all be red? What makes them all classifiable as red things? What makes them all of the same kind (in this respect, if not in others)?

We met with another version of this problem in Chapter 1 when we wondered how Locke's idea-theory of meaning can account for general terms. How can an idea—an image—which is particular serve as the idea of a general category, each of whose members differs from the others in some way?

We can put the question yet another way: terms like 'human being' and 'red' and 'six-legged' are general terms—they have application to many things, in contrast to singular terms like proper names and definite descriptions, which have application to single individuals. What is it that justifies our application of a general term to certain things and our refusing its application to certain others?

Traditionally, there are, broadly speaking, two kinds of answers to this question (though there are multiple variations on the two kinds of answers): *realism* and *nominalism*. The term 'realism', unfortunately, has an array of other applications in philosophy, and it is best not to get them confused, even though there are issues that link them.[24] What is intended by it here is the view that particulars fall into categories because they *share* certain general or *universal* characteristics, where we are to think of these *universals* as real, existing things. It is the presence of these universals that justifies the application of certain general terms to the individuals which instantiate the universals. Typically, two types of realism are distinguished: *transcendent* (or Platonic) realism, which holds that universals may exist uninstantiated, perhaps in "Platonic heaven" or what Frege called the "third realm"

24 For example, 'realism' is also used to refer to (i) the contention that the nature and existence of the world of things and events are independent of what we believe about it, in contrast with 'idealism'; (ii) the contention that the truth-conditions of sentences of natural language transcend our abilities to recognize those conditions, in contrast with 'anti-realism'; (iii) the related contention that an adequate theory of meaning must treat the meanings of sentences as given by their truth-conditions, rather than by their conditions of warranted assertibility, again in contrast with 'anti-realism'; (iv) the view that unobservable entities posited by the natural sciences really exist and are not merely convenient fictions (as is contended by *instrumentalism*). And these probably do not exhaust the doctrines known as realism.

(after the material and mental realms),[25] and *immanent* (or Aristotelian) realism, which holds that universals always inhere in particular objects that instantiate them.

Nominalists recoil from the idea of postulating the existence of anything but particulars. Of the transcendent realist, the nominalist may ask, "Where is this magical third realm, and how can we earth-bound mortals know anything about it?" Of both the transcendent realist and the immanent realist, she may ask, "What is the relation of 'instantiation' or 'participation' that is supposed to obtain between particulars and their universals? Do particulars resemble universals? If so, then we seem to need a further universal instantiated by those particulars and their universals to explain this resemblance, and this can lead only to an infinite regress. Does a universal exist in its entirety in the things that instantiate it? If so, then it seems, oddly, to be in more than one place at the same time. If not, then could the parts of the universal be used up? This seems to entail that there is a limit, for example, to the number of red things that could exist before there is no redness left over. And if all the red things are destroyed, has redness itself been destroyed?—Not if it continues to exist in Platonic heaven, but if it does not, how could some new red thing then come into existence?"

We may follow David Armstrong in distinguishing several different kinds of nominalism:

> Class Nominalism
> Natural Class Nominalism
> Concept Nominalism
> Predicate Nominalism
> Resemblance Nominalism.[26]

According to Class Nominalism, the instances that fall under a general term have nothing in common but the fact that they are all members of a particular class. Since any combination of things at all can be members of an arbitrarily chosen class, the actual general terms that we use pick out only a tiny number of the classes into which things could be grouped.

---

25 Gottlob Frege, "The Thought: A Logical Inquiry" in *Logicism and the Philosophy of Language*, edited by Arthur Sullivan (Peterborough, ON: Broadview Press, 2003), 201–18 at 211.

26 See D.M. Armstrong, *Universals: An Opinionated Introduction* (Boulder: Westview Press, 1989), Chapter 1. Armstrong also discusses varieties of nominalism that allow the existence of "tropes"—that is, properties that are uniquely possessed and, indeed, cannot be possessed by more than one thing. This complication is not important for my purposes here.

Both Predicate Nominalism and Concept Nominalism differ from Class Nominalism in the following respect: Class Nominalism makes category-membership an objective feature of the world in the sense that it is utterly independent of the actual categories that we bother to employ. By contrast, Predicate Nominalism and Concept Nominalism both make category-membership dependent on what predicates and concepts we actually have at our disposal. Predicate Nominalism (Armstrong, 10) says that all instances of a particular type share nothing in common other than the fact that they are called by the same name. Concept Nominalism (11) says that all instances of a particular type share nothing in common other than the fact that they are grouped together under the same concept, where a concept is thought of as a mental representation of some sort.

However, both of these views share with Class Nominalism a picture of categories as fundamentally arbitrary. We can make up as many predicates or concepts as we like and stipulate that any combination of things at all falls under the concept or predicate.

Someone who feels uncomfortable with the arbitrariness of these views may want to find a way of being a nominalist without giving up on the idea that some concepts or categories are more objective than others—that some classes tell us something about the nature of things, rather than generate arbitrary descriptions. One way to do this is to be a Natural Class Nominalist. Such a nominalist just takes the naturalness of certain classes as a kind of brute, irreducible fact about the world.

However, the brute irreducibility of the distinction between natural and non-natural classes may itself seem arbitrary. If so, then it will be tempting to become a Resemblance Nominalist (or a realist, of course). The Resemblance Nominalist says that there are objective resemblances among things and that those objective resemblances let us group things into natural classes. Such a view remains nominalistic because, although it postulates something objective in virtue of which our categories can be grounded, it does not suppose that that objective thing has the features of a universal. A resemblance is a relation that obtains between objects; it is not something that is shared in its entirety by several objects (which is not to say that several objects cannot resemble each other, just that each resemblance is a particular relation between two things).[27]

27 Note that being a resemblance nominalist need not commit one to thinking that there are natural classes. One might hold that which objective resemblances seem "natural" is partly determined by facts about our human perceptual systems—facts that might have been different, in which case the "natural" classes and the "objective" resemblances would have been different.

4.9 BEYOND REALISM AND NOMINALISM

The debate between realists and nominalists is a very old debate indeed. And it is a good example of the kind of problem that Wittgenstein thinks arises when we are misled by "certain analogies between the forms of expression in different regions of language" (PI §90), and which may be remedied—treated, but not *solved*—by obtaining a synoptic overview of the uses of language that mislead us in the first place. The temptation that we may feel to treat all words as names and also to overlook the many different ways in which names function seems like a potent source of philosophical confusion here. Crudely put, if a name gets its meaning from the object for which it stands, then it seems that there must be an object of some sort for which a meaningful term like 'red' stands, the universal redness.

By itself, this diagnosis may seem too simple. Surely, we want to say, philosophers are smarter than that! Perhaps, and perhaps not. But there are other reasons that help to explain why this problem survives the observation that not all words are names.

> Our craving for generality has another main source: our preoccupation with the method of science. I mean the method of reducing the explanation of natural phenomena to the smallest possible number of primitive natural laws; and, in mathematics, of unifying the treatment of different topics by using a generalization. Philosophers constantly see the method of science before their eyes, and are irresistibly tempted to ask and answer questions in the way science does. This tendency is the real source of metaphysics, and leads the philosopher into complete darkness. (BB 18)

We have already encountered fragments of this passage in the course of exploring Wittgenstein's conception of philosophical method and his account of family resemblances. It seems especially relevant to the problem of universals, for what seems to keep this debate going is an interest in giving a simple explanation of the applicability of certain concepts to particulars—in uncovering the hidden essence that unifies the objects of our attempts at categorization, at least when we get things right, when we carve nature at the joints.

Now it may seem that neither of these diagnoses captures the attitude of the nominalist, but Wittgenstein thinks that the nominalist shares certain basic assumptions with the realist, in particular, the assumption that realism (or perhaps, resemblance nominalism, which postulates objective resemblances that cut nature at the realist's joints) would have to be right if we are to avoid the conclusion that our application of general terms is simply arbitrary.[28] One may have doubts about such strange objects as universals, but as long as one fails to attain a perspicuous representation of the grammatical conventions that lie implicit in our linguistic practice, then it will be tempting to hold that the use of general terms like 'red' is simply arbitrary. "Nominalists," like realists, "make the mistake of interpreting all words as *names*, and so of not really describing their use, but only, so to speak, giving a paper draft on such a description" (PI §383).

Following through on the project of describing the use of colour terms (for example) would require examining the sorts of language-games in which those terms are taught and learned—games like the one played by the builders. In those games, as we saw earlier, a description of the way a term like 'red' is used requires no reference to universals. The use of 'red' is taught by pointing out particular red things—by pointing to their colour, rather than their shape or their number. How does one do that? By drawing attention to the similarities between different red things, similarities that do not obtain between red squares of cloth and blue squares of cloth, or between this one red apple and that one green apple, and so on. By insisting on the similarities between this red apple and that red fire hydrant and this red-headed child and that red-faced man about to lose his temper. In short, by drawing attention in particular contexts to "a complicated network of similarities overlapping and criss-crossing" (PI §66).

Does this make Wittgenstein a kind of nominalist, after all—a Resemblance Nominalist? I think it does not. The Resemblance Nominalist, remember, is troubled by the arbitrariness of other kinds of nominalism and hopes to guard against it by insisting that some resemblances are objective, whereas others are not. But Wittgenstein takes the objectivity of a resemblance, I think, to be exhausted by its teachability. What the presence of similarities between instances does is make it possible for certain classifications to be applied. But this is compatible with there being a vast number of similarities that we overlook—and, hence, with there being multiple systems of classification, each of which is *objective* insofar as it can be taught and learned. However, those similarities do not by themselves *justify* anything, contrary to the view of the Resemblance Nominalist—only *a practice of making judgments about classification* can do that. That is, only a convention can confer justification on our applications of a concept to particular instances. And although conventions are contingent, they are not simply arbitrary, as we saw in

28 This point has been made by Renford Bambrough in a justly influential paper called "Universals and Family Resemblances," *Proceedings of the Aristotelian Society* 61 (1960–61): 207–22. Bambrough oversimplifies the debate between realists and nominalists, but ultimately I find his reading of Wittgenstein persuasive and the position he attributes to Wittgenstein defensible.

Chapter 3. To think so is to ignore "the *deep* need for the convention" (RFM I §74). That we find certain conventions "natural" is, Wittgenstein suggests, the result of "extremely general facts of nature: such facts as are hardly ever mentioned because of their great generality" (PI 56)—for example, the fact that human beings are bipedal, that we require food, companionship, and shelter from the elements, that we reproduce sexually, that we are vulnerable to certain diseases and kinds of injury, etc.

> I am not saying: if such-and-such facts of nature were different people would have different concepts (in the sense of a hypothesis). But: if anyone believes that certain concepts are absolutely the correct ones, and that having different ones would mean not realizing something that we realize—then let him imagine certain very general facts of nature to be different from what we are used to, and the formation of concepts different from the usual ones will become intelligible to him. (PI II §xii; 230)

4.10 THE FAMILY OF NUMBERS

It is easy to be so mesmerized by Wittgenstein's discussion of games that one overlooks his second example of a concept that is characterized by family-resemblances, the concept of "number": "Why do we call something a 'number'? Well, perhaps because it has a—direct—relationship with several things that have hitherto been called number; and this can be said to give it an indirect relationship to other things we call the same name" (PI §67).

I remarked above that Wittgenstein's treatment of family-resemblances gestures at a story about linguistic change and development, and I sketched an imaginary history of the use of the word 'game'. A similar story about linguistic change and development applies here, but we do not have to invent intellectual history in the case of the concept "number." We know, for example, that the Romans had no numeral for zero and that it was brought into European mathematics from the Arabic world. We know that negative numbers, imported from India, were long resisted by European mathematicians, but that they were eventually accepted as genuine numbers. We know that irrational numbers, logarithms, complex numbers, matrices, and quaternions all at one time were no part of anyone's mathematics and then, in each case, at some later time were incorporated into the concept of number.[29]

29 See Morris Kline, *Mathematics: The Loss of Certainty* (New York: Oxford University Press, 1980).

In each of these instances, the application of the term 'number' (or its linguistic ancestor) was extended to include new cases that had not been thought of before, and, in the story that Wittgenstein's way of thinking suggests, the concept of "number" was itself changed and broadened to include new instances. "[w]e extend our concept of number as in spinning a thread we twist fibre on fibre" (PI §67). In each case, we recognize some similarity between the new candidate for number-hood and the established cases. We discover, for example, that we can calculate with negative numbers as smoothly as with positive ones, and this undermines our resistance to the idea of making use of them. We discover that a coherent technique can be employed for manipulating numbers (such as matrices and quaternions) that fail to obey the law of commutativity ("*a* x *b* = *b* x *a*") and this convinces us that they are as much numbers as are more familiar cases.

In the story that Platonists—i.e., transcendent realists about numbers—tell about the development of mathematics, mathematicians gradually come to know more and more about a pre-existing realm of abstract objects. They merely discover transcendent truths that already awaited them. By Wittgenstein's lights such a story involves unnecessary extravagance. We can make sense of the meaningfulness of words for natural numbers by pointing to the roles that they play in language-games like that of PI §8. There is pressure to think of numbers as transcendent objects only if we persist in thinking of all words as names (on a narrow model of naming) or allow ourselves to be driven by our craving for generality to look for the essence that lies hidden beneath our number-talk, instead of focusing on getting a clear view of the ways in which we teach and learn language-games with number-words.

Consider, then, how we move beyond the simplest employments of number-words that we find in the builders' language-game. The use of words for numbers of things that *cannot* be taken in at a glance can be taught by learning counting-games and by being introduced to the basic concept of addition—which can itself be taught ostensively by using groups of objects that *can* be taken in at a glance. Among the techniques that can be learned in conjunction with this training are the techniques of manipulating written symbols. I learn to write '1, 2, 3, 4...' and so on, as I count off objects; I learn to write '2' after I have counted off the objects in a surveyable group of two objects; I learn to write '+' when I take two readily surveyable groups of objects and put them together; I learn to write '4' upon counting the objects in the new, surveyable group; and I learn to write '2+2=4' in conjunction with combining these two groups of objects. Once I have been trained in the technique, then I learn to write '2+2=4' without combining any actual groups of objects. Groups of objects that are not so easily surveyed I learn to break up into smaller groups. At the same time I learn symbols for numbers that

I cannot take in at a glance, and in the process my calculating-techniques become more sophisticated.

In the background of all this training lies the possibility of tracing these calculations back to operations involving actual groups of objects that can be taken in at a glance. These objects function as samples employed in teaching and learning, and, as we have seen, "It is most natural, and causes least confusion, to reckon the samples among the instruments of the language" (PI §16). As such, any written calculation that I carry out—given this much training—could be replaced by the manipulation and counting of actual objects.[30]

However, at some point in the development of my use of the word 'number' the possibility of tracing my calculations back to the use of actual samples is no longer so clear. Perhaps this begins with the introduction of negative integers, perhaps with the introduction of zero, or perhaps when I get to the point of considering sums of objects that are uncountable—not in the mathematical sense, but in the practical sense. But certainly by the time I come to talk of irrational numbers, imaginary numbers, or logarithms, I have gone past the point at which I could substitute the manipulation, grouping, and counting of actual objects for the manipulation of symbols. (If this is not the case, then so much the worse for talk of abstract objects.)

It is here that the treatment of "number" as a family-resemblance concept gets its interest. It seems that I come to regard these new calculations with imaginary numbers and such as *calculations* because they resemble *old* calculations in some way. Talk of the square root of -4 does not simply extend the pre-existing techniques of grouping and counting actual objects. I begin to calculate with complex numbers on the basis of an analogy with calculations that involve real numbers, and as this new set of techniques is developed, I learn to comport myself in accordance with a new norm of calculation—a new convention. (Such extended number-talk begins as metaphor, I am tempted to say, which gradually dies into literal use.[31]) At no point in this process is there any need to speak of "abstract

30 Philip Kitcher (*The Nature of Mathematical Knowledge* [Oxford: Oxford University Press, 1983], 107ff.) makes a similar claim but then moves in a very non-Wittgensteinian direction. W.V. Quine (*From a Logical Point of View*, 2nd ed. [Cambridge, MA: Harvard University Press, 1980]) allows the nominalist a related proposal but complains that "this expedient has the shortcoming that it cannot guarantee the infinite multiplicity of numbers which classical arithmetic demands" (128). The nominalist, of course, lacks a story about family-resemblances.

31 But, as in science, not just *any* metaphor will prove fruitful in mathematics. Consider, for example, the childhood fear of Rilke's Malte Laurids Brigge "that some number may begin to grow in my brain until there is no room for it inside me." In the same passage Rilke writes of "the fear that I might not be able to say anything, because everything is unsayable..." See Rainer Maria Rilke, *The Notebooks of Malte Laurids Brigge*, translated by Stephen Mitchell (*Continued*)

objects." I become familiar with what it means to say that -4 *has* a square root, that *there is* such a thing. But what I know here does not consist in my being confirmed in *positing* the existence of an abstract object, as though it were a special kind of unobservable entity—like the electron, but even smaller. We do talk of numbers, but such talk gets its meaning from techniques for counting and manipulating real "concrete" objects and from techniques for calculating. We may even want to say—or prove—that there *are* two prime numbers between 20 and 30. But what that *means* is shown by what counts as a proof of such a statement and how the claim functions in our calculating practices.

We could vary the point of these observations about the concept "number" by observing that the concept "existence" is likewise a family-resemblance concept. We speak without much confusion about the existence of tables and chairs, but mathematics does not simply apply the same concept to a new kind of "object"; rather it gives the concept of "existence" a new sense by making a calculation a criterion for the concept's proper application. As Wittgenstein cautions in *The Blue Book*, we should not be "misled ... by the different meanings of the word 'exist'" (BB 31).

This is not to say that the term 'exist' and its cognates suffer from full-blown semantic ambiguity.[32] 'Exist' is not like 'bank' in having two utterly distinct standard meanings. Wittgenstein clarifies a parallel point about the word 'good' in his lectures of 1932–33: "When there is an argument about whether a thing is good, the discussion shows what we are talking about. In the course of the argument the word may begin to get a new grammar" (WLC II 33).[33] Instances of "goodness," he argues, display what he later calls a "family resemblance," and because of this, he thinks that the word 'good' lacks a "general meaning," but this, he clarifies, does not mean that 'good' is ambiguous:

> In view of the way we have learned the word "good" it would be astonishing if it had a general meaning covering all of its applications. I am not saying it has four or five different meanings. It is used in different contexts because there is a transition between similar things called "good", a transition which continues, it may be, to things which bear no similarity to earlier members of the series. (WLC II 33)

(New York: Vintage International, 1990), 64. Just before the start of the Great War Wittgenstein inherited a huge fortune (which he later gave to his siblings) from his father and decided to donate a substantial sum to the support of needy artists. One of them was Rilke. See Ray Monk, *Ludwig Wittgenstein: The Duty of Genius* (London: Jonathan Cape, 1990), 106–10.

32 Thanks to Rob Stainton for this objection.

33 Ludwig Wittgenstein, *Wittgenstein's Lectures, Cambridge, 1932–35*, edited by Alice Ambrose (Amherst, NY: Prometheus Books, 2001).

To say that 'good' has no "general meaning" is to say that the criteria for its proper application vary significantly from context to context. Much the same can be said, I believe, about 'exist'.

4.11 THE VOICES OF THE *INVESTIGATIONS*

I remarked at the beginning of this chapter that Wittgenstein does not write in a single, unified voice in the *Investigations*. A number of important commentators have emphasized the importance of this stylistic feature of the book. Stanley Cavell, in his 1962 essay "The Availability of Wittgenstein's Later Philosophy," suggests that we see the *Investigations* as a confession written in dialogue form (71).[34] "The voice of temptation and the voice of correctness," writes Cavell, "are the antagonists in Wittgenstein's dialogues" (71). Both the voices, temptation as much as correctness, belong to Wittgenstein, and so neither is properly *the* voice of Wittgenstein. Cavell thinks that we must not underestimate the importance of this aspect of Wittgenstein's writing:

> In confessing you do not explain or justify, but describe how it is with you. And confession, unlike dogma, is not to be believed but tested, and accepted or rejected. Nor is it the occasion for accusation, except of yourself, and by implication those who find themselves in you. There is exhortation ... not to belief but to self-scrutiny. And that is why there is virtually nothing in the *Investigations* which we should ordinarily call reasoning; Wittgenstein asserts nothing which could be proved, for what he asserts is either obvious (§126)—whether true or false—or else concerned with what conviction, whether by proof or evidence or authority, would consist in. Otherwise there are questions, jokes, parables, and propositions so striking (the way lines are in poetry) that they stun mere belief. (71)

Cavell is right to emphasize the importance of the voice of temptation in the *Investigations*. Work in philosophy, as we saw in Chapter 3, "is really more work on oneself" (CV 24; *cf.* BT 300), and so what Cavell calls "the method of self-knowledge" (Cavell, "The Availability," 70) has a central role to play in Wittgenstein's investigations.

34 Stanley Cavell, "The Availability of Wittgenstein's Later Philosophy" in *Must We Mean What We Say?* (Cambridge: Cambridge University Press, 1976), 44–72.

However, it is easy to be led by these considerations to overemphasize the lack of what "we should ordinarily call reasoning" (Cavell, "The Availability," 71) in the *Investigations*. Cavell's concern, perhaps, is that if Wittgenstein's method, as I have agreed, prevents him from taking sides in traditional philosophical disputes, then to attribute arguments or "views" to him is to catch him in a contradiction. This, of course, depends on what the arguments are supposed to show and what the "views" are. If the arguments are taken to show only that elaborate philosophical claims about the possibility of a "private language," for example (see Chapter 5), are unmotivated or that theories of X fail (where 'X' stands in for such would-be objects of theoretical knowledge as meaning (see Chapter 5) or knowledge (see Chapter 6)), then no contradiction arises, for reasoning in favour of such conclusions is consistent with the claim that traditional philosophical problems arise "when language *goes on holiday*" (PI §38), when we fall into confusion about the grammatical norms implicit in our linguistic practices.

It is true enough that, e.g., when Wittgenstein urges us to "*look and see*" (PI §66) whether there is anything common to all games that plays the role of justifying our calling them all games, he is engaged in exhortation and not explicit reasoning. But there are moments of exhortation in the *Investigations* when the point has much to do with a piece of reasoning that is obliquely gestured at. If there need be no such common element in order for our application of a concept to its instances to be justified, then we seem to be given an invitation to draw for ourselves a conclusion about the traditional debate between realists and nominalists, even if that conclusion is never explicitly stated. This reasoning is aimed at the *dissolution* of a problem, but it is reasoning nonetheless. And other passages in the *Investigations*, including a number discussing the problem of "private language" (which I shall take up in Chapter 5), seem clearly to be engaged in explicit reasoning, though what conclusion is reached and how we should understand it in the context of Wittgenstein's inquiry demand careful scrutiny.

In short, it *is* of deep importance for understanding Wittgenstein's task in the *Investigations* that he does not speak with a unified voice. But this need not deter us from attributing arguments to Wittgenstein any more than the fact that an author of fiction is not identical with any of her characters or narrative voices need automatically prevent us from attributing views to her. (Boris Pasternak was not Yuri Zhivago or Strelnikov or Lara Antipova, but this is no barrier to reading *Dr. Zhivago* as a criticism of the Bolshevik revolution.)

Indeed, the idea that there are just *two* voices in the *Investigations*—temptation and correction—may oversimplify the text, as David Stern has argued. The *Investigations*, he writes, "is not straightforwardly identifiable as a dialogue, a confession, therapy, or philosophy of language, though it certainly contains elements of all these" (WPII 24).[35] Stern thinks that there are *three* prominent types of voices in the text: "interlocutory voices," which raise various philosophical temptations, the voice of "Wittgenstein's narrator," which advances various arguments in response to the interlocutory voices, and a voice which "provides an ironic commentary" on the exchanges between narrator and interlocutor, "a commentary consisting partly of objections to assumptions the debaters take for granted, and partly of platitudes about language and everyday life they have both overlooked" (22). The voice of the commentator, thinks Stern, comes the closest to being Wittgenstein's own (23).

Stern's reading seems to me to capture the spirit of the *Investigations* quite well. But as he notes, the voices of the commentator and the narrator are "not always clearly distinct" (WPII 22). Wittgenstein's presentation of the method of language games, for example, is best thought of on the reading I have advanced here as given in something like his own voice, but that voice is neither ironic nor simply given to "platitudes about language and everyday life," though it does seem concerned to draw our attention to such platitudes as we may have forgotten or taken out of context. In this respect, like the narratorial voice, it seems engaged in a project of argumentation, albeit one that spans the *Investigations* instead of locating itself in particular exchanges with an interlocutory voice. (Stern, of course, is well aware that there is both "small-scale" and "large-scale" argumentation at work in the *Investigations.*) This observation is compatible, I think, with Stern's insistence that the argumentative and therapeutic aspects of the book "are actually complementary and interwoven" (5).

Of course, there is one claim that my reading of Wittgenstein's later works cannot refrain from attributing to him, and that is the claim that I have repeated about philosophical problems having their source in confusions about grammatical norms. Is that a philosophical claim, and is Wittgenstein committed to an inconsistency by his acceptance of it?

Perhaps it *is* a kind of philosophical claim, but it is certainly not a traditional one. It would be a mistake to think that 'philosophy' is the name of a natural or metaphysical kind if we take Wittgenstein's discussion of family resemblances seriously, and so there is room to say of certain philosophical claims that they succumb to Wittgenstein's method while also saying that his own metaphilosophical pronouncements do not so succumb. It is a further question, to which I shall return in Chapter 7, whether Wittgenstein himself is tempted to essentialize philosophy.

---

35 David G. Stern, *Wittgenstein's Philosophical Investigations: An Introduction* (Cambridge: Cambridge University Press, 2004), 24.

5

RULES AND PRIVATE LANGUAGE

In the preceding chapter I presented the method of language-games and tried to show how Wittgenstein employs it to remind us of the variety of words that we classify as names and the variety of their uses, as well as the variety of words and of linguistic activity generally that we engage in. These reminders serve to undermine the *Tractarian* thesis that language has a hidden essence that might be uncovered by the unifying techniques of natural science, by presenting in explicit form the kinds of conventional norms of usage that are implicit in our linguistic practices. The rejection of this *Tractarian* thesis was further underwritten by Wittgenstein's figure of "family resemblances." That metaphor, together with Wittgenstein's discussion of names in the context of the builders' language-game of PI §8,[1] served also to diagnose and treat (but not solve) the traditional problem of universals, offering, in particular, a way of thinking about number-talk that avoids committing us to thinking that numbers are special "abstract objects" of some sort.

In this chapter I shall turn first to Wittgenstein's discussion of understanding and following a rule and then to his treatment of the suggestion that the meanings of sensation-terms like 'pain' and 'pleasure' are derived from our individual acquaintance with objects or events situated in a private inner space. The examination of rule-following, I shall argue, shows that mastery of techniques that

1 Ludwig Wittgenstein, *Philosophical Investigations*, 2nd ed., translated by G.E.M. Anscombe (Oxford: Basil Blackwell, 1968).

one does not learn to describe is necessary for learning a language, because the alternative would involve an explicit grasp of all linguistic norms, and this would lead us into an infinite regress. The rule-following passages are thus deeply significant for Wittgenstein's whole conception of philosophy. The treatment of the idea of a private language for our sensations, I shall then argue, depends crucially on the discussion of naming that is the focus of the opening sixty or so remarks of the *Philosophical Investigations*. Although Wittgenstein makes many interrelated points here, a central one is that the idea of a private sensation language arises from failing to take a synoptic view of how naming works, and of how sensation-terms are taught and learned. It is tempting to look for a categorical refutation of the very possibility of a private language in these sections of the *Investigations*, but I contend that, consistent with Wittgenstein's account of philosophical method, no such argument is to be found. Neither, however, is one needed.

5.1 KRIPKE'S PROBLEM

It is difficult to embark on any discussion of the rule-following passages in the *Philosophical Investigations* without taking into consideration the interpretation of these passages that has been forcefully presented by Saul Kripke. This is not just because Kripke provocatively purports to discover a new form of scepticism in these remarks, but because the treatment of these remarks as a unified object of interpretation is largely the result of Kripke's examination. Before Kripke they received little in the way of systematic discussion (there are exceptions, of course), but since Kripke, they have been the focus of a sustained and exhausting debate, not just amongst scholars of Wittgenstein, but amongst philosophers of language and mind, who have descended on this new form of scepticism like the fabled wolf on the fold.[2] I shall begin by presenting Kripke's reading and then offer a critique

---

2 *Some* notable responses to Kripke include G.P. Baker and P.M.S. Hacker, *Scepticism, Rules and Language* (Oxford: Blackwell, 1984); John McDowell, "Wittgenstein on Following a Rule" in *Mind, Value and Reality* (Cambridge, MA: Harvard University Press, 1998), 221–62; Crispin Wright, "Kripke's Account of the Argument Against Private Language," *Journal of Philosophy* 81 (1984): 759–78; Warren Goldfarb, "Kripke on Wittgenstein on Rules," *Journal of Philosophy* 82 (1985): 471–88; Paul Boghossian, "The Rule-Following Considerations," *Mind* 98 (1989): 507–49; Ruth Millikan, "Truth Rules, Hoverflies and the Kripke-Wittgenstein Paradox," *Philosophical Review* 99, no.3 (1990): 323–53; Meredith Williams, "Blind Obedience" in *Meaning Scepticism*, edited by Klaus Puhler (New York: Walter de Gruyter, 1991), 93–125; Gary Ebbs, *Rule-Following and Realism* (Cambridge, MA: Harvard University Press, 1997), Chapters 1 and 3; Marie McGinn, *Wittgenstein and the* Philosophical Investigations (London: Routledge, 1997), Chapter 3; David

of it, both as a philosophical position and as a reading of Wittgenstein—though given the aims of this book, the two tasks will be intimately related.

According to Kripke, Wittgenstein is preoccupied with the question of what my understanding or following a rule consists in—or, in Kripke's terms, with the question of what "*fact* about me" (WRPL 21)[3] makes it the case that I understand or follow a rule. If we take language to be a rule-governed phenomenon, in the sense that there are rules governing the correct combination and application of words, this question has obvious consequences for the question of what my understanding a word or other linguistic expression consists in. Kripke embellishes on an example that appears at PI §185, concerning a pupil who has been taught the series of natural numbers and is now introduced to new series:

> Now we get the pupil to continue a series (say + 2) beyond 1000—and he writes 1000, 1004, 1008, 1012.
>
> We say to him: "Look what you've done!"—He doesn't understand. We say: "You were meant to add *two*: look how you began the series!"—He answers: "Yes, isn't it right? I thought that was how I was *meant* to do it."—Or suppose he pointed to the series and said: "But I went on in the same way."—It would now be no use to say: "But can't you see..?"—and repeat the old examples and explanations. (PI §185)

Kripke takes the point of this passage to be a sceptical one concerning our abilities to know which rule another person has been following up to any given time.[4] In Wittgenstein's example, if we have never tested the pupil's grasp of the series beyond 1000, we do not know that he has been following some other rule than the one that we follow, because up to now his behaviour—by which Kripke means his bodily movements described in the sorts of non-intentional terms we apply equally to rolling stones and orbiting planets—has been in no way different from our own.[5]

G. Stern, *Wittgenstein's Philosophical Investigations: An Introduction* (Cambridge: Cambridge University Press, 2004), Chapter 6.

3 Saul Kripke, *Wittgenstein on Rules and Private Language* (Cambridge, MA: Harvard University Press, 1982), 21.

4 In fact, Kripke does not discuss this passage. Rather, he introduces another example involving an eccentric rule for "quaddition" which is indistinguishable from the rule for addition except where one or both of the terms to be added is greater than or equal to 57 (though any arbitrarily large number would do). But Wittgenstein's example serves well enough and seems to be the obvious inspiration for Kripke's. See WRPL 9.

5 Kripke is eager to insist (WRPL 14) that Wittgenstein does not restrict us to behavioural facts when it comes to saying what fact about me might count as a candidate for determining whether I am doing addition or some other operation, but the data to be explained need to be behavioural (*Continued*)

However, this sceptical point seems to generalize in an unsettling way, for each of us has only ever applied the rule 'add 2' in a finite number of cases. For each of us there is some number that is the highest number to which we have ever proceeded by adding 2 to another number. So how can I know of *anyone* that after some arbitrarily large number she will not prove to have been following some bizarre rule that diverges from 'add 2' only for very large numbers? The hypothesis that she follows the bizarre rule fits her behaviour to date just as adequately as the hypothesis that she follows the rule 'add 2'.

As if this consequence were not strange enough, Kripke presses the argument further. How can I tell *in my own case* that I have not been following some rule other than the rule 'add 2' and that my bizarre rule would distinguish itself from 'add 2' only if I were confronted with some arbitrarily large number which, to date, I have not encountered? "In the past I gave myself only a finite number of examples instantiating this function.... The sceptic claims (or feigns to claim) that I am now misinterpreting my own previous usage... under the influence of some insane frenzy, or a bout of LSD..." (WRPL 8–9).

So far this looks simply like a point about self-knowledge: that if the sceptical worry is right, I cannot *know* what rules I follow. But Kripke means to present us with a sceptical worry about the very determinacy of the rules we follow. This "ontological" scepticism has it that I do not know what rules I follow, because there is no fact of the matter here for me to find out. And there is no fact of the matter for me to find out because even if I had God-like access to all the facts about my past behaviour and my mind, I would still not be able to settle the question of which rule I had been following (WRPL 21). So it is neither true nor false that I follow the rule 'add 2', or any other rule, for that matter. And since the use of language is supposed to be a rule-governed practice, it follows that there is no fact of the matter about what anyone's words mean. "It seems," says Kripke, "that the entire idea of meaning vanishes into thin air" (WRPL 22).

Before this puzzle can seem worrying, we need to be persuaded that there really is no fact about me that constitutes my having understood and applied the rule 'add 2', so we must ask ourselves, "What sort of fact might constitute my following this rule rather than some other?"

It cannot be that someone else has given me, or that I have in some way given myself, explicit instructions concerning every case in which 2 may be added. The infinite applicability of addition rules that out. But could it be that in a sense I have given myself *implicit* instructions in the form of an *intention*? According to

---

if the sceptical puzzle is to get going. In particular, we cannot take the relevant behaviour to consist in *doing addition*.

this view, "'The right step is the one that accords with the order—as it was *meant*'" (PI §186). When I intended to add 2, I did not have to represent explicitly to myself every application of the rule. It is enough that I intended to go on *in the same way* as I had in previous cases. The problem here is that what counts as "going on in the same way" is determined by what rule I am following (WRPL 10–11). "The use of the word 'rule' and the use of the word 'same' are interwoven" (PI §225), as Wittgenstein puts it. If I am doing addition, then continuing the series, "1002, 1004, 1006..." counts as going on in the same way, but if I am following some bizarre Kripkean rule, then continuing the series, "1004, 1008, 1012..." may count as going on in the same way. Since what is at issue is whether I have been adding 2 up to now, I cannot appeal to the facts about what rule I was following in order to explain what my having intended to go on in the same way amounted to.

My behaviour to date will not do, since the problem turns on precisely the fact that my behaviour is finite. No extension of my behaviour into the future will fix this apparent defect, because any such extension will itself remain finite and, so, will always be compatible with rival hypotheses concerning just what rule it is I follow—perhaps I shall begin to give unexpected results only once I continue the series beyond numbers with 20 digits.

But if my finite behaviour serves merely to reinforce the sceptical worry, perhaps my *disposition* to behave in one way rather than another under appropriate circumstances makes it the case that I follow this rule rather than that (WRPL 22). It is true (let us suppose) that I shall never add 2 to 2,000,000,000, but it might be that *were* I asked to do so, then I *would* respond by saying or writing '2,000,000,002'.

Such dispositional facts are familiar from other contexts. When we confidently assert that a given wineglass is fragile, we seem to be saying that *if* it were struck or dropped, then it *would* break. This *subjunctive* fact ("if it were..., then it would be...") can be true, even if the glass is never actually struck or dropped. Similarly, as long as the right subjunctive facts are true about me, then it could be said that I follow the rule 'add 2', and that, therefore, there is a fact of the matter about which rule I follow that transcends my actual behaviour.

However, as Kripke observes, even though my disposition to behave in some sense outruns my actual behaviour, it is still finite (WRPL 26). It may well be, for example, that there are some numbers that are simply too large for my limited brain to handle, regarding which I would have no disposition to respond in any particular way because I could not finish the calculation without falling into confusion (WRPL 27). If so, then my disposition leaves it indeterminate what rule I follow. And this is not a problem that can be solved by adding that, if I had a bigger brain, then I would give the right answer in the case above, since even a bigger brain will have its limitations. Even if this were not so, it remains the case that the only way of specifying a disposition with *infinite* applicability seems to be by describing it as, for example, *the disposition to add 2*. But it helps us none to be told that if I am disposed to add 2, then I follow the rule 'add 2'. Dispositions were supposed to tell us what following the rule 'add 2' consists in. They cannot do that by invoking the rule to identify the disposition (WRPL 28).

Perhaps the most serious problem with the dispositional account, however, is that it fails to account for the *normativity* of meaning—for the possibility of making mistakes. If, when I come to add 2 to 200,000, I write '200,004', because I am getting bored or sleepy or irritated with the philosophically-minded arithmetic teacher who is putting me through this dreary exercise, then the dispositionalist must reckon this response as indicative of my disposition, and her conclusion must be that I am not following the rule 'add 2', but some eccentric rule instead. Given the explanation for my writing '200,004', this seems wrong. Clearly, we want to say, I am doing addition and have *made a mistake* (deliberate or not), but the only way that the dispositionalist can recognize my latest move as a mistake is by assuming some *independent* way of identifying the rule I am following, and that identification is just what the dispositionalist was trying to give us the means to carry out (WRPL 28–30).

Wittgenstein illustrates this point (among others) by comparing rule-following to the operation of a machine which is designed with a disposition to behave in a certain way:

> The machine as symbolizing its action: the action of a machine—I might say at first—seems to be there in it from the start. What does that mean?—If we know the machine, everything else, that is its movement, seems to be already completely determined.
>
> We talk as if these parts could only move in this way, as if they could not do anything else. How is this—do we forget the possibility of their bending, breaking off, melting, and so on? Yes; in many cases we don't think of that at all. (PI §193)

This, says Wittgenstein, is because when we use a machine to symbolize its action, we are using it as a stand-in for the procedure that we intend or want it to help us accomplish. The purpose of an electronic calculator, for example, is to help us carry out mathematical calculations, and we may fall back on the results we get using it, when we do not trust our calculating ability without it. So it can be tempting—and in many contexts harmless—to think that the right result just is the one that we get using an electronic calculator. But we do not suppose that whatever result the calculator displays *has* to be right. If its batteries are low, or if it has been dropped, it may give the wrong result. And 'wrong result' here presupposes some independent reference to mathematical rules, so we cannot use the results obtained by using an electronic calculator to say what counts as the right result.

If neither behaviour nor dispositions to behave can answer the sceptic, perhaps we might appeal to facts about my mind to say what my following or understanding the rule 'add 2' consists in. Maybe my understanding of a rule or of a word consists in some mental process that takes place when I hear or speak the word, or when I apply the rule. But it is hard to see how any such process could *be* my understanding. It may be that whenever I add 2, I get an itch behind my right ear, but this surely does not *make it the case* that I am adding 2 and not applying some bizarre alternative rule. It may be that whenever I add 2, I have a vivid mental image of holding two blocks on top of a pile of others. "But are the processes which I have described here *understanding*?" (PI §152), Wittgenstein asks. It seems not. Having such an image or sensation does not seem necessary for me to understand the rule or to be applying it in a particular case (WRPL 42). Having such an image or sensation seems, rather, to be an experience that I contingently associate with the application of the rule. The right sorts of experiences might lead me, with equal vividness, to see a mental image of a stern Austrian schoolmaster whenever I add 2, and we certainly would not say that *this* counts as my understanding.

If such an associated image is not necessary for my understanding or applying a particular rule, then neither is it sufficient (WRPL 42–43). When I experience the mental image of holding two blocks on top of a pile, how do I know that I am to leave them there and not to take them away? The image itself does not tell me this. Instead, it seems that I must first understand how to apply the image before it can in any way count as my understanding or applying the rule 'add 2'. In that case, I would need yet another image, whose correct application would itself need to be explained. An infinite regress looms, and the first step down this endless path was the wrong one.

It is no help to suppose that instead of the image of two blocks, a mathematical formula occurs to me, such as '$x + 2 = y$', because the usefulness of this formula likewise presupposes that I understand how to apply it. And it should be equally clear that we cannot appeal here to my being given a *rule* that tells me how to apply the image or the formula, because precisely what we were trying to understand was what my grasp of a rule consists in. Another rule is merely an interpretation of the original rule, my grasp of which we were trying to explain, and as Wittgenstein remarks, "any interpretation still hangs in the air along with what it interprets, and cannot give it any support" (PI §198).

So understanding does not consist in any fact about my non-intentionally described behaviour to date, nor in any fact about my dispositions to behave. It does not consist in my receiving or giving myself explicit instructions about how to apply the rule in every case, nor in my intending to go on in the same way. And it does not consist in any mental process, such as my having a particular sensation or my "seeing" an image or a formula in my mind, nor still in my being given an interpretation of the rule. Perhaps we have overlooked some possible solution, but it is by no means clear that we have any way left of defeating the sceptic's doubts.

5.2 KRIPKE'S "SCEPTICAL SOLUTION"

This then is the new form of scepticism that Kripke takes Wittgenstein to have invented—scepticism about the very possibility of meaning. If we cannot defeat it, what are we to do?

Kripke argues that Wittgenstein should be understood to respond to the problem of rule-scepticism in much the way that Hume responds to his own sceptical doubts about the justifiability of inductive reasoning—by offering "A Sceptical Solution of these Doubts."[6] A sceptical solution, unlike a straight solution, says Kripke, is one that concedes that "the sceptic's negative assertions are unanswerable" (WRPL 66), but which then argues that "our ordinary practice or belief is justified because—contrary appearances notwithstanding—it need not require the justification the sceptic has shown to be untenable" (WRPL 66). On Kripke's reading, then, Wittgenstein concedes the force of rule-scepticism, but offers an alternative justification for our ordinary belief that we generally continue to follow the same rules, whether we are engaged in solving problems of arithmetic or making use of any number of linguistic expressions.

Wittgenstein's alternative, according to Kripke is to say that we are warranted in saying that someone follows this rule rather than that one (or none at all) only insofar as she is a member of a linguistic community—or rather, only insofar as she is *thought of* as a member of a community. "Our community can assert of any individual that he follows a rule if he passes the tests for rule following applied to any member of the community" (WRPL 110). However, our being warranted in saying that someone follows a rule does not entail that she actually does follow that rule. Indeed, given that the sceptical solution accepts the sceptic's conclusion, *it is neither true nor false* that anyone follows any rule. Let's try to make some sense of this.

6 David Hume, *An Enquiry Concerning Human Understanding*, edited by Eric Steinberg (Indianapolis: Hackett Publishing, 1977), Section V, Part I.

According to Kripke, Wittgenstein is *not* claiming that whether or not a person is following a particular rule depends upon whether or not her community *says* she is. That would be an attempt to *defeat* the sceptic by saying that some kind of community consensus makes it the case that I *do* follow this rule and *not* another. "Such a theory would be a theory of the *truth* conditions" (WRPL 111) of assertions about what rules people follow, but a sceptical solution assumes that all such assertions *lack* truth-values and are, therefore, not true (or false) under any conditions. Wittgenstein, thinks Kripke, is instead offering a theory of the *assertibility-conditions* of propositions about what rules people follow. A proposition's assertibility-conditions are those conditions under which we are licensed in asserting that proposition, and we may be so licensed even if that proposition lacks a truth-value (or so the sceptical solution has it). Wittgenstein, on Kripke's reading, tries to answer the rule-sceptic by focusing on the assertibility-conditions for statements *about* meanings and rules, with the proviso that those conditions have some role to play in our lives. Thus, we are told:

> All that is needed to legitimize assertions that someone means something is that there be roughly specifiable circumstances under which they are legitimately assertible, and that the game of asserting them under such conditions has a role in our lives. (WRPL 77f.)

These assertibility-conditions, thinks Kripke, are bound up with the fact that the members of a community tend to agree in what constitutes a correct application of a rule to a new case. We are warranted in attributing to you the ability to carry out addition if in sufficiently many cases you give the same answer as we would, or at least appear to be applying the same procedure as we would, even if you are making a mistake. We will not be warranted in withdrawing our assessment, unless you consistently give an answer that we would not give, or unless your mistakes seem especially bizarre to us.

But does this really deal with the sceptical worry that Kripke attributes to Wittgenstein? Shouldn't the rule-sceptic simply respond that we are warranted in attributing to you an understanding of the rule 'add 2', only if we are not equally warranted in attributing to you an understanding of some eccentric rule? Precisely the same conditions which, according to Kripke, would warrant our assertion that you have followed the rule 'add 2' in the past would warrant another assertion that you have followed the rule 'add 2 until you reach 1000; then add 4' in the past. And as long as we contingently never face 4-digit numbers, we will find that you are inclined to give just the same answers as we are.

I suspect that it is this objection which Kripke hopes to anticipate and deflate by adding the specification that the particular "language-game" in question—attributing certain concepts to others—must have "a role in our lives" (WRPL 78; see also WRPL 108). Attributions of an understanding of eccentric rules do not normally have any role to play in our lives, whereas attributions of an understanding of such rules as the rule for addition do. However, should someone begin producing solutions radically different from the ones that we are inclined to give, then attributions of a different concept would acquire a point and, hence, a justification. Until that happens, however, it is of no actual consequence for our judgments about the understanding of others.

5.3 CONTRA KRIPKE

It is not clear that the sceptical solution is viable. On Kripke's account, when a speaker *S* says that 2+2=4, there is no fact of the matter concerning what she means by '+'. But we are supposedly justified in *asserting* that she means *plus* by '+' because she gives the answer that we would be inclined to give and because attributions of understanding addition have a role to play in our lives. But if we are justified in asserting that she means *plus* by '+', then we are likewise justified in asserting that it is *true* that she means *plus* by '+'. After all, the practice of judging it to be true that *P* whenever we judge that *P* surely has a role to play in our lives. In that case, we are also justified in asserting that there is some fact of the matter concerning what *S* means by '+', since there is a fact of the matter concerning *P* if and only if it is either true or false that *P*. However, the sceptical solution that Kripke offers us seems to turn on *rejecting* the thought that we are justified in saying that there is any fact of the matter about what *S* means by '+'. Indeed, the sceptical reasoning seems to *justify* us in *asserting* that there is *no* fact of the matter. So it seems that if we follow Kripke, we must hold that we are justified in asserting both that there is some fact of the matter here and that there is not.

Now perhaps this is not an outright contradiction. Perhaps it is merely a tension that can be resolved by, for example, distinguishing two different senses of our being justified in asserting something. Someone might hold, for example, that moral claims lack truth-values and are merely expressions of approval or disapproval of certain actions. So if I say, "Torture is wrong," then I do not say something that is either true or false but express my disapproval of torture. Because it is neither true nor false, according to this view, that torture is wrong, I cannot be justified in believing or asserting that torture is wrong. Nonetheless, one might hold, compatibly with this noncognitivist view of moral discourse, *that my expressions of feeling* are themselves justified in some way—perhaps because they contribute to social cohesion, and members of my society collectively approve of social cohesion. Similarly, we might be justified in uttering the sentence "It is true that *S* means *plus* by '+'" if such utterances have a role in our practices and if *S* typically gets the same results we do. But we might not be justified in *believing* that it is true that *S* means *plus* by '+' or even in believing that *S* means *plus* by '+' because such beliefs purport to have a determinate meaning or content. (The form of our utterance might be justified even if the content is not.)

However, even if the ethical non-cognitivism I described above is a viable view, Kripke's meaning-scepticism encounters special problems precisely because it concerns claims about *meaning*. If there is to be any content to the idea of *assertion*, then it ought not to amount merely to making certain noises, and if we are never justified in believing that anyone means anything in particular by her words, then it is not clear that asserting of someone that she means *plus* by '+' amounts to anything but making a certain noise in a certain context. So this reply does not show us why, even if our belief that *S* means *plus* by '+' is not justified, we can be justified by the sceptical argument in *asserting* that there is no fact of the matter concerning what *S* means *plus* by '+'.[7]

Of greater importance for my purposes, however, is the fact that Kripke's reading of Wittgenstein's text is fundamentally flawed. The idea that Wittgenstein is advocating a "sceptical solution" to a sceptical paradox from which he can see no escape should seem instantly implausible in the light of our earlier examination of Wittgenstein's conception, on the one hand, of the origin and nature of philosophical problems and, on the other, of the appropriate way of responding to those problems—therapeutically. Only by ignoring his methodological remarks can we be led to attribute such a sceptical view to Wittgenstein. Nevertheless, Kripke is right, I think, to portray Wittgenstein as rejecting the various proposals canvassed concerning the essence of rule-following and understanding.

Where, then, does Kripke go wrong? By starting with the wrong questions: *What does my understanding of a word consist in? What fact about me makes it the case that I meant "add 2" rather than "add 2 for numbers less than 1000; add 4 for numbers greater than or equal to 1000"?* Those questions seem to presuppose that there is something more fundamental than my understanding itself to which my understanding might in some way be reduced—that my understanding has some kind of hidden essence that demands investigation by framing the right, or at least a good, explanatory hypothesis. And this seems plausible to us. It makes us vulnerable to the philosophical puzzles that Kripke examines because we are tempted to

7 This objection is inspired by Wright's discussion. See Wright (1984), 766–71.

think that my understanding the rule "add 2" serves as an *explanation* for my getting the right answer in so many cases. So it makes sense to us to see understanding as something hidden from view—a state or process hypothesized to explain the manifest data. "But what exactly is it?" we wonder, just as we wonder what exactly the basic constituents of matter are. The sceptical problem begins here because it seems as though there are alternative hypotheses that fit the observable data, alternative explanations for my getting the "right" results when I am told to add 2, explanations that cite my understanding of some eccentric rule.

But saying that I got the right result *because* I understood addition, thinks Wittgenstein, is like saying that some people have a lot of money because they are wealthy.[8] The latter is not the *cause* of the former; nor is it a *good explanation* for the former. Being wealthy just *is* having a lot of money, and getting the right result (consistently, with room for occasional error) just *is* understanding addition. But the form of expression here— "... *because* I understand ..."—makes it look as though my getting the right result were something that needed explanation by appeal to some hypothesis or other, and it is that move that opens the door to the sceptic, who readily takes this opening as an invitation to come inside (like someone selling vacuum-cleaners or handing out evangelical religious tracts).

The rule-following passages thus present us with an exemplary case of how a preoccupation with the method of science—of hypothesis and confirmation, in particular—"is the real source of metaphysics, and leads the philosopher into complete darkness" (BB 18).[9] Indeed, we could see Wittgenstein's discussion of the proposals that Kripke examines as an extended *reductio ad absurdum* of the application of a scientific explanatory model to the various phenomena of understanding. If my understanding a rule or a word has some hidden essence, then that essence must be given by one of the answers proposed. However, each of these answers leads to absurdities: finite behaviour is compatible with applications of many different rules; behavioural dispositions can be identified only by presupposing rules and on their own cannot distinguish following a rule from failing to follow it; the same type of image can be associated with indefinitely many different words or rules; no image could direct my application of a rule without its own application first being grasped, and this threatens to lead to an infinite regress of rules to interpret rules; interpretations hang in the air with what they interpret

8 See Stuart Shanker, *Wittgenstein's Remarks on the Foundations of AI* (London: Routledge, 1998), 205 for a parallel point about interpreting 'because'.

9 Ludwig Wittgenstein, *The Blue and the Brown Books*, 2nd ed. (Oxford: Blackwell, 1969).

and can provide no foundation. So the original assumption that following a rule or understanding a word consists in something more basic must be mistaken. But this is an assumption that the sceptic shares with the metaphysician.

I said that Kripke goes wrong by beginning with the wrong questions. These questions are not Wittgenstein's. We might say that he wants to replace them with other questions: *When do we normally say that someone who is learning a language or a game within a language has understood a word? When do we allow that a pupil has learned the rule that we are trying to teach her?* If we can get a clear picture of our use of terms like 'understand', Wittgenstein thinks, then any philosophical difficulties that may seem to attend the term should disappear.

Consider, for example, how one use of the term 'understand' and related expressions can get us into difficulty by leading us to mistake the various "characteristic *accompaniments*" (PI §152) of a person's understanding for her understanding itself. Although we test whether someone knows the meaning of a term by checking to see whether or not she can apply it correctly in a range of standard cases, "... there is also this use of the word 'to know': we say 'Now I know!'—and similarly 'Now I can do it!' and 'Now I understand!'" (PI §151). We speak as though knowing or understanding a meaning is something that occurs at an instant, the moment when I suddenly "get it," so that understanding seems like an event or a process:

> [W]e *understand* the meaning of a word when we hear or say it; we grasp it in a flash, and what we grasp in this way is surely something different from the 'use' which is extended in time!
>
> When someone says the word "cube" to me, for example, I know what it means. But can the whole *use* of the word come before my mind, when I *understand* it in this way? (PI §§138–39)

It seems that it cannot—that whatever comes before my mind when I understand in an instant must be something that endures only an instant—a sensation or an image, perhaps. And this conflicts with the ostensibly intuitive observation that "For a large class of cases—though not for all—in which we employ the word 'meaning' it can be [explained] thus: the meaning of a word is its use in the language" (PI §43).

But as we have seen, the occurrence of such an image, or of any other mental process, cannot *be* my understanding, because I can experience the process without being able to apply the word or the rule, and I may be able to apply the word or rule without experiencing any such process. The fact, if it is a fact, that some image occurs to me whenever I hear and understand a word, or the fact that I feel like saying "Now I see!" when I finally come to understand something, shows only that there are certain experiences that characteristically accompany my "sudden understanding" (PI §321):

> Try not to think of understanding as a 'mental process' at all.—For *that* is the expression which confuses you. But ask yourself: in what sort of case, in what kind of circumstances, do we say, "Now I know how to go on," when, that is, the formula *has* occurred to me?—
>
> In the sense in which there are processes (including mental processes) which are characteristic of understanding, understanding is not a mental process.
>
> (A pain's growing more and less; the hearing of a tune or a sentence: these are mental processes.) (PI §154)[10]

And whether or not I have *really* understood is something that is decided by how I apply the rule in question (see PI §146):

> [F]or us it is *the circumstances* under which he had such an experience that justify him in saying in such a case that he understands, that he knows how to go on. (PI §155)

What sorts of circumstances are these? Someone tries to teach me the technique of adding 2. I add 1, instead. "Do it again," she instructs me. I add 1 again, and she says, "Okay, now you've added 2. That's just like adding 1 twice. Try again." I go through a list of numbers, adding 1 twice to each, and then suddenly I feel as though I understand. "I can do it!" I exclaim. My teacher gives me another list of numbers. "Let's see," she says. I successfully add 2 to each number on the list. "Okay! You've got it!" she agrees. *Those* are the kinds of circumstances that justify saying that I know how to go on. Of course, if later on I start making frequent mistakes, the circumstances *may* be enough to undermine that justification. "You could do this yesterday. I thought you understood," my teacher may say to me. But perhaps she will say, "You're not paying attention. You know how to do this. Just be careful." And then perhaps I shall stop making mistakes, affirming her original judgment about my ability, and the confidence I expressed, when I said, "I can do it!"

10 "'What happens when a man suddenly understands?'—The question is badly framed. If it is a question about the meaning of the expression 'sudden understanding', the answer is not to point to a process that we give this name to.—The question might mean: what are the tokens of sudden understanding; what are its characteristic psychical accompaniments?" (PI §321).

Wittgenstein does not deny or even doubt in any of these passages that we *do* understand rules. Rather—to repeat the point I have been emphasizing—he means to deny that understanding is the sort of phenomenon with a hidden essence that we might come to know more about by formulating the right explanatory hypothesis. We can look at this point from another angle. Applying the term 'understands' and related expressions is a language-game, albeit a sophisticated one, that we learn like countless others by being presented with clear examples of understanding. In order to become proficient in making judgments of understanding, we do not require a grasp of its allegedly hidden nature, any more than we require a grasp of the hidden nature of games in order to be able to categorize an activity as a game. Here, too, we are trained in the technique of making such judgments (and that training can go on a long time—how do I decide whether or not a student has understood the central themes of Descartes's *Meditations*?), and our training teaches us to look at the application that a person makes of the word or expression in question. "The application," as Wittgenstein likes to say, "is ... a criterion of understanding" (PI §146).

Commentators have disputed at length about what exactly Wittgenstein means by 'criterion'. According to one view, the satisfaction of a criterion logically entails the truth of some statement for which the criterion is a criterion.[11] This view would have it that if I consistently give the correct answer to a long list of sums, then my correct application of the rule for addition logically entails that I grasp and follow the rule for addition. It is hard to see how such a view can deal with cases in which I give the right answers because I am being given them secretly by a fellow student or because I have memorized them as part of my lines in a play. Here the criterion is satisfied, but it may well be false that I understand addition.

According to a more influential view,[12] if *X* is a criterion for *Y*, then *necessarily*, *X* is evidence for *Y*. That is, it is a necessary truth that *X* is evidence for *Y*. A criterion is, therefore, supposedly unlike a normal piece of empirical evidence, whose evidentiary relation to an explanatory hypothesis is only contingent. Customary evidence is evidence only relative to some set of background assumptions. Perturbations in Mercury's orbit are evidence for the existence of an undiscovered planet, Vulcan, only relative to the general assumptions of Newtonian physics. Relative to the general assumptions of Einstein's general theory of relativity, such perturbations provide no support for postulating the existence of an unnoticed

11 See Rogers Albritton, "On Wittgenstein's Use of the Term 'Criterion'" in *Wittgenstein: The Philosophical Investigations*, edited by George Pitcher (Garden City, NY: Doubleday, 1966), 231–50.

12 See, among others, W.G. Lycan, "Noninductive Evidence: Recent Work on Wittgenstein's 'Criteria,'" *American Philosophical Quarterly* 8, no.2 (1971): 109–25 and Gordon Baker, "Criteria: A New Foundation for Semantics," *Ratio* 16, no.2 (1974): 156–89.

planet at all. By contrast, on this view, (X), my correct application of a rule, being a criterion for (Y), my understanding the rule, is *necessarily* evidence that I understand the rule. It follows that there is no circumstance in which my correct application of the rule would not give someone else a reason to think that I understood the rule. Of course, it would not be a *conclusive* reason, because there might be better evidence for thinking that I did not really understand—for example, evidence that I was being surreptitiously fed the right answers by a fellow student or manifest evidence that I was merely pretending to understand (because I was acting in a play, perhaps). But it would still be *evidence*, and my correct application would remain a criterion, regardless of the circumstances.

The main rival to this view has it that if X is a criterion for Y, then the satisfaction of that criterion is *sufficient* for Y, but only in appropriate circumstances.[13] That is, the satisfaction of the criterion does not provide *evidence* for Y; it is *definitive* of Y under the right sorts of circumstances. What sort of circumstances are those? The sorts of circumstances in which the rule or the concept is taught and learned, as we saw above. According to this view, my giving correct answers to a series of addition questions would not satisfy a criterion for my understanding addition if the circumstances in which I gave the answers included my being fed the answers by someone else or my performing in a play. Cases in which it seems as though the criterion was fulfilled, but in which the corresponding judgment was false, are not cases in which the evidence is defeated by conflicting evidence. Rather, they are cases in which the criterion was not really satisfied to begin with, despite our having thought it was. Thus, someone who begins to add 4 once she reaches 20-digit numbers was not really getting the right answer up to this point. She was doing something else that led us incorrectly to think she was getting the right answer, or she has now forgotten how to apply the rule correctly.

This third interpretation of 'criterion' seems to me to be the most plausible one. For one thing, it fits the textual evidence very well. For example, it fits nicely with Wittgenstein's use of the phrase 'defining criterion' (BB 25) in the *Blue Book*. (The same cannot be said for the "necessary evidence" interpretation.) But, more importantly, the definitional interpretation of 'criterion' is clearly consistent with Wittgenstein's methodological remarks. The necessary-evidence view is not consistent with those remarks, for it is clear that Wittgenstein means to contrast a criterion for a judgment with empirical evidence for it. If my consistently correct answers on addition-tests were merely empirical evidence for my understanding

---

13 See, e.g., John V. Canfield, *Wittgenstein, Language and World* (Amherst: University of Massachusetts Press, 1981) and John McDowell, "Criteria, Defeasibility, and Knowledge," *Proceedings of the British Academy* 68 (1982): 455–79.

of addition, then they could also be construed as evidence that I grasp some other eccentric rule instead. However, if we try to avoid this problem by insisting that the satisfaction of a criterion for my grasping the rule of addition *necessarily* provides evidence that I do addition rather than some eccentric Kripkean operation, then we seem merely to be begging the question by stipulating that *this* kind of behaviour will count as evidence for following *this* rule, but not for following *that* rule. We are still operating with the model of hypothesis-and-confirmation whose misapplication Wittgenstein thinks of as one of the roots of philosophical confusion. As I remarked above, Wittgenstein thinks that my consistently getting the right answers in the appropriate circumstances *just is* my understanding addition. That is what it means to say that my application is a *criterion* for the judgment that I understand.

If Wittgenstein is not promulgating a new form of scepticism, why is Kripke so sure that he is? Let's consider two passages that seem especially important for Kripke's interpretation. He begins by citing a part of PI §201:

> This was our paradox: no course of action could be determined by a rule, because every course of action can be made out to accord with the rule. The answer was: if everything can be made out to accord with the rule, then it can also be made out to conflict with it. And so there would be neither accord nor conflict here. (PI §201)

This looks like a way of summarizing the claim that all the plausible answers to the question "What does my understanding a rule consist in?" lead to trouble. None of them allows us to distinguish understanding a rule from failing to understand it, or from understanding some eccentric alternative rule. But as other commentators have observed,[14] it is odd that Kripke pays no attention to the rest of this section of the *Investigations*, which continues:

> It can be seen that there is a misunderstanding here from the mere fact that in the course of our argument we give one interpretation after another; as if each one contented us at least for a moment, until we thought of yet another standing behind it. What this shews is that there is a way of grasping a rule which is *not* an *interpretation*, but which is exhibited in what we call "obeying the rule" and "going against it" in actual cases. (PI §201)

---

14 See especially Baker and Hacker (1984); McDowell (1998), 229; Robert Brandom, *Making It Explicit* (Cambridge, MA: Harvard University Press, 1994), 21.

If grasping a rule amounted to interpreting it—to "the substitution of one expression of the rule for another" (PI §201)—then we would be faced with the infinite regress that we encountered above. But, like the terms 'block' and 'pillar', 'addition' and 'plus' are terms I come to understand not by being given *interpretations* of them, not by being given explicit verbal definitions, but by being trained in the practice of applying them—by becoming "master of a technique" (PI §199). This is a way of grasping a rule that is not an interpretation. "The application," to repeat, "is ... a criterion of understanding" (PI §146).

Indeed, we can find in Wittgenstein's discussion of rule-following a further motivation for his mature views about philosophical method (beyond the motivation provided by an example of how the model of hypothesis-and-confirmation leads us into darkness). For the regress argument shows us why philosophy, insofar as it takes an interest in the normative, must take an interest in the synopsis of trivialities—in giving a perspicuous representation of norms implicit in our practices. The reason is that at least some of those norms *must be* implicit in our practices if we are to have any norms at all.[15] That is, there must be a way of grasping a rule that is not an interpretation if it is to be possible to give interpretations of rules—explicit verbal definitions.

A second passage that may seem to support Kripke's interpretation is the one that introduces the example of the pupil who, when asked to continue a series by adding two beyond 1000, "writes 1000, 1004, 1008, 1012" (PI §185). We encountered this passage earlier. What is Wittgenstein doing here if not presenting a sceptical problem? The remainder of PI §185 suggests an alternative. Wittgenstein continues:

> —In such a case we might say, perhaps: It comes natural to this person to understand our order with our explanations as *we* should understand the order: "Add 2 up to 1000, 4 up to 2000, 6 up to 3000 and so on."
>
> Such a case would present similarities with one in which a person naturally reacted to the gesture of pointing with the hand by looking in the direction of the line from finger-tip to wrist, not from wrist to finger-tip. (PI §185)

Wittgenstein takes such bizarre behaviour to be a logical possibility, but a logical possibility is no ground for sceptical doubt. Such extraordinary doubt requires an *explanatory* possibility—an hypothesis that would give an alternative account of some manifest phenomenon that puzzles us. But as we have seen, my

15 *Cf.* Brandom (1994), 20: "Norms that are *explicit* in the form of rules presuppose norms *implicit* in practices."

understanding addition is not the explanation for my getting the right answers when asked to add 2; it *is* my getting the right answers in the appropriate circumstances (with allowance for occasional error).

What this passage also draws attention to, however, is the remarkable fact that we do not encounter such bizarre behaviour. Perhaps if we travelled to some distant arm of the galaxy, we might find intelligent creatures who found it natural to add 4 after 1000, 6 after 2000, and so on, just as we might find creatures who found it natural to "point" backwards. Many practices that we take for granted—arithmetic, pointing, gesturing, the whole wide and variable array of activities interlaced with uses of language—are contingent through and through. They rest on implicit conventions that could well have been different. But in at least some of these cases—arithmetic is a good example—here on planet Earth, we seldom, if ever, confront such alternatives.[16]

This note recalls a theme that we played in Chapters 3 and 4: that the conventions that replace the transcendental logical form of the *Tractatus* may be *contingent*, but they are not thereby made *arbitrary*, because "certain very general facts of nature" (PI II §xii; 230) constrain the range of possible conventions that we find reasonable, plausible, or useful to adopt. Human conventions, contingent though they are, are woven into what Wittgenstein calls a "form of life" (PI §19). They are practices that are typical of organisms like us. This is not to reduce our conceptual repertoire to something strictly biological—human beings are *cultural* beings—but it is to recognize contingent constraints on which conventions human beings regard as plausible or worth adopting. Perhaps if human beings had long, boney protuberances on their shoulders or differently organized visual systems, we might find it natural to "point" in a different way. And perhaps changing other "extremely general facts of nature: such facts as are hardly ever mentioned because of their great generality" (PI 56)—indeed, facts so general that we find it difficult to think what they might be—might make eccentric rules of calculation look more plausible or useful to us. But as it is, we find it difficult to envision what alternatives to our existing arithmetical conventions there might be—though we *can* think of simple language-games that we play with numbers, and we can be surprised by the complicated systems of calculation that come into higher mathematics.[17]

---

16 This is not to deny obvious cultural variation, for example, in the significance of certain gestures, but rather to stress that even some practices that seem to rest on "necessary truths," such as arithmetic, are contingent. We might not have developed them at all.

17 Perhaps human beings do not have to have systems of calculation at all—it has been argued that some, such as the Pirahã of the upper Amazon, do not. See Daniel Everett, "Cultural Constraints on Grammar and Cognition in Pirahã," *Current Anthropology* 46 (2005): 621–46.

5.4 KRIPKE ON PRIVATE LANGUAGE

At PI §243 Wittgenstein introduces a topic that has generated an extraordinarily large secondary literature and a great deal of puzzlement, the topic of the possibility of a private language. Such a private language is not to be confused with the evident fact that language-users can speak to themselves:

> A human being can encourage himself, give himself orders, obey, blame and punish himself; he can ask himself a question and answer it. We could even imagine human beings who spoke only in monologue; who accompanied their activities by talking to themselves.—An explorer who watched them and listened to their talk might succeed in translating their language into ours. (This would enable him to predict these people's actions correctly, for he also hears them making resolutions and decisions.) (PI §243)

These are linguistic phenomena with which we are all familiar. A language that is in the relevant sense "private" is something else:

> But could we also imagine a language in which a person could write down or give vocal expression to his inner experiences—his feelings, moods, and the rest—for his private use?—Well, can't we do so in our ordinary language?—But that is not what I mean. The individual words of this language are to refer to what can only be known to the person speaking; to his immediate private sensations. So another person cannot understand the language. (PI §243)

Wittgenstein is concerned here with what may be loosely termed the "Cartesian" conception of subjectivity and self-knowledge (we could as well say "Lockean"). According to this view, I have determinate concepts of my own inner experiences independently of having learned to speak a public language like English or Urdu. My consciousness is like an inner theatre in which various objects and events are arrayed, and in which I am the sole audience member. No one else can experience the inner workings of my consciousness because it is, after all, *my* consciousness, shut up and locked away from other consciousnesses. So only I can know what my experiences are like, and no public language can capture all there is to be captured about my sensations. No amount of instruction on my part or diligent study on the part of another would enable her to learn the meanings of terms in my private sensation-language. Wittgenstein seeks to reject this Cartesian picture as a philosophical illusion, but before examining what his reasons are, I want to say something about what his reasons are *not*. This requires taking one last look at Kripke's interpretation.

Kripke thinks that the anti-realist account of meaning that is supposed to supply a sceptical solution to the sceptical puzzle about rules also provides us with what he calls "the real 'private language argument'" (WRPL 3). That argument, according to Kripke, looks something like this. Remember that, according to Kripke's sceptical solution, "All that is needed to legitimize assertions that someone means something is that there be roughly specifiable circumstances under which they are legitimately assertible, and that the game of asserting them under such conditions has a role in our lives" (WRPL 77f.). The roughly specifiable circumstances in which it is legitimate for us to assert that you have grasped the rule for addition are those in which in sufficiently many cases you give the same answers to addition-problems as we would. But, plainly, such circumstances presuppose that there is a community of judges against whose responses your performance can be assessed. Take away the community, and you take away the circumstances necessary for legitimate attributions of meaning and understanding: "if one person is considered in isolation, the notion of a rule as guiding the person who adopts it can have *no* substantive content" (WRPL 89). So no person considered in isolation can justifiably be held to be a speaker of a language, and this, thinks Kripke, is what Wittgenstein has in mind when he argues against the possibility of a "private" (PI §243) language.

The dependence of this reasoning on the sceptical solution to rule-scepticism makes it immediately suspect as a reading of Wittgenstein for reasons I have already presented. But, additionally, the opening passage of Wittgenstein's discussion of private language, which we glanced at above, draws a sharp distinction between our ability to talk to ourselves and the speaking of a language that "another person cannot understand" (PI §243), and this difference is conflated by Kripke's reading, which simply contemplates a person "considered in isolation."

5.5 SOME ARGUMENTS AGAINST PRIVATE LANGUAGE

So we are now left with the difficult task of trying to make some sense of what the so-called private language argument is supposed to amount to. In fact, as other commentators have observed,[18] there is really more than one argument against private language, but if there is a recurrent theme in these arguments it concerns the dubiousness of modelling words for sensations on names for publicly observ-

18 See, e.g., P.M.S. Hacker, *Wittgenstein: Meaning and Mind, Part II* (Oxford: Blackwell, 1993), Chapter 1.

able spatio-temporal objects and events. The problem here should be immediately obvious in light of Wittgenstein's treatment of naming and ostensive teaching and learning, examined in Chapter 4. A language that referred only to my private sensations would have to be very different from any of the simple language-games by means of which Wittgenstein illustrates the variety of terms that we call names. In particular it would be remarkably different from the language-game of the builders, whose terms 'block', 'slab', etc. are taught and learned ostensively in the context of learning to follow various commands. Indeed, as we have seen, terms for colours and even numbers are also taught ostensively by means of simple language-games like that of the builders. No such ostension is available in the case of terms for my "immediate private sensations" (PI §243), and it is on this ground that such terms are claimed to be private. But given that what we understand of *naming* rests on ostensive teaching, there is no clear reason to think that naming can be successfully carried out where there can be no ostensive teaching. This general theme recurs in a number of Wittgenstein's arguments.

If the meanings of sensation-terms really were fixed by some mysterious procedure of inner ostensive definition, then they could have no use in the public language that we share with each other. Or—what amounts to the same thing—if sensation-terms have a use in our public language (and they clearly do), then their meanings are not fixed by inner ostensive definition. The success of such definitions would depend on the possibility of others' being able to learn the use of sensation terms by acquaintance with other people's sensations, but it is unclear what it would mean to acquaint someone else with my pain, for example, unless it were to express it to her in some way. But such expressions are part of our public language, not examples of inner ostension. The alleged definition would be playing no role in bringing the term into the language. The point is illustrated by Wittgenstein's example of the beetle in a box. Imagine, he says, that each of us had a box that contained something we call a "beetle":

> No one can look into anyone else's box, and everyone says he knows what a beetle is only by looking at *his* beetle.—Here it would be quite possible for everyone to have something different in his box. One might even imagine such a thing constantly changing.—But suppose the word "beetle" had a use in these people's language?—If so it would not be used as the name of a thing. The thing in the box has no place in the language-game at all; not even as a *something*: for the box might even be empty.—No, one can 'divide through' by the thing in the box; it cancels out, whatever it is.

> That is to say: if we construe the grammar of the expression of sensation on the model of 'object and designation' the object drops out of consideration as irrelevant. (PI §293)[19]

If sensation-terms are not used, taught, and learned in the same way as terms like 'block' and 'slab', then how are they used, taught, and learned? Wittgenstein makes it clear that he sees this question as equivalent to the question of how sensation terms manage to refer to sensations:

> How do words *refer* to sensations?—There doesn't seem to be any problem here; don't we talk about sensations every day, and give them names? But how is the connexion between the name and the thing named set up? This question is the same as: how does a human being learn the meaning of the names of sensations?—of the word "pain" for example. Here is one possibility: words are connected with the primitive, the natural, expressions of the sensation and used in their place. A child has hurt himself and he cries; and then adults talk to him and teach him exclamations and, later, sentences. They teach the child new pain-behaviour.
>
> "So you are saying that the word 'pain' really means crying?"—On the contrary: the verbal expression of pain replaces crying and does not describe it. (PI §244)

Notice, first, the tentative character of Wittgenstein's proposal: "Here is one possibility," he says. Perhaps it is wrong. Perhaps it fails to capture clearly the conventions of use that are implicit in our linguistic activities, or perhaps it captures them only in part. But language-games serve their purpose if they are acting as "*objects of comparison*" (PI §130), and this one would go some distance toward clarifying how we could come to learn how to use sensation-terms without imagining extraordinary, private acts of inner ostensive definition. If "my words for sensations [are] tied up with my natural expressions of sensation," says Wittgenstein, then "my language is not a 'private' one. Someone else might understand it as well as I" (PI §256).

To say that a child learns "new pain-behaviour" when she learns how to use sensation-terms is to say that her basic use of sensation-terms is not to *describe* her

19 For a nuanced reading of this passage see David G. Stern, "The Uses of Wittgenstein's Beetle: *Philosophical Investigations* §253 and Its Interpreters" in *Wittgenstein and His Interpreters: Essays in Memory of Gordon Baker*, edited by Guy Kahane, Edward Kanterian, and Oksari Kuusela (Oxford: Blackwell, 2007), 248–68.

inner states, as though her ability to identify them came first and were followed by a search for the right way of representing them. She first learns to *express* her sensations and *in doing so* learns to identify them. Of course, once she has mastered the technique of expressing her inner episodes, she is in a position to learn the language-game of describing them—of saying whether her pain is sharp or dull, burning or tingling, and so on. But it would be puzzling how sensation-terms would ever be learned at all if they lacked the public accessibility that goes with Wittgenstein's *expressivist* view. As Wittgenstein says later in the *Investigations*, "An 'inner process' stands in need of outward criteria" (PI §580). (I'll return to this point below.)

The suspicion may linger, however, that even if sensation-terms do have a public component to their meaning, their full meaning is a vector-sum of this public meaning and a private one that we might get at by imagining what it would be like if we had sensations without any means of publicly expressing them: "—But suppose I didn't have any natural expression for the sensation, but only had the sensation? And now I simply *associate* names with sensations and use these names in descriptions.—" (PI §256). At PI §257 Wittgenstein goes on to imagine a child-genius who "invents a name for the sensation" of toothache, but who then cannot "make himself understood" when he uses the term because he has no way of "explain[ing] its meaning to anyone." Isn't such a case logically possible?

Wittgenstein responds:

> —But what does it mean to say that he has 'named his pain'?—How has he done this naming of pain?! And whatever he did, what was its purpose?—When one says "He gave a name to his sensation" one forgets that a great deal of stage-setting in the language is presupposed if the mere act of naming is to make sense. And when we speak of someone's having given a name to pain, what is presupposed is the existence of the grammar of the word "pain"; it shews the post where the new word is stationed. (PI §257)

Everything we know about naming, Wittgenstein seems to say, suggests that it takes place in a public context—that is, in a context where it is possible to teach or learn a term ostensively. And that, remember, does not simply consist in pointing at something and saying its name, for learning the use of a term involves coming to understand the role it plays in a nexus of human activities. "One has already to know (or be able to do) something in order to be capable of asking a thing's name" (PI §30). Precisely what is missing in the case of the child-genius is any account of "the overall role of the word in language" (PI §30), and without that we have no reason to believe that an act of naming takes place when the child "*associate*[s] names with sensations" (PI §256).[20] This does not show that it is *impossible*, but the burden of proof is on the philosopher who wants to insist that the customary stage-setting that we rely on as a matter of course when we assign names—the grammar of the word 'pain' in this case—can be removed without interfering with the child-genius's ability to bestow a name.

5.6 A REFUTATION OF THE POSSIBILITY OF PRIVATE LANGUAGE?

It is tempting to think, however, that there is a further argument against the very logical possibility of private language to be found in the *Investigations*. Consider the diary-example of PI §258. Here Wittgenstein's interlocutor has us consider the case of someone who records a certain type of sensation in a diary by writing an "S" on every day that he has a sensation of that type. Would it not be possible for me to name my sensations in this way? Could I not, for example, focus my attention inward on the sensation at the time I write "S" in my diary, thereby establishing a link between name and sensation? This would be analogous to pointing to an object and giving an ostensive definition, thinks the interlocutor. It would be an *inner* ostensive definition. Wittgenstein will have none of this:

> —But what is this ceremony for? for that is all it seems to be! A definition surely serves to establish the meaning of a sign.—Well, that is done precisely by the concentrating of my attention; for in this way I impress on myself the connexion between the sign and the sensation.—But "I impress it on myself" can only mean: this process brings it about that I remember the connexion *right* in the future. But in the present case I have no criterion of correctness. One would like to say: whatever is going to seem right to me is right. And that only means that here we can't talk about 'right'. (PI §258)

It is easy to be perplexed by this passage if one reads it as an attempt to show that a private language is logically impossible, and such perplexity has resulted in some curious reconstructions of the argument. The most notorious, perhaps, is due to A.J. Ayer.[21] The problem, Ayer takes Wittgenstein to be saying, is that I cannot

20 See David G. Stern, "A new exposition of the 'private language argument': Wittgenstein's 'Notes for the "Philosophical Lecture"'," *Philosophical Investigations* 17, no.3 (1994): 552–65.

21 See A.J. Ayer, "Can There Be a Private Language?" in *Wittgenstein: The Philosophical Investigations*, edited by George Pitcher (Garden City, NY: Doubleday: 1966), 251–66.

verify at a later time whether I am applying the name to the same kind of sensation, because all I have to go on here is my ability to recognize or remember the sensation. However, I may be misremembering the connection that I set up between sensation and name, and so I cannot be sure that I am using the name correctly.

According to Ayer's reconstruction, the argument of the diary example looks roughly like this:

> 1. My private sensation-term 'S' is meaningful only if its application can be justified.
>
> 2. The application of 'S' can be justified only if there is some "test for determining that the sign is being used correctly" that is "independent ... of the subject's recognition, or supposed recognition, of the object which he intends the sign to signify" (Ayer 256).
>
> 3. No private test could satisfy the independence condition of premise 2.
>
> 4. Therefore, my private sensation-term 'S' is meaningful only if its application can be justified by some public test—i.e., 'S' is meaningful only if it is not private.

As Ayer correctly points out, if this argument works at all, then its application is too broad. *All* testing depends ultimately on our capacity for recognition, says Ayer, so if premise 2 is true, then I can be no more confident that my applications of a name for a *public* object or event are justified. My memory may as easily play me false here as in the imagined case of a private ostensive definition. All that this amounts to is scepticism about memory.

Many commentators have found Ayer's interpretation implausible. It seems, for example, to place an inappropriate emphasis on the verification of apparent memories when Wittgenstein tells us that what is missing is any "criterion of correctness"—anything that would render determinate whether I had remembered correctly or not. The problem seems to be not that my memory or capacity for recognition might fail me, but that nothing here would *count* as remembering correctly.[22] That, in turn, seems to be connected specifically with the nature of the example—it is not a point that generalizes to include objects and events that are publicly accessible.

---

22 See, e.g., Rush Rhees, "Can There Be a Private Language?" in Pitcher (ed.), 26; Stewart Candlish "The Real Private Language Argument," *Philosophy* 55 (1980): 85–94; Hacker (1993), 64.

P.M.S. Hacker offers a much more nuanced reading of the diary case. As he sees it, the trouble with a private ostensive definition lies in the fact that there is no way in which some future occurrence of a sensation can be compared with the original sensation that served as the sample by which 'S' was to be defined. When I give an ostensive definition of, say, 'one metre', I can point to the standard metre bar in Paris (let's suppose), and subsequent applications of the term 'one metre' can be checked for their correctness by comparing the lengths of the objects so described with the standard metre. Or, at least, the standard metre can be used to calibrate other metre sticks to which the objects can be compared to justify the judgment that these objects are one metre long. However, my current sensation cannot be compared with the past sensation that was supposedly used to define the term 'S' (Hacker 47–48).

It may seem once again that there is no difference here from the case of public objects. If I designate some stick to be the standard metre and then destroy it, surely I can make no further comparisons with it, but we don't think that this makes meaningful application of the term 'one metre' impossible. Hacker's point is more subtle than this, however. The reason that my original sensation cannot serve as a standard of comparison by means of which future applications of the term 'S' might be justified is that my only way of *identifying* that sensation to begin with is by applying the term 'S' to it (Hacker 48–49). I cannot say to myself, "This *sensation* I shall call 'S'," because these are all words belonging to a public language (PI §261). Unfortunately, I seem to have no further way of picking out the sensation that is to serve as a standard. By contrast, I can identify the standard metre bar *as a bar*, as being made of a certain kind of metal, as being smooth or rough, as having a certain shape, colour, etc. It is not *just* the standard metre, because it can be described in other ways. The would-be private linguist has no comparable resources at her disposal when it comes to identifying her original sensation, and so it cannot serve as a standard of comparison. 'S' cannot be meaningful.

This is a powerful argument, I think, but I am not convinced that a dedicated proponent of the logical possibility of a private language need be swayed by it. Why shouldn't she simply insist that it is possible to have a brute capacity to recognize one's sensations on different occasions? This may seem like magic, but magic is not *impossible*; it just fails to conform to what we take to be the actual course of nature.

It seems to me that attempts to extract from this passage (and others) an outright refutation of the logical possibility of a private language fail to take sufficient heed of Wittgenstein's explicit pronouncements about philosophical problems and philosophical method.[23] The task of the philosopher is to assemble reminders for a particular purpose, to help prevent us from falling into confusion by reminding us of what we already know. It is *not* to provide categorical refutations of alleged logical possibilities.

Of course, Hacker might respond here that we need not think of his reconstruction of the argument in such strong terms. We could say, instead, that any instance of naming with which we are acquainted allows for the possibility of independently identifying the sample used to define a term ostensively. Because the sensation in the diary case cannot be independently identified, we have no grounds for thinking that any comparison is made when the diarist has some later sensation and no grounds for thinking that the term 'S' is meaningful.

However, there is a further problem with Hacker's reading, identified by John Canfield. As Canfield observes, we should not treat PI §258 as an argument that the private diarist fails to name her sensation because it lacks the appropriate "stage-setting"—the argument presented in PI §257—because this would commit Wittgenstein to a piece of circular reasoning (Canfield 2001, 383). The diary example cites as the *reason* for the failure of private ostensive definition the fact that there is no criterion of correctness for the application of 'S' to future cases. So it had better not be the case that the reason for there being no criterion of correctness is that no ostensive definition has been given to start.

It seems, rather, that the diary case grants for the sake of argument that the diarist gives a private ostensive definition and then tries to cast doubt on her ability to understand it, to "remember the connexion *right* in the future." Naming is supposed to establish a use for the word, and that is done by showing how the word fits into some practical activity. Here, we have stripped the context of any practical activity, and our usual criteria for the attribution of understanding are unavailable to us. It is a criterion of my understanding how to use a word that I be able to apply it correctly in an unlimited variety of standard cases—in other words that I remember from one occasion to the next how to use it. My asserting on a single occasion, "This is called 'S'" is not by itself a criterion for my understanding the use of 'S'—remember the discussion of rule-following and understanding. So by all our normal standards of teaching and learning, there is no reason to say that I have understood an application for the term 'S' or that I have established a meaning for 'S' by concentrating my attention inwards. Again, it is not *impossible* that I have done so, but the burden of proof is on the philosopher who wishes to

23 Indeed, conversations with Bob Martin and John Canfield have persuaded me that such attempts are doomed to failure. See John V. Canfield, "Private Language: The Diary Case" *Australasian Journal of Philosophy* 79, no.3 (2001): 377–94.

maintain such an extravagant thesis. She must convince us that the extraordinary story that she imagines is one which warrants the description "naming"—that the act there described is sufficiently similar to clear and uncontroversial cases of naming to warrant extending the term to include that act—and she needs also to convince us that this story then has some special significance for us as philosophers and is not merely an idle exercise.[24]

Far from offering an outright refutation of the possibility of a private language, Wittgenstein is simply reminding us of the implicit conventions that govern our uses of names and of the variety and complexity of the category 'name' in the hope that we will avoid confusing the language-game of object-and-designation with that of naming sensations.[25]

5.7 "ROBINSON CRUSOE"

Philosophers have been interested in Wittgenstein's discussion of private language for reasons that go beyond a concern about the grammar of sensation-language or the viability of Cartesian views about the mind. For they have also thought that if Wittgenstein really does refute the possibility of a private language, then he has shown something of fundamental importance concerning the social character of language. This interest has been reinforced by Kripke's interpretation of the *Investigations*, because in his view the discussion of private language is essentially connected to the discussion of rule-following in the sense that the sceptical solution to the rule-following puzzle is one that rules out not only a private sensation-language, but the very possibility of regarding someone "considered in isolation" (WRPL 89) as speaking any language whatsoever.

Interest in the (im)possibility of a solitary language-user, in the context of Wittgenstein's *Investigations*, goes back at least as far as Ayer's article, which first

24 Barry Stroud and David Stern agree that no categorical refutation of the possibility of private language is to be found in §258, but they are not convinced of the circularity that Canfield identifies and read §258 as re-emphasizing the point of §257, as I understand it: there is insufficient stage-setting to make it plausible that the would-be private linguist succeeds in giving a definition of 'S' by our normal standards of naming. See Barry Stroud, "Wittgenstein's 'Treatment' of the Quest for 'a language which describes my inner experience and which only I myself can understand'" in *Meaning, Understanding, and Practice: Philosophical Essays* (Oxford: Oxford University Press, 2000), 67–79, at 74–78, and Stern (2004), 184–85.

25 Notice in this connection that when Wittgenstein introduces the idea of a private sensation-language at PI §243, he does not ask, "Is it logically possible for anyone to speak a private language?" but "Can we *imagine* such a language?" An answer to the latter question need not be an answer to the former. "There is a lack of clarity about the role of *imaginability* in our investigation" (PI §395).

appeared in 1954. There Ayer speculates on whether it would be logically possible for a "Robinson Crusoe," who had spent his entire life in isolation on a desert island, to speak a language.[26]

If Wittgenstein offers no refutation of the logical possibility of a private sensation-language, then I do not think we should expect him either to offer any decisive refutation of such a life-long Robinson Crusoe. There is nothing to prevent us from imagining that young Robinson somehow manages to survive his childhood and develops a system of markings for recording the numbers and kinds of various tropical fruit that grow on his island. Were we to discover him at work in his hut making such markings, the hypothesis that they were meaningful would be difficult to resist. What our observations would have to establish, of course, is whether his behaviour satisfied criteria of the sort that we ordinarily associate with understanding a rule. We would look for patterns in his behaviour that made sense to us, and we might investigate whether we were able to learn how to follow his would-be rules and, perhaps, whether he were able to learn any of our own rules. Affirmative answers to these questions would, I think, be persuasive reasons for thinking that he did, prior to our intervention, satisfy criteria for understanding rules. No doubt, it would be an empirical mystery how such an extraordinary thing could come about, but that does not demonstrate that a life-long Crusoe is a logical impossibility.

> We can indeed imagine a Robinson [Crusoe] using a language for himself but then he must *behave* in a certain way or we shouldn't say that he plays lang[uage] games with himself.[27]

There are, to be sure, many reasons for thinking that when Wittgenstein writes about language he has in mind something that is paradigmatically social. His examples of rudimentary language-games are frequently interwoven with discussions of how children are trained to participate in these games by adults. And it is no secret that he thinks of rule-following as a custom or an institution (see PI §§198–99). But we have also seen that Wittgenstein rejects categorically the idea that language has a hidden essence, and only the idea that language is *essentially* social is compatible with thinking that Wittgenstein aims to refute

26 Philosophers have long played fast and loose with Defoe's proto-capitalist hero, who was marooned as an adult on an island that was deserted only in the sense that it was devoid of other Europeans. Marx was already making fun of the popularity of such examples in the first volume of *Capital*, published in 1867.

27 Ludwig Wittgenstein, "Notes for Lectures on 'Private Experience' and 'Sense Data,'" translated and edited by David G. Stern, in *Philosophical Occasions 1912–1951*, edited by James Klagge and Alfred Nordmann (Indianapolis: Hackett Publishing, 1993), 237.

the possibility of a life-long Crusoe. As John Canfield remarks, "[This] Crusoe is a borderline case of language use."[28] Language is a family-resemblance concept, and what we choose to allow into its fold will depend on our purposes in raising cases for consideration. If we choose to exclude life-long Crusoe from the set of language-users, then that will be a decision that we make for special purposes, not a carving of language at its natural joints.

5.8 EXPRESSIVISM

I said earlier that Wittgenstein seeks to reject the Cartesian picture of the mind as a philosophical illusion. One of the sources of that illusion, we can now see, is our being misled by "certain analogies between the forms of expression in different regions of language" (PI §90)—our failing to distinguish, as types, names for sensations from names for building materials, for example. But does the expressivist story that Wittgenstein tentatively advances succeed in making explicit to us the implicit conventions governing our uses of sensation terms?

We were given hints of Wittgenstein's expressivism before encountering the problem of private language. When we considered earlier the phenomenon of "sudden understanding," we saw that it can be tempting to confuse the characteristic accompaniments of understanding with the understanding itself, and my expression "I can do it!" or "I understand!" is one such accompaniment. But it is also an *expression*—an expression of my confidence, in contrast to my teacher's judgments about my ability. When I say, "I can do it!" I am not making a *judgment* about my ability. I am not *reporting* on something I have seen or otherwise witnessed and wish to share with the world. I have not looked within myself and *discovered* my understanding. How could I? When I look within myself I discover, for example, associated images or sensations, which, as we have seen, are not my understanding itself. When I say, "I can do it!" I might as well say, "Aha!" because what I share with the world in this expression is simply my confidence. My teacher, by contrast, may well be confident of my ability, but she makes a report on something she has observed. She might be wrong, because she might be mistaken concerning whether I have really fulfilled the criteria for understanding. But I cannot be similarly mistaken about whether or not I am confident (though I may, of course, display *false* confidence).

As we have briefly seen, Wittgenstein takes much the same story to apply to fundamental first-person uses of sensation terms. When a child says, "I am in

28 John V. Canfield, "The Community View," *The Philosophical Review* 105 (1996): 469–88 at 485.

pain," or, more idiomatically, "It hurts," clutching at her skinned knee, she is not in the first instance giving a report about how she has discovered things to be with her. Rather, she is giving spontaneous expression to her pain. She might simply have clutched her knee and cried. Adults ask her, "Does it hurt? Have you hurt yourself?" and she learns to respond to such questions by giving her pain a new kind of expression.

Some critics have supposed that this is the end of the story as far as Wittgenstein is concerned—that all first-person uses of sensation-terms take the form of *avowals*, rather than of reports or descriptions, and this has seemed implausible for two reasons: first, it seems clear that we *can* describe or report on our sensations; second, if first-person, present-tense uses of sensation-terms are always expressive and never descriptive, then it is tempting to say that they differ in meaning from second- and third-person uses, and from uses that concern one's past sensations, which seem typically to be descriptive.[29]

However, this interpretation of Wittgenstein is based on inattention to other remarks that we find later in the *Investigations*. Consider the following discussion of expressive and descriptive uses of psychological terms:

> But here is the problem: a cry, which cannot be called a description, which is more primitive than any description, for all that serves as a description of the inner life.
>
> A cry is not a description. But there are transitions. And the words "I am afraid" may approximate more, or less, to being a cry. They may come quite close to this and also be *far* removed from it.
>
> We surely do not always say someone is *complaining*, because he says he is in pain. So the words "I am in pain" may be a cry of complaint, and may be something else.
>
> But if "I am afraid" is not always something like a cry of complaint and yet sometimes is, then why should it *always* be a description of a state of mind? (PI II §ix; 189)

Wittgenstein clearly recognizes that there are non-expressive first-person uses of psychological terms, including sensation-terms. I can express my fear or pain in words, but I can also utter a sentence like "I am in pain" or "I am afraid" as an explanation for my behaviour: "Why don't you tell her how you feel?"—"I am afraid to! I don't know how she would react." "Why are you walking so strangely?"—"I am in pain!" I can use first-person psychological terms in hypothetical constructions:

29 See P.F. Strawson, *Individuals* (London: Methuen, 1959), 134.

"Let's pretend that I am afraid of you," I say, initiating a game of make-believe or a bit of improvisational theatre. Or I can give a description of changes in my frame of mind or in the state of my sensations: "I was in quite a lot of pain yesterday," I tell my doctor, "but today I am feeling much better." "I was afraid that you had gotten lost, but now I am just relieved to see that you are all right."

Wittgenstein's concern is not to deny that such uses exist, but to insist that they do not exhaust the first-person uses of psychological terms, and it is crucial that they do not exhaust those uses, because the expressive use of psychological terms is needed to make sense of how psychological terms get to refer to our inner episodes. We need not suppose, as I put the point earlier, that I first identify my inner episodes and then learn what to call them, as the Cartesian model would suggest. Rather, in learning to express my inner states using the vocabulary of sensation-talk, I learn to identify (i.e., categorize) those inner states—that is, my identification of them just is my expression of them in sensation-language. So my ability to categorize them is something I get from learning a public language. If I do not understand this *fundamental* expressive use of sensation-talk, it is tempting to say, then I do not understand sensation-talk at all.

Does this leave a residual problem concerning whether first-person and other-person uses of sensation-terms and other psychological terms have the same meanings?[30] The worry here is that if they do not, then they suffer from systematic semantic ambiguity, much in the way that terms like 'bank' and 'bill' do, and there is a strong intuition that there is no such ambiguity. After all, it might be argued, it is not as though we get confused when someone says "I am in pain" as to whether she is *expressing* her pain or *reporting* it, in the way that we might at times be confused by someone who says, "I lost my wallet down by the bank."

Notice, first, that according to Wittgenstein we *do* get confused quite systematically here—we get misled by surface features of English grammar into thinking that all first-person uses of psychological terms are reports on inner states. That is one of the sources of temptation that leads to the Cartesian picture of the mind. Second, it is a genuine feature of first-person uses of psychological terms that they differ from second- and third-person uses. That is part of the explanation for Moore's paradox—the paradox that G.E. Moore thought was to be found in the grammatical possibility of saying,

(MP) It's raining, but I don't believe it.[31]

---

30 See Strawson (1959), 134.

31 See G.E. Moore, "Moore's Paradox" in *G.E. Moore Selected Writings*, edited by Thomas Baldwin (London: Routledge, 1993), 207–12.

If "I don't believe it" were nothing but a report of my inner states, then there would be nothing odd about an utterance like MP. But the fact is that MP is pragmatically self-defeating. "It's raining" may be a report about the state of the weather, but in making that report I also express a belief—a belief whose expression I then withdraw by expressing my lack of belief. I seem at one and the same time to be committing myself to something and withholding commitment. So although it is perfectly possible that it should be raining even though I do not believe that it is raining, a first-person (present-tense, indicative) statement to that effect sounds like a contradiction.[32] (The paradox disappears in the past tense: "It was raining, but I didn't believe it"; in the second- or third-person: "It's raining, but she doesn't believe it"; and in hypothetical formulations: "Imagine that it's raining but I don't believe it." Of course, one can use MP to express astonishment that it is raining, but that idiomatic usage does not exhaust the field of possibilities.)[33]

Third, the first- and other-person uses of psychological terms can be tied together in the teaching and learning of psychological talk. I learn to replace crying with "It hurts!" in response to questions from others: "Does that hurt?" "Where does it hurt?" Second-person uses are important in teaching first-person uses, and second-person uses are in turn readily connected with third-person uses. The first-person uses of psychological terms are no more (and no less) remarkable than the first-person uses of various predicates that are specially suited to the performance of certain distinctive speech-acts. "I promise," for example, is not usually a report about an undertaking that I make to another, but an expression of the undertaking itself. That fact, however, does not prevent there being a clear connection between the meaning of "I promise" and "She promises." As Wittgenstein later remarks, "Not every *use*, you want to say, is a meaning."[34] That is, not every difference in use marks a difference in meaning, even though meaning can often be explained by use. The "games" we play with such words are "not everywhere circumscribed by rules; but no more are there any rules for how high one throws the ball in tennis, or how hard; yet tennis is a game for all that and has rules too" (PI §68).

---

32 Wittgenstein makes roughly this argument about Moore's paradox at PI II §x.

33 For more on Wittgenstein on the expression of belief see Béla Szabados, "Wittgenstein on Mistrusting One's Own Belief," *Canadian Journal of Philosophy* 11, no.4 (1981): 603–12.

34 Ludwig Wittgenstein, *Last Writings on the Philosophy of Psychology*, Vol. I, edited by G.H. von Wright and Heikki Nyman, translated by C.G. Luckhardt and Maximilian A.E. Aue (Oxford: Blackwell, 1990), §289.

5.9 OTHER MINDS

If Wittgenstein's expressivism is part of his attempt to avoid the Cartesian picture of the mind by reminding us of the conventions implicit in our use of sensation-terms, the avoidance of that Cartesian picture also has consequences for how we think of other minds than our own. One of the consequences of thinking of minds as private inner spaces to which others can have no access is that I have a certain "Privileged Access"[35] to the contents of my own mind, but a corollary is that I can never really know what is going on in someone else's mind because those goings-on are private. Indeed, as we have seen, her terms for her inner episodes, according to this view, are terms that I cannot in principle understand. However, my inability to understand her private sensation-language and my inability to have direct access to her private thoughts together raise the sceptical worry that there is really nothing there for me to wish I had access to. Perhaps mine is the only mind in the universe.

Just as Wittgenstein offers us no refutation of rule-scepticism or of the logical possibility of private language, I maintain, he offers us in the *Investigations* no categorical refutation of solipsism and the problem of other minds. What he does offer us is a way of talking that prevents these problems from getting a foothold in our language. There are two clear reasons for saying this. First, solipsism and the problem of other minds depend crucially on the Cartesian picture of the self. Getting rid of that picture entails getting rid of these sceptical worries. If we need not think of inner episodes as essentially private, then there is no principled problem in having knowledge of someone else's. Indeed, sometimes another person's sensations are manifest to us: "Just try—in a real case—to doubt someone else's fear or pain" (PI §303).

To someone impressed by the Cartesian picture this will seem implausible. *Can't* I be mistaken about whether or not someone else is in pain? Can't I mistake certain facial expressions? Can't I be fooled by the deceitful behaviour of another? Well, of course, I can. But the possibility of mistakes and deceit does not entail the possibility of always being mistaken or deceived. And we might counter these questions with another: Could I ever learn how to apply sensation-terms to another human being (let alone to animals or, in a game of make-believe, to dolls or puppets) unless I were acquainted with genuine expressions of pain? Perhaps that question invites too much idle speculation about possibility and impossibility, or sounds too much like an attempted refutation of scepticism about other minds, so let us consider another: Does anyone *in fact* ever learn how to apply sensation-terms to

35 Gilbert Ryle, *The Concept of Mind* (Harmondsworth: Penguin, 1963), 148.

other human beings without being acquainted with genuine expressions of pain? It may not be impossible that this should happen, but it is difficult to believe that it ever does. This is the second reason for saying that Wittgenstein's way of talking helps us avoid certain sceptical puzzles (without thereby refuting them). The learning of second- and third-person uses of psychological vocabulary occurs in the presence of sincere expressions of inner states and episodes. When I teach a child that another person is in pain, I rely on genuine instances of other people's pain. Playacting, puppetry, and so on can help. But the fact that we draw the distinction between playacting and sincere expressions of pain (for example), is, in the absence of prior commitment to Cartesianism, a reason to think that we have learned to use sensation-terms by being presented with sincere instances of their expression.

The *Philosophical Investigations* pursues many related themes and explores them in greater depth than my sketch in this and the preceding chapter might suggest. My goal here has not been to give a comprehensive reading of the book, but to illustrate how the remarks on method discussed in Chapter 3 are important to understanding what *kind* of pursuit Wittgenstein is engaged in. In the next chapter I want to turn away from Wittgenstein's highly polished employment of his methods in the *Investigations* to his much rougher application of them to some of the central problems of epistemology: scepticism and the nature of knowledge. His late reflections on these topics will lead us to think once again about his conventionalism and its importance for his mature methodological views.

6

SCEPTICISM, KNOWLEDGE, AND JUSTIFICATION

Although the *Philosophical Investigations* was not published during Wittgenstein's lifetime, it was in his mind as close as he could get to a completed book, and he did for a time have plans of trying to have it published.[1] But the rest of Wittgenstein's later published work has been cobbled into books by his literary executors, and much of it would probably have had to pass a good deal more stern scrutiny before Wittgenstein himself would have offered it up for publication. So it may well be appropriate to have some grains of salt ready to hand when sampling this work. This advice applies to some of the last remarks that Wittgenstein ever wrote, which have been collected together under the title *On Certainty*.

The salt that best seasons *On Certainty*, I think, comes from those explicit pronouncements about philosophical method and the nature of philosophical problems that we have already examined and applied to some key problems in the *Philosophical Investigations*.[2] In this chapter I want to examine some of the anti-sceptical themes of *On Certainty* with an eye to arguing that they are best thought of not as attempts to give a decisive refutation of epistemological scepticism, but as attempts to remind us of grammatical conventions with which we are already

1 See Ray Monk, *Wittgenstein: The Duty of Genius* (London: Jonathan Cape, 1990), 457.

2 I thus set myself against the recent contention that in *On Certainty* Wittgenstein becomes a more systematic and less therapeutic philosopher. See Danièle Moyal-Sharrock's "Introduction" in *The Third Wittgenstein*, edited by Danièle Moyal-Sharrock (Aldershot: Ashgate, 2004), as well as her *Understanding Wittgenstein's* On Certainty (New York: Palgrave Macmillan, 2004).

familiar concerning our talk of knowledge and justification. Those conventions, Wittgenstein is suggesting, avoid commitment to the kinds of premises that epistemological scepticism depends on. It is only a failure to command a clear view of our linguistic practices that makes scepticism look like a serious philosophical problem. The task of acquiring such a clear view, however, reveals a variety of epistemic and linguistic contexts each of which is marked by its holding certain propositions immune from doubt. And as we shall see, it looks as though there are some propositions that must be held immune from doubt in *all* epistemic contexts.

6.1 MOOREAN PROPOSITIONS AND SCEPTICAL DOUBTS

On Certainty consists largely of remarks that Wittgenstein wrote in response to two articles by G.E. Moore, "A Defense of Common Sense" and "Proof of an External World."[3] In the former article Moore enumerates a long series of "common-sense" propositions that he takes himself to know "with certainty"—for example, that "there exists at present a living human body, which is *my* body" and that "there have also existed many other things, having shape and size in three dimensions" (Moore 107). His goal here is to distinguish his own philosophical views from those of idealists, who think that the world has no mind-independent existence, and from those of sceptics, who doubt our ability to have any knowledge of a mind-independent reality.

In the latter article Moore offers what may seem like a question-begging attempt to refute the sceptic about the external world. Such a refutation could be carried out, thinks Moore, if only it could be proved that objects exist in space outside his mind. That, in turn, can be established if it can be shown that there are two such objects. A human hand would count as such an object, and so, says Moore—with what seems to the philosophically initiated like tiresome flat-footedness:

> I can prove now, for instance, that two human hands exist. How? By holding up my two hands, and saying, as I make a certain gesture with the right hand, 'Here is one hand', and adding, as I make a certain gesture with the left, 'and here is another'. And if, by doing this, I have proved *ipso facto* the existence of external things, you will all see that I can also do it now in numbers of other ways: there is no need to multiply examples. (Moore 165–66)

3 G.E. Moore, *Selected Writings*, edited by Thomas Baldwin (London: Routledge, 1993), 106–33 and 147–70.

The philosophically initiated will find this tiresome because it will seem as though Moore is just begging the question against the Cartesian sceptic,[4] who casts doubt on my ability to have any knowledge of objects and events that exist independently of my own consciousness. Such a sceptic might be taken to argue as follows:

S1. If I know that I have two hands, then I know that I am *not* a brain in a vat.

S2. I do not know that I am not a brain in a vat.

S3. Therefore, I do not know that I have two hands.

But perhaps there is more to Moore than at first meets the eye. We could take his proof of an external world to be aimed at the sceptic's second premise.[5] In particular, we could take Moore to be saying that we can be no more certain of the sceptic's second premise than we can be of the sceptic's conclusion. But the conclusion of an argument can never be any more certain than its premises. So we have a kind of stand-off:

M1. If I know that I have two hands, then I know that I am *not* a brain in a vat.

M2. I know that I have two hands.

M3. Therefore, I know that I am not a brain in a vat.

Is there any way of breaking this stalemate in favour of either Moore or the sceptic?

At least one more recent philosopher—Robert Nozick—has thought that the sceptical argument consisting in S1-S3 relies on a general principle of *epistemic closure*.[6] According to that principle, if I know that some proposition *p* obtains,

4 The Cartesian sceptic casts doubt on our knowledge of an external world—as I explain below—by invoking a kind of underdetermination argument. By contrast, the ancient sceptic invokes some version of what Michael Williams has called "Agrippa's trilemma." See Michael Williams, *Unnatural Doubts: Epistemological Realism and the Basis of Scepticism* (Princeton: Princeton University Press, 1996), 60 (hereafter UD). I shall be focusing on Cartesian scepticism, which will prove more than enough to keep us busy. Of course, Descartes's own scepticism was entirely methodological, but his inability to rescue his own knowledge from radical doubt suggests an argument whose implications go beyond what Descartes intended.

5 This reading of Moore was suggested to me by Bruce Hunter.

6 See Robert Nozick, *Philosophical Explanations* (Cambridge, MA: Belknap Press, 1981), 204–11.

and I know that *p* materially implies another proposition *q*, then I also know that *q* obtains. So the sceptic's argument, made explicit, looks something like this:

> S1′. If I know that I have two hands and that my having two hands implies that I am not a brain in a vat, then I know that I am not a brain in a vat.
>
> S2a. I do not know that I am not a brain in a vat.
>
> S2b. I know that my having two hands implies that I am not a brain in a vat.
>
> S3. Therefore, I do not know that I have two hands.

Nozick thinks that the way to avoid the sceptic's conclusion is to deny the principle of epistemic closure, thereby denying premise S1′. But this has counterintuitive consequences, because that principle seems quite plausible. If, for example, I know that this wine is a Chardonnay, and if I know that this wine's being a Chardonnay entails that it is not a Pinot Noir, then I know that it is not a Pinot Noir. If I protest that I do not know that it is not a Pinot Noir, but that I nonetheless know that it is a Chardonnay, then you would be justified in saying, "You don't *really* know that it's a Chardonnay because you don't know the difference between a Chardonnay and a Pinot Noir! For all *you* know, it might *be* a Pinot Noir!"

As Michael Williams has argued (UD 332), however, the principle of epistemic closure is actually irrelevant to what the sceptic wants to argue, because the sceptic really needs a stronger principle—call it the principle of *epistemic presupposition*. According to this principle, if I am to know that *p*, then if I know that *p* implies *q*, I must *first* know that *q*. That is, if I am to know that I have two hands, then I must *first* know that I am not a brain in a vat. But this principle is not very plausible. It entails, for example, that if I am to know that there is snow on the ground, then if I know that there being snow on the ground entails that it has not been 30°C for the past week, I must first know that it has not been 30°C for the past week. But this is false. I can discover that there is snow on the ground by stepping outside.

Without the principle of epistemic presupposition, we are returned to the stalemate between Moore and the sceptic. "I do know that I am not a brain in a vat," I can say, "because I know that I have two hands, and I know that if I have two hands then I am not a brain in a vat."

At this juncture it should be obvious, however, that the Cartesian sceptic is really relying on another kind of argument. "You don't know that you are not a brain in a vat," she will say, "because all the experiences that you have had as if of a world of happenings and things beyond your senses could be explained just as well by another hypothesis—the hypothesis that you have always been a brain in a vat, attached to some experience-simulating machine by electrodes, or the hypothesis that you are being deceived by some powerful, evil demon who has the ability to control your inner experiences." In other words, the Cartesian sceptic presents an *underdetermination* argument, which purports to show that a certain body of evidence—my experiences as if of a world beyond my senses—could be explained just as well by some sceptical hypothesis as by the hypothesis of an external world. If that is so, then, the sceptic insists, I am not justified in any of the beliefs I am disposed to hold regarding the sources of my experiences. So the philosophically initiated are right: Moore really is begging the question after all, but for much more complicated reasons than it might have first appeared.

6.2 DEFINITIVE REFUTATION?

> Though he admired Moore's exactitude of expression, and would occasionally make use of it to find the precise word he wanted to make a particular point, Wittgenstein had little respect for him as an original philosopher. 'Moore?'—he once said—'he shows you how far a man can go who has absolutely no intelligence whatever.' (Monk 262)

Wittgenstein does not trace the dialectical steps outlined in the preceding section, but he does hint in the very first remark of *On Certainty* that Moore begs the question against the Cartesian sceptic: "If you do know that *here is one hand*, we'll grant you all the rest" (OC §1).[7] More explicitly, Moore's belief that he has given a proof of the external world seems to assume exactly what he needs to show, for the sceptic has already argued that it might merely *seem* to Moore as though he has two hands, when he really does not. "From its *seeming* to me—or to everyone—to be so, it doesn't follow that it *is* so" (OC §2). Of course, neither does it follow from the fact that such and such merely seems to me to be so on a particular occasion, that *everything* that seems to me to be so might *merely* seem to be so—but Wittgenstein is under no illusions about this (as we shall see). The point for the moment is that Moore is being dogmatic by ignoring the sceptic's underdetermination argument.

7 Ludwig Wittgenstein, *On Certainty*, translated by Denis Paul and G.E.M. Anscombe (New York: Harper Torchbooks, 1972).

This is clear from a later remark: "Moore's mistake lies in this—countering the assertion that one cannot know that, by saying 'I do know it'" (OC §521).

Immediately after making this criticism of Moore, however, Wittgenstein hints at an alternative argument that he seems to think is relevant to Moore's concerns: "From its *seeming* to me—or to everyone—to be so, it doesn't follow that it *is* so. What we can ask is whether it can make sense to doubt it" (OC §2). Michael Williams has argued that Wittgenstein's alternative constitutes an attempt at what he calls a "*definitive refutation*" (UD 32) of Cartesian scepticism. Such a refutation, if successful, would show not merely that the sceptic's doubts are answerable, but that those doubts could not possibly be correct because they are a sophisticated form of *nonsense*. A number of passages can be cited that seemingly hint at something like the argument that Williams envisages:

> If you are not certain of any fact, you cannot be certain of the meaning of your words either. (OC §114)

> If I wanted to doubt whether this was my hand, how could I avoid doubting whether the word "hand" has any meaning? So that is something that I seem to *know* after all. (OC §369)

> The argument "I may be dreaming" is senseless for this reason: if I am dreaming, this remark is being dreamed as well—and indeed it is also being dreamed that these words have any meaning. (OC §383)

> If, therefore, I doubt or am uncertain about this being my hand (in whatever sense), why not in that case about the meaning of these words as well? (OC §456)

> "If my memory deceives me *here* it can deceive me everywhere."
>
> If I don't know *that*, how do I know if my words mean what I believe they mean? (OC §506)

If there is an attempted definitive refutation to be gleaned from these remarks, I think it goes something like this:

> DR1. Any reason that I could have for doubting the existence of a world beyond my senses is a reason for thinking that I do not understand the meanings of my own words.

DR2. If I do not understand the meanings of my own words, then I cannot doubt the existence of a world beyond my senses.

DR3. Therefore, any reason that I could have *for* doubting the existence of a world beyond my senses is a reason for thinking that I *cannot* doubt the existence of a world beyond my senses.

DR4. Therefore, doubt about the existence of a world beyond my senses is nonsense.[8]

Premise DR2 appeals to the thought that a doubt that cannot be in some way expressed is no doubt at all. We might see this as a corollary of the arguments against private language that we examined in Chapter 5. So the premise that needs examination here is DR1. I submit that the best way of understanding DR1 is to see it as another reminder concerning linguistic conventions with which we are already acquainted. Recall the simple language-games in which children are trained in the uses of language—the language-game of the builders, for example. It is essential to such games that uses of words are embedded in practical activity—the bringing of slabs and pillars, for example. Taking away the external world would plainly deprive us of slabs and pillars and the activities we engage in with them (not to mention other human beings). "Every language-game is based on words 'and objects' being recognized again. We learn with the same inexorability that this is a chair as that 2x2=4" (OC §455). There would, in short, be no language-game left for us to learn from, and our paradigms of what it is to learn and *understand* the use of a word rest on the playing of such language-games. Deprived of them, we have no clear sense of what it would mean to say that someone understood the meaning of a word. And so any reason to doubt the existence of the external world is a reason to think that we do not understand the very words with which that doubt is formulated. The sceptic's doubt proves to be a sophisticated form of nonsense.

If we take this argument as aiming at a definitive refutation of the Cartesian sceptic, then it surely fails. For it presupposes empirical knowledge of the language-games that we make use of in teaching and learning the uses of words. Moreover, as Williams complains, the sceptic's doubts *seem* to make sense, and

8 A similar argument is to be found in Chapter 1 of Hilary Putnam's *Reason, Truth and History* (Cambridge: Cambridge University Press, 1981); however, I think it is a mistake to interpret Putnam as trying to refute scepticism—much as, I shall argue, it is a mistake to think that Wittgenstein is trying to refute scepticism.

any argument to the effect that they do not is in danger of relying on premises that are as controversial as the sceptic's conclusion (see UD 153). Clever though our arguments may be, it is difficult to persuade ourselves that we do not really understand what the sceptic is saying.

6.3 REMINDERS AND DIAGNOSES

I think it is better—both interpretatively and philosophically—to read the argument I have extracted from *On Certainty* as offering no such definitive refutation. Wittgenstein is not attempting to refute the sceptic but to suggest how we might avoid a confrontation with the sceptic. This much is hinted at by my suggestion above that Wittgenstein is reminding us of grammatical conventions with which we are implicitly familiar. Let me expand on the hint. First, inasmuch as premise DR2 is a corollary of the arguments against private language considered in Chapter 5, it is not advanced as an airtight reason for denying the truth or the intelligibility of the sceptic's conclusion. Rather it is better seen as the observation that given our ordinary practices of language-learning, there is no reason to think that it is possible to entertain doubts without being able to speak and understand a language. That observation might be vulnerable to sceptical doubt, but it seems that the sceptic must rely not merely on the uncertainty of this observation, but on a *positive* thesis to the effect that it is possible to formulate relevant doubts—doubts about knowledge of the world around us—without understanding a public language. If our ordinary practices do not commit us to that consequence, then we need not be troubled by the sceptic's reasoning.

Second, much the same point can be made about premise DR1. All our experience with learning a language suggests that we need to be able to interact with objects in public space and time if we are to learn how to apply words. This experience is, on the face of it, vulnerable to sceptical doubt, but again, the sceptic about the external world seems to assume a positive thesis to the effect that interaction with objects in a public space and time is *not* necessary for the acquisition of a language[9]—unless, that is, she falls back on the controversial assumption that language is unnecessary for the formulation of relevant doubts.

---

9 Notice that even Chomsky, who insists that our capacity to speak a language is rooted in our native grasp of a finite set of grammatical principles, insists that it is experience (albeit of an "impoverished" sort) that sets the parameters left open by these principles and that our "language organ" will not develop without external stimulus. Without experience, there would be no linguistic performance or competence. See Noam Chomsky, *New Horizons on Language and Mind* (Cambridge: Cambridge University Press, 2000), Chapter 1.

The conclusion of the argument is, accordingly, weaker than Wittgenstein's expression of it would suggest. None of this proves that scepticism is either false or *nonsense*, but it does suggest that the sceptic is assuming without argument that her doubts have been clearly expressed and that in making that assumption, she is helping herself to one or more controversial assumptions about the possibility of formulating a doubt about knowledge of the world around us without having acquired a public language.

If this reading of Wittgenstein's argument is plausible, then it has the effect of blurring a distinction that Williams invokes between "therapeutic" and "theoretical diagnoses" of the sceptic's doubts (UD 31–40).[10] According to Williams, a therapeutic diagnosis—which is what one would expect from someone who likens philosophical activity to a form of therapy—is one which assumes that

> The problem of scepticism must be *dissolved* by showing the sceptic doesn't or can't mean what he seems to mean, perhaps even that he does not succeed in meaning anything at all. It is not enough to show that the case for scepticism is less than compelling: he has to show that no coherent problem was ever presented. (UD 32)

By contrast, a theoretical diagnosis attempts

> *a shifting of the burden of theory.* We must show that sceptical arguments depend essentially on theoretical commitments that are *not* forced on us by our ordinary ways of thinking about knowledge, justification and truth. (UD 31–32)

Williams's own theoretical diagnosis, which I find both original and compelling, consists in arguing that Cartesian sceptical doubts rely on assuming that there are certain classes of beliefs which, by their very nature—their very content—are better justified than others, beliefs that arise from perception, for example. Without that assumption, no invidious distinction can be drawn between, for instance, my warranted perceptual beliefs about how the world *seems* to be and the less certain hypothesis that there is a world of doings and beings that exists beyond my senses.

But if Wittgenstein is "assembling reminders for a particular purpose" (PI §127), then he is, if consistent, seeking a clear overview of "our ordinary ways of thinking

10 Williams has more recently acknowledged that the distinction is not hard and fast. See Michael Williams, *Problems of Knowledge* (Cambridge: Cambridge University Press, 2001), 146; hereafter PK.

about knowledge, justification and truth" (UD 32)—or, at least, of our customary ways of *talking* about these things, the conventions implicit in our talk about things epistemic. So in effect he does aim to shift the "burden of theory" onto the shoulders of the would-be sceptic by trying to show that only a choice, conscious or otherwise, to deviate from our standard grammatical norms can make us vulnerable to the doubts of the sceptic.

What sort of overview of our uses of terms like 'knowledge' and 'certainty' does Wittgenstein have to offer us? For one thing, it is an incomplete overview. As I remarked at the beginning of this chapter, *On Certainty* is a collection of remarks from Wittgenstein's notebooks that he did not have time to subject to selective editing. (Indeed, the last remark in the book was written two days before Wittgenstein died [Monk 579].) And he would surely have had more to say on the topic than his short time allowed him. Furthermore, I shall offer below only an incomplete overview of that incomplete overview. But a number of features stand out as especially important: (i) First-person uses of the verb 'to know' are, like first-person uses of psychological terms, often avowals, not reports on what one has observed or determined, but, unlike psychological avowals, their sincere expression is not normally sufficient for us to say that the person avowing her knowledge actually knows. (ii) We typically express avowals of knowledge or make attributions of knowledge to others only when there is some chance of error, some room for doubt. (iii) The possibility of what we understand to be doubt rests on not calling everything into question at once. (iv) Holding a proposition or a belief immune from doubt helps to define a context of inquiry or even a world-view. What is held immune from doubt in that context may be called into doubt in another context. Standards of justification thus vary across such contexts. (v) There are some propositions concerning which we can find no context for intelligible doubt. I shall spend the rest of the chapter exploring these features.

6.4 'I KNOW'

We saw in Chapter 5 that one of the characteristic accompaniments of sudden understanding is the utterance of "I understand!" or "I get it!" or "I *know* how to go on!" Such utterances, we saw, are avowals of one's confidence—or, we could say, of one's subjective *certainty*—and in this respect they are like expressions of pain or pleasure or belief or consternation. But in another respect they differ from such psychological avowals because it is always a possibility that my confidence in my own understanding or knowledge is misplaced. It may make sense for another to doubt my sincere avowal of understanding but not my sincere avowal of pain and, usually, not my sincere avowal of belief.[11]

This theme re-emerges in Wittgenstein's discussion of Moore's list of common-sense propositions that he takes himself to know.

> Moore's view really comes down to this: the concept 'know' is analogous to the concepts 'believe', 'surmise', 'doubt', 'be convinced' in that the statement "I know..." can't be a mistake. And if that *is* so, then there can be an inference from such an utterance to the truth of an assertion. And here the form "I thought I knew" is being overlooked.—But if this latter is inadmissible, then a mistake in the *assertion* must be logically impossible too. And anyone who is acquainted with the language-game must realize this—an assurance from a reliable man that he *knows* cannot contribute anything. (OC §21)

'I know that I have never been on the moon', in a list of Moorean common-sense propositions, makes the same claim as 'I have never been on the moon' (and it expresses the same conviction, albeit more emphatically). So if the former cannot be false, then neither can the latter. But plainly the latter *can* be false (even if it is unlikely to be), and so the former must likewise be vulnerable to error. This is another way of saying that 'I know...' is not typically a report *about oneself* but about the subject matter whereof one claims to know. Of course, it *can* be a report about oneself. "Don't kill me! I know certain things that you might find valuable!" says the petty thief to the mobster. "What do you know about our investments in Hong Kong?" asks the business executive, hoping to avoid having to explain too much. Her underling may reply, "I know that ...," thereby reporting on herself—but she could as easily respond by saying, "They have been unstable ever since the outbreak of bird-flu," without adding explicitly that she *knows* this.

Second- or third-person uses of the verb 'to know' differ here:

> For it is not as though the proposition "It is so" could be inferred from someone else's utterance: "I know it is so". Nor from the utterance together with its not being a lie.—But can't I infer "It is so" from my own utterance

11 Matters get complicated here rapidly because we sometimes attribute beliefs or withhold their attribution if we think that a person's behaviour in some way belies her avowals. But we do not simply disregard everything a person says about what she believes. We take it to have a special relevance. See Béla Szabados, "Wittgenstein on Mistrusting One's Own Belief," *Canadian Journal of Philosophy* 11, no.4 (1981): 603–12.

> "I know etc."? Yes; and also "There is a hand there" follows from the proposition "He knows that there's a hand there". But from his utterance "I know…" it does not follow that he does know it. (OC §13)

I can infer that it is so from my utterance that I know it to be so, because each is an expression of my conviction that it is so, but you cannot. And if I claim of someone else that she knows something to be so, then I can conclude from this that it is so since in order for her to *know* it to be so, it must *be* so. Avowals of knowledge and attributions of knowledge are two different things.[12]

Now Wittgenstein thinks that when Moore lists the many things that he takes himself to know with certainty, he is in some way misusing the expression "I know":

> Now, can one enumerate what one knows (like Moore)? Straight off like that, I believe not.—For otherwise the expression "I know" gets misused. And through this misuse a queer and extremely important mental state seems to be revealed. (OC §6)

What exactly is the misuse in question here? I think Wittgenstein's complaint, in part, is that avowals of knowledge, such as Moore's, are appropriate only in certain kinds of linguistic contexts and that the listing of a series of common-sense propositions fails to determine a context for their interpretation. So whether Moore says "I know" or not, it is still unclear how to take his remarks. But, additionally, for Moore to say explicitly that he *knows* these things is to use 'I know' in an unusual way, because we do not customarily say "I know" except in cases in which it makes sense to have certain doubts. Let me deal with each of these points further.

Wittgenstein hints at the latter point in the *Philosophical Investigations* when he discusses first-person avowals of pain and other sensation states. The Cartesian tradition has it that I cannot be mistaken about my having certain sensations, such as pain, and that, therefore, I have a special kind of infallible *knowledge* of my sensations. In an exchange with an imagined interlocutor Wittgenstein's narrator[13]

---

12 Considerations such as these prompt Robert Brandom to describe knowledge as "a complex hybrid deontic status" (*Making It Explicit* [Cambridge, MA: Harvard University Press, 1994], 201). That is, roughly, to attribute knowledge to someone else is to allow that *she* is *entitled* to draw certain consequences from her belief and at the same time to avow *one's own commitment* to the correctness of her belief.

13 See David G. Stern, *Wittgenstein's Philosophical Investigations: An Introduction* (Cambridge: Cambridge University Press, 2004), 173. See my discussion of Stern in Chapter 4, §4.11.

dismisses this view, which—as we have seen—he takes to be modelled on the naming of certain kinds of public objects:

> In what sense are my sensations *private*?—Well, only I can know whether I am really in pain; another person can only surmise it.—In one way this is wrong, and in another nonsense. If we are using the word "to know" as it is normally used (and how else are we to use it?), then other people very often know when I am in pain.—Yes, but all the same not with the certainty with which I know it myself!—It can't be said of me at all (except perhaps as a joke) that I *know* I am in pain. What is it supposed to mean—except perhaps that I *am* in pain? (PI §246)

It seems odd to suppose, for example, that I might be in excruciating agony and doubt that I am (unless I do not understand what 'excruciating agony' means), but typically when we talk about knowing that something is the case, we allow that doubt is a possibility.[14] Knowledge of particular facts is something that one can acquire or fail to acquire as long as the facts obtain. But I do not learn or discover that I am in pain after having carried out an extensive—or even a cursory—investigation. I cannot try to find out whether or not I am in pain. Nothing would count as evidence for me of my being in pain, and I could not believe, comprehendingly, that I was in excruciating agony and then be convinced by hitherto unnoticed evidence that I had been wrong. The only kind of error or doubt that we know how to make sense of here is error or doubt that casts suspicion on my grasp of the concept "excruciating agony."

This theme re-emerges early in *On Certainty*, but with some additional nuances:

> "I know that I am a human being." In order to see how unclear the sense of this proposition is, consider its negation. At most it might be taken to mean "I know I have the organs of a human". (E.g. a brain which, after all, no one has ever yet seen.) But what about such a proposition as "I know I have a brain"? Can I doubt it? Grounds for *doubt* are lacking! Everything speaks in its favour, nothing against it. Nevertheless it is imaginable that my skull should turn out empty when it was operated on. (OC §4)

14 I speak of excruciating agony here to make the case as plausible as possible. Could I have doubts about lesser pains? It is worth distinguishing between doubting *whether* I am in pain and doubting, when I *am* in pain, *that* I am in pain. The former kind of doubt will be familiar to anyone who has run hands numb with cold under hot water, but the latter is harder to make sense of—what would a pain be like that I could not feel?

Here it seems that doubt is in some way bizarre or inappropriate, but error is not completely unimaginable in the way it seems to be in the case of my own excruciating agony. It is a logical possibility that there is no brain inside my skull, and this is something that could be subjected to empirical testing. So what is the weaker sense in which there is something wrong with doubting whether or not I have a brain? We get a hint at OC §10:

> I know that a sick man is lying here? Nonsense! I am sitting at his bedside, I am looking attentively into his face.—So I don't know, then, that there is a sick man lying here? Neither the question nor the assertion makes sense. Any more than the assertion "I am here", which I might yet use at any moment, if suitable occasion presented itself.... And "I know that there's a sick man lying here", used in an *unsuitable* situation, seems not to be nonsense but rather seems matter-of-course, only because one can fairly easily imagine a situation to fit it, and one thinks that the words "I know that..." are always in place where there is no doubt, and hence even where the expression of doubt would be unintelligible. (OC §10)

I take the key point here to be one that we might easily find in the *Philosophical Investigations*: that until a context of use has been specified, it is difficult to say what conclusions can be drawn from an isolated occurrence of a sentence like 'I know that a sick man is lying here' or 'I know that I have a brain' or 'I know that I have two hands'. This is because it is difficult to say what conclusions can be drawn from an isolated occurrence of *any* sentence: "it is only in use that the proposition has its sense" (OC §10). If I confront you in the street and say, out of the blue, "I know that I have a brain" or "I know that I have two hands," you may doubt my psychological stability—unless, perhaps, you know that I am a philosopher (see OC §467).

It takes special circumstances for my avowal, "I know that I have two hands," to be readily understandable:

> If I don't know whether someone has two hands (say, whether they have been amputated or not) I shall believe his assurance that he has two hands, if he is trustworthy. And if he says he *knows* it, that can only signify to me that he has been able to make sure, and hence that his arms are e.g. not still concealed by coverings and bandages, etc. etc. My believing the trustworthy man stems from my admitting that it is possible for him to make sure. (OC §23)

By comparison, if I am sitting at the bedside of a sick man, watching over him, the assertion "There is a sick man lying here" lacks any point, as does my explicit avowal "I know that there is a sick man lying here." This is not to say, I think, that either of these utterances is meaningless in the way that twiddling one's lips with one's fingers and saying "bzbzbzbzbz" is. They are syntactically well-formed, and their component parts are meaningful. So expressions of doubt are, likewise, not devoid of meaning, but they, too, lack a point. They are troubled by what J.L. Austin would have called a pragmatic "infelicity" of sorts.[15]

Suppose, for example, that a woman tried to vote in a Canadian federal election before 1918. She might have gone to a polling station, filled out a ballot and cast it for the candidate of her choice, but because women did not have the right to vote in federal elections in Canada until 1918, her ballot-casting would not *count* as a vote. This is not to say that her action would be *meaningless*. It might well count as a protest on behalf of women's suffrage, but it would not be a *vote*. The context needed for her action to count as a vote is absent, and this makes her attempt infelicitous.[16]

The infelicity that spoils expressions of doubt in the case of my sitting at an ailing man's bedside is similar to the case of failed voting insofar as my words remain meaningful but fail to express a doubt. The difference between the two cases is that, first, my failure to doubt is not the result of there being an unjust law that makes it impossible for me to doubt and, second, my attempt to doubt in this context, in effect, *undermines* that context. To see the point of this claim, consider some similar but slightly varied contexts.

I am sitting at the bedside of a sick man, watching over him, when a group of children rush in, laughing and shouting. "Shhh!" I say. "There is a sick man lying here!" "I know!" says one of the children. My utterance serves either to remind the children, who have forgotten, or to inform them, because they did not know—both cases in which doubt and error can likewise get a foothold. The child's response is defensive. She is embarrassed, either because she forgot, or because she did not know and thinks she should have. Doubt and error are possibilities here.

I am sitting at the bedside of a sick man, watching over him, and I fall asleep. When I awake, I have been dreaming and feel disoriented. "There is a sick man lying here," I say, rediscovering my surroundings. But then doubt enters my mind,

---

15 See J.L. Austin, *How to Do Things with Words* (New York: Oxford University Press, 1965), 14 *et passim*. The reading of contextual immunity from doubt that I present below differs somewhat from one that I have suggested elsewhere. See "Putnam and the Difficulty of Renouncing All Theory," *International Studies in Philosophy* 35, no.4 (2003): 55–82.

16 The example is inspired by Rae Langton, "Speech Acts and Unspeakable Acts," *Philosophy and Public Affairs* 22, no.4 (1993): 293–330.

as I struggle to overcome my grogginess. "Am I still dreaming?—No, I know there is a sick man lying here! I brought him to the hospital last night."

I am sitting at the bedside of a man, watching over him, worried about his illness. Someone walks onto the theatre stage and shakes me by the shoulders. "The rehearsal is over!" she says. "Snap out of it!" "There is a sick man lying here..." I begin to say before realizing how absorbed I have become in playing my theatrical role. Doubt and error are possibilities here.

In contexts like these doubt has a point, and, accordingly, so does saying "I know...." By contrast, Moore's assertions lack any clear context, and so it remains unclear whether either doubting or claiming to know has any point.

> Only in certain cases is it possible to make an investigation "is that really a hand?" (or "my hand"). For "I doubt whether that is really my (or a) hand" makes no sense without some more precise determination. One cannot tell from these words alone whether any doubt at all is meant—nor what kind of doubt. (OC §372)

Because we can readily imagine contexts in which there *would* be some point in saying—or doubting—"I have two hands" or "I have never been to the moon," it can seem as though claiming to know these things and expressing doubts about them are speech-acts that can be performed in any context (see OC §10). However, somebody who tries to express doubt that there is a sick man lying here in the case Wittgenstein sketches or who tries to claim, in the way Moore does, that he knows that he has never been very far from the Earth, is somebody who misunderstands the context or who is actively trying to change it.[17] Wittgenstein hints at this immediately after a passage we have already considered:

> If I wanted to doubt whether this was my hand, how could I avoid doubting whether the word "hand" has any meaning? So that is something I seem to *know* after all.
>
> But more correctly: The fact that I use the word "hand" and all the other words in my sentence without a second thought, indeed that I should stand before the abyss if I wanted so much as to try doubting their meanings—shews that absence of doubt belongs to the essence of the language-game, that the question "How do I know..." drags out the language-game, or else does away with it. (OC §§369–70)

17 Perhaps *this* is not so different from the political protest imagined above after all.

6.5 DOUBT REQUIRES CERTAINTY

We can travel some distance toward clarifying what it means to undermine a context by trying to entertain certain doubts within it, if we focus on the following remark: "If you tried to doubt everything you would not get as far as doubting anything. The game of doubting itself presupposes certainty" (OC §115). I take this remark to support my reading of Wittgenstein's argument against Cartesian scepticism, presented in §§6.2–6.3 above, by drawing a link between the language-games used to teach children and the absence of any clear conception of what doubt that was not publicly expressible would "look" like. *One* of the things that I cannot call into doubt if I am to be able to *have* doubts is that I understand the words with which I express my doubt. Learning a language, remember, begins with a lot of *training*, not with explicit definitions or explanations of the meanings of words. Understanding those explanations would presuppose the very abilities that they are supposed to impart.

> We say: if a child has mastered language—and hence its application—it must know the meaning of words. It must, for example, be able to attach the name of its colour to a white, black, red or blue object without the occurrence of any doubt.
>
> And indeed no one misses doubt here; no one is surprised that we do not merely *surmise* the meaning of our words. (OC §§522–23)

However, possibilities for doubt are not constrained *only* by the absence of doubt concerning the meanings of the words in which I formulate my doubt. That words have the meanings they do is just one empirical fact:

> [I]n order for you to be able to carry out an order there must be some empirical fact about which you are not in doubt. Doubt itself rests only on what is beyond doubt.
>
> But since a language-game is something that consists in the recurrent procedures of the game in time, it seems impossible to say in any *individual* case that such-and-such must be beyond doubt if there is to be a language-game—though it is right enough to say that *as a rule* some empirical judgment or other must be beyond doubt. (OC §519)

So, in addition to the general semantic constraint on doubt, there may also be other constraints imposed by the need to hold "some empirical judgment or other ... beyond doubt."

Those other constraints are made manifest if we ask what happens once a child has learned enough language to start asking questions. Could she not then start doubting what her teachers tell her? She could, but part of Wittgenstein's point is that how much she calls into doubt will have consequences for how much she is able to learn.

> The child learns by believing the adult. Doubt comes *after* belief. (OC §160)

> The schoolboy *believes* his teachers and his schoolbooks. (OC §263)

> For how can a child immediately doubt what it is taught? That could mean only that he was incapable of learning certain language games. (OC §283)

> A pupil and a teacher. The pupil will not let anything be explained to him, for he continually interrupts with doubts, for instance as to the existence of things, the meaning of words, etc. The teacher says "Stop interrupting me and do as I tell you. So far your doubts don't make sense at all". (OC §310)

> ... And it would be just the same if the pupil cast doubt on the uniformity of nature, that is to say on the justification of inductive arguments.—The teacher would feel that this was only holding them up, that this way the pupil would only get stuck and make no progress.—And he would be right.... (OC §315)

> When a child learns language it learns at the same time what is to be investigated and what not. When it learns that there is a cupboard in the room, it isn't taught to doubt whether what it sees later on is still a cupboard or only a kind of stage set.
>
> Just as in writing we learn a particular basic form of letters and then vary it later, so we learn first the stability of things as the norm, which is then subject to alterations. (OC §§472–73)

One of the lessons of the discussion of rule-following in Chapter 5 was that a child who found it natural to continue the expansion of a rule in a way different from that taken by the rest of us would have difficulty learning our rule. A similar point can be made here. If I try to teach a child basic multiplication, and she is linguistically skilled enough to ask how I *know* that 2x2=4 and will not accept the equation unless I can justify it, then my efforts are probably doomed to failure. Part of understanding multiplication is that one does not routinely doubt the multiplication-tables that are used in the classroom. But, likewise, part of learning natural science is that one does not routinely doubt the uniformity of nature. Anyone who did that "would only get stuck and make no progress" (OC §315), because the attempt to discover and describe natural laws would then be unmotivated.

Less general but analogous considerations apply to particular forms of inquiry within and without the natural sciences. Part of understanding geography is that one does not continually doubt the existence of faraway lands—that one does not think their existence is "just a conspiracy of cartographers," as Stoppard's Guildenstern puts it.[18] Part of understanding history is that one does not doubt the reality of the past. "What we call historical evidence points to the existence of the earth a long time before my birth ..." (OC §190). Part of understanding palaeontology is that one does not doubt the *ancient* prehistoric existence of the Earth. That nature is uniform, that there are faraway lands, that the past is not an illusion, that the Earth is older than 6000 years—these are all empirical propositions, but they have special roles to play within their respective disciplines. "Our 'empirical propositions' do not form a homogeneous mass" (OC §213). Some of them are what Wittgenstein calls *norms of description*:

> Think of chemical investigations. Lavoisier makes experiments with substances in his laboratory and now he concludes that this and that takes place when there is burning. He does not say that it might happen otherwise another time. He has got hold of a definite world-picture—not of course one that he invented: he learned it as a child. I say world-picture and not hypothesis, because it is the matter-of-course foundation for his research and as such also goes unmentioned. (OC §167)

The "foundation" here—that there is regularity in nature—is a "norm of description" (OC §167) for Lavoisier, because descriptions that entail or presuppose its falsehood violate the norm and so fail to be good scientific descriptions.

18 Tom Stoppard, *Rosencrantz and Guildenstern Are Dead* (London: Faber and Faber, 1967), 78.

Such norms of description serve as the "hinges" (OC §341) on which particular kinds of inquiry, debate, or conversation turn:

> We know, with the same certainty with which we believe *any* mathematical proposition, how the letters A and B are pronounced, what the colour of human blood is called, that other human beings have blood and call it "blood".[19]
>
> That is to say, the *questions* that we raise and our *doubts* depend on the fact that some propositions are exempt from doubt, are as it were like hinges on which those turn.
>
> That is to say, it belongs to the logic of our scientific investigations that certain things are *in deed* not doubted.
>
> But it isn't that the situation is like this: We just *can't* investigate everything, and for that reason we are forced to rest content with assumption. If I want the door to turn, the hinges must stay put.
>
> My *life* consists in my being content to accept many things. (OC §§340–44)

Wittgenstein writes here of the "logic of our scientific investigations," but the example of "how the letters A and B are pronounced" suggests that similar considerations apply beyond any strictly disciplinary context. Not just science, but "my *life*" is of interest here. In this connection, consider once again the example that provoked us to wonder how certain doubts can undermine the context in which they are raised—the example of my claiming to know that there is a sick man lying before me. The claim about 'I know' that I attributed to Wittgenstein was that such claims have a point only when doubt is not only semantically possible, but also possible in that sense that it would not undermine the context of its formulation. We now have an idea of what such undermining consists in for special disciplines like the natural sciences or history. Doubts that undermine the context of their expression are doubts that violate the norms of description typical of that context by entailing or presupposing their falsehood.

But similar considerations, I think, apply to contexts like the one in Wittgenstein's example of the sick man. In order to make those doubts appear

19 Notice that there is some ambivalence displayed by Wittgenstein here, for he remarks that we *know* these things that serve as "hinges" or as norms of description, and yet he chastises Moore for saying much the same thing. But I take the broader point to be that certain empirical propositions can play a role in certain contexts analogous to the role often played by mathematical propositions of being held beyond doubt.

relevant, I had to change the original example by introducing the uninformed or forgetful children or by imagining myself falling asleep at the patient's bedside or becoming wrapped up in my theatrical role. The relevant norm of description that these changes call into question is something like "Person S sees a sick man lying on the bed" or "I see a sick man lying on the bed." In the variations on the example that I presented, the removal or suspension of such a norm of description makes doubt and knowledge-claims alike readily intelligible—it gives them a point. But so long as the norm of description remains in place, we inhabit a context in which doubt has no point.

And that is what is special about Moorean propositions—we are well acquainted with contexts in which those propositions serve as norms of description, and in which doubts and knowledge-claims about them alike lack any point. So when Wittgenstein says that "The game of doubting itself presupposes certainty" (OC §115), 'certainty' does not refer to a psychological state of conviction, but to the *logical* status of the propositions that cannot be doubted without undermining the contexts of which they are constitutive. Wittgenstein's complaint with Moore is, in effect, that he fails to distinguish psychological certainty from logical certainty:

> When Moore says he *knows* such and such, he is really enumerating a lot of empirical propositions which we affirm without special testing; propositions, that is, which have a peculiar logical role in the system of our empirical propositions. (OC §136)

Some of these propositions get to be norms of description because they serve as "piece[s] of instruction" (OC §36). "This is a hand," I say to a young child—or better, "Hand!" as I point to it, teaching her the use of the word 'hand'. I probably do this at the same time as I teach her how to use 'arm' and 'leg' and 'foot' and 'head' and 'tummy'. Then I say to her, "Show me your hands!" And when we start to play number-games, I rely on this earlier piece of instruction and ask her, "How many hands do you have?"

I teach her all these things under particular sorts of circumstances. I do not do it when she is falling asleep, for example, and I do not first tell her to close her eyes or hide her face in a pillow. Those are circumstances that neither she nor I need ever be very good at describing, but we can often tell when circumstances depart from this standard. Remember this passage, which we considered in Chapter 3:

> One learns the word "think", i.e. its use, under certain circumstances, which, however, one does not learn to describe.

> But I can teach a person the use of the word! For a description of those circumstances is not needed for that.
>
> I just teach him the word under particular circumstances. (Z §§114–16)

Substitute the word 'hand' for the word 'think' in this passage and the point remains the same, even if the use of 'hand' is simpler and less puzzling than the use of 'think'. And the result is an explanation for Moore's conviction that he *knows* a great many things that in contexts of teaching and learning are beyond doubt:[20] he lacks a perspicuous representation of the role of these propositions as norms of description and so conflates their invulnerability to doubt as such norms with their knowability and dubitability in *other* contexts.[21]

But some of the propositions that Moore enumerates are not typically pieces of instruction. For example:

> There exists at present a living human body, which is *my* body. (Moore 107)
>
> "[C]ats do not grow on trees" (OC §282), and "motor cars don't grow out of the earth". (OC §279)
>
> People do not remove their heads when they go to sleep at night.
>
> The Eiffel Tower is not made of cheese.

The fact that propositions like these may be beyond doubt in certain contexts helps to show something important about how we should classify Wittgenstein's view. Let me explain why in the next section.

20 And maybe also an explanation for Wittgenstein's ambivalence at OC §340.

21 Is philosophical discussion itself a context that might give a point to Moore's claims? (See Williams [UD 155] for this suggestion.) Wittgenstein seems to overlook this possibility here, but to the extent that such a context gives a point to Moore's claims, it also gives a point to doubts about them (but only in that context), and it becomes unclear that Moore's affirmations then do anything more than beg the question against the sceptic.

6.6 CONTEXTUALISM

Wittgenstein uses the term 'foundation' in a number of places to describe the role played by hinge propositions or norms of description. But we should not be misled by this into thinking that Wittgenstein was therefore a *foundationalist* about epistemic justification.[22] There are two reasons for saying this.

First, the foundationalist is offering a theory about the *nature* of epistemic justification, suggesting that there is more to it than meets the observant eye so that when we speak of knowledge as justified true belief, we are saying something non-trivial and philosophically exciting about propositional knowledge. However, this is the last thing we should expect from Wittgenstein. What we should expect, instead, is what I have already suggested—that Wittgenstein would try to give us a clear overview of our uses of terms like 'knowledge' and 'justification'.

Second, recall from Chapter 1 that the foundationalist thinks that there is a certain class of beliefs or propositions—call them *basic*—whose justification cannot be traced to any other beliefs or propositions, but which are, nonetheless, justified all on their own. Basic beliefs or propositions, in turn, play the role of ultimate justifiers for all beliefs or propositions that are justified, but not basic. However, Wittgenstein's hinge propositions do not themselves play the role of justifiers for other propositions:

> The child learns to believe a host of things. I.e. it learns to act according to these beliefs. Bit by bit there forms a system of what is believed, and in that system some things stand unshakeably fast and some are more or less liable to shift. What stands fast does so, not because it is intrinsically obvious or convincing; it is rather held fast by what lies around it. (OC §144)

> No one ever taught me that my hands don't disappear when I am not paying attention to them. Nor can I be said to presuppose the truth of this proposition in my assertions etc., (as if they rested on it) while it only gets sense from the rest of our procedure of asserting. (OC §153)

---

22 Avrum Stroll advances an interpretation of Wittgenstein as a kind of foundationalist, but it is clear that Stroll has a very non-standard kind of foundationalism in mind. I find the term 'foundationalism' quite misleading given the considerable lack of resemblance that Wittgenstein's view has to, say, Locke's or Descartes's. See Avrum Stroll, "Wittgenstein's Foundational Metaphors" in Moyal-Sharrock (ed.) (2004), 13–24. See also Moyal-Sharrock, *Understanding Wittgenstein's* On Certainty. For an extension of this misleading use of 'foundationalism' to the rest of Wittgenstein's intellectual *corpus* see Daniel Hutto, "Two Wittgensteins Too Many: Wittgenstein's Foundationalism" in Moyal-Sharrock (ed.) (2004), 25–41.

> I have arrived at the rock bottom of my convictions.
>
> And one might almost say that these foundation-walls are carried by the whole house. (OC §248)

Peculiar foundations these are, which do not hold anything up! But to say that they are carried by the rest of the house is not to say that *they* are justified by some *other* propositions or beliefs in the context for which they are fundamental: "At the foundation of well-founded belief lies belief that is not founded" (OC §253). When a proposition serves as a hinge on which our questions and doubts turn—to switch metaphors—it is not itself something that can be known in that context, something for which reasons can be given, because it is not itself something that can be called into doubt in that context. Moreover, as we have already seen, norms of description may not be propositions that we ever explicitly learn or think about.

> I should like to say: Moore does not *know* what he asserts he knows, but it stands fast for him, as also for me; regarding it as absolutely solid is part of our *method* of doubt and enquiry.
>
> I do not explicitly learn the propositions that stand fast for me. I can *discover* them subsequently like the axis around which a body rotates. This axis is not fixed in the sense that anything holds it fast, but the movement around it determines its immobility. (OC §§151–52)

Call it a "hinge," call it an "axis," call it a "foundation-wall"—a norm of representation, when it is not a "piece of instruction," is often a norm that is *implicit* in our epistemic practices:

> Giving grounds, however, justifying the evidence, comes to an end;—but the end is not certain propositions' striking us immediately as true, i.e. it is not a kind of *seeing* on our part; it is our *acting*, which lies at the bottom of the language-game. (OC §204)

> "We could doubt every single one of these facts, but we could not doubt them *all*."
>
> Wouldn't it be more correct to say: "we do not doubt them *all*".
>
> Our not doubting them all is simply our manner of judging, and therefore of acting. (OC §232)

But if Wittgenstein is not a foundationalist, it would be equally wrong to think of him as a coherentist about justification—someone who thinks that a given belief is justified insofar as it belongs to a coherent set of beliefs—because the coherentist essentially holds that ultimately there is just one context of justification to which all candidates for knowledge must be traced if they are to pass muster. Coherence is a property or set of properties that an *entire system* of beliefs has in virtue of the relationships that obtain amongst all members of the system.

Wittgenstein is rather a *contextualist* about justification in a sense of that term that comes very close to the view that has been defended recently by Michael Williams.[23] That is, he thinks that "standards for correctly attributing or claiming knowledge are not fixed but subject to circumstantial variation" (PK 159). He thinks that there is no complete, coherent system of beliefs, but many clusters of beliefs that are knit together in a variety of different ways, falling well short of the standards of a coherent system. This should be amply clear from our examination of *contexts* of doubt and norms of description above. To call him a contextualist, however, is not to ascribe to him a third theory of the *nature* of epistemic justification that stands as an alternative to foundationalism and coherentism. It is, more accurately, to attribute to him the view—already noted—that knowledge and justification do not have hidden natures waiting to be captured by the right philosophical theory. As Williams puts it, the contextualist does not have a theory of knowledge but a theory of "the concept of knowledge" (UD 112), a story to tell about the role played by terms like 'knowledge' and 'justification' in our linguistic practices.

One of the distinctive features of this kind of contextualism is its rejection of what Williams calls the "Prior Grounding Requirement" (PK 24). What that requirement says, roughly, is that every knowledge-claim or belief must be assumed to be unjustified until reasons have been given in support of it. Of course, those reasons themselves will stand in need of further reasons if they are to provide any justification at all, and an infinite regress looms. Stopping seems to require a foundationalist theory of justification, if one is to avoid being dogmatic. Conversely, one might hold that the regress is irrelevant because a belief or claim gets to be justified by belonging to a coherent set. Because contextualism rejects either of these options, it must either respond in some other way to this kind of ancient sceptical argument or show why the argument need not be confronted. Williams takes the latter course, suggesting that every belief or claim is justified by *default*—a status that it loses only when it is subject to reasonable challenge.

23 This view should not be confused with another that has been advanced under the title "contextualism" by such thinkers as Stewart Cohen and Keith DeRose. See Michael Williams's UD and PK. Williams's insightful discussion of *On Certainty* in *Unnatural Doubts* has strongly influenced my reading.

A reasonable challenge does not amount merely to asking "Why?" or "How do you know?" Rather, it presents positive *reasons* for thinking that the claim or belief is likely to be false. That Wittgenstein accepts something like this is illustrated by his insistence that doubt presupposes certainty. A number of remarks make the point explicitly:

> ... But what about such a proposition as "I know I have a brain"? Can I doubt it? Grounds for *doubt* are lacking! Everything speaks in its favour, nothing against it. Nevertheless it is imaginable that my skull should turn out empty when it was operated on. (OC §4)

> Can one say: "Where there is no doubt there is no knowledge either"?
> Doesn't one need grounds for doubt? (OC §§121–22)

> I cannot at present imagine a *reasonable* doubt as to the existence of the earth during the last 100 years. (OC §261; my emphasis)

> One doubts on specific grounds. The question is this: how is doubt introduced into the language-game? (OC §458)

However, insofar as Wittgenstein does not think that hinge propositions are themselves justified in the contexts for which they are hinges, he does not accept Williams's claim that *every* proposition is default-justified. Only those that do not function as norms of representation seem to enjoy this status in the story that Wittgenstein tells.

6.7 THE RIVERBED OF THOUGHT

The possibility of changing the context of justification makes it clear that the distinction between norms of description and hypotheses is a fluid one. That is *not* to say that there is no distinction to be drawn, nor that the distinction is an unimportant one. Already in the *Philosophical Investigations* Wittgenstein was cautioning against conflating the two—albeit with different terminology:[24]

---

24 Indeed, the point is to be found even earlier in BB 25. See also Z §438. Such passages suggest, I think, that what Moyal-Sharrock calls the "grammaticalization of experience"—the treatment of empirical-looking propositions as norms of representation—is already present well before *On Certainty* and does not distinguish yet a "third Wittgenstein" from what I have been calling the "later Wittgenstein." Obviously, Wittgenstein's discussion of these matters is more extensive

> The fluctuation in grammar between criteria and symptoms makes it look as if there were nothing at all but symptoms. We say, for example: "Experience teaches that there is rain when the barometer falls, but it also teaches that there is rain when we have certain sensations of wet and cold, or such-and-such visual impressions." In defence of this one says that these sense-impressions can deceive us. But here one fails to reflect that the fact that the false appearance is precisely one of rain is founded on a definition. (PI §354)

Norms, we could say, express criteria, while empirical propositions express symptoms. From the mere fact that we can think of contexts in which it makes sense to doubt visual impressions, it does not follow that such doubt has any point in the context in which I look out the window to determine whether or not it is raining.

This fluidity of the distinction between norm and empirical proposition is brought out dramatically when Wittgenstein describes our "world-picture" (OC §95) as a kind of "mythology," consisting of propositions that we do not learn explicitly, but which we come to accept nonetheless. At different times different propositions may be accepted implicitly, serving as "channels" (OC §96) through which ordinary empirical propositions flow:

> The mythology may change back into a state of flux, the river-bed of thoughts may shift. But I distinguish between the movement of the waters on the river-bed and the shift of the bed itself; though there is not a sharp division of the one from the other.
>
> But if someone were to say "So logic too is an empirical science" he would be wrong. Yet this is right: the same proposition may get treated at one time as something to test by experience, at another as a rule of testing.
>
> And the bank of that river consists partly of hard rock, subject to no alteration or only to an imperceptible one, partly of sand, which now in one place now in another gets washed away, or deposited. (OC §§97–99)

Wittgenstein's focus here is primarily on norms of representation that have a broad cultural significance. He is concerned here more with "world pictures" than with variations in context of the sort exemplified by the different settings

---

in *On Certainty*, but that is because he is writing on *knowledge*, which was at most a secondary topic in the *Blue Book* and the *Investigations*. See Danièle Moyal-Sharrock, "*On Certainty* and the Grammaticalization of Experience" in Moyal-Sharrock (ed.) (2004), 43–62 and Moyal-Sharrock (2004), 163–65.

considered earlier for "There is a sick man lying before me." Propositions that belong to my "world picture" are like "rules of a game" (OC §95) insofar as they make it possible for me to pass true or false judgment, but they need not be explicit rules—norms implicit in practice will do. Nonetheless, which propositions get to play this important role is something that varies with time and place. Prior to the advent of space travel, of the airplane, of the hot-air balloon, it was unmentioned, but taken for granted, that human beings cannot fly (the mythological case of Icarus notwithstanding). Now we confidently reject that assumption. Europeans in the Middle Ages—the story goes—assumed without thought that the Earth was flat, whereas most people everywhere now take it for granted that it is roughly spherical:

> We form *the picture* of the earth as a ball floating free in space and not altering essentially in a hundred years. I said "We form the *picture* etc." and this picture now helps us in the judgment of various situations....
>
> The picture of the earth as a ball is a *good* picture, it proves itself everywhere, it is also a simple picture—in short, we work with it without doubting it. (OC §§146–47)

It is important to see that Wittgenstein is not suggesting any kind of relativism about truth here. To say that certain propositions that we now take to be false once served as norms of representation is not to say that those propositions were in some sense "true" for the people whose world-picture they typified (though, of course, those people presupposed the truth of those propositions in their acting). It is, instead, to say that in the contexts in which those propositions served as norms, an absence of doubt about them was a precondition for a claim's being justified. But a claim can be justified without being true. Wittgenstein tells us that a world picture is "the inherited background against which I distinguish between true and false" (OC §94). He is commenting on what I, a fallible epistemic agent, need to have standing fast if I am to be able to distinguish propositions that I take to be true from propositions that I take to be false. But my fallibility entails that I can make mistakes about some of those propositions and, indeed, that my world picture can be, in part, mistaken.[25]

25 Why only "in part"? Because it is not clear, for example, what it would mean for me to be completely mistaken about the meanings of the words I use. See Sections 6.2 and 6.3 above.

6.8 THE HARD ROCK OF THE RIVERBED

Recall the last remark from the long passage that I quoted in the preceding section:

> And the bank of that river consists partly of hard rock, subject to no alteration or only to an imperceptible one, partly of sand, which now in one place now in another gets washed away, or deposited. (OC §99)

This remark makes it clear that Wittgenstein is not drawing a simple, if fluid, binary distinction between empirical propositions (movement of the waters) and norms of representation (the riverbed).[26] The riverbed itself is more or less stable, some of it changing, some of it "subject to no alteration or only to an imperceptible one." That the Earth is flat, that human beings cannot fly, that there are no gaps in nature—these were all relatively stable norms of representation, but they belonged only to the sandy deposit of the riverbed, not its hard rock. The same is true of such propositions as "Human beings are biological creatures" and "Stars are balls of fiery gases." We do not expect those propositions to be washed away any time soon, but we can *imagine* what it would be like to find out that they were false. Doubts about them have *no point* in any ordinary context in which we might encounter these propositions explicitly stated, but such doubts are not *unintelligible*—we could imagine contexts in which they would have a point. (In the first case, as Donna Haraway points out, science-fiction writers have already helped us to think of ways in which the boundary between the biological and the technological can be blurred, and with it, a lot of customary thinking about sexuality and gender.[27] In the second case, imagine a new physical theory that reclassifies the building blocks of matter in such a way that gas, liquid, and solid are no longer seen as sufficiently rigorous categories of phase-classification.[28])

The hard rock of the riverbed, it seems, must be different. Like the sand, the hard rock does not serve as a justificatory foundation, but as "the inherited background against which I distinguish between true and false" (OC §94). But its stability suggests that it consists of propositions that serve as norms of representation that are free from doubt in *every context*. And these propositions—if Wittgenstein

26 This point has been made by Roger Shiner, "Wittgenstein and Heraclitus: Two River-Images," *Philosophy* 49 (1974): 191–97.

27 Donna Haraway, "A Cyborg Manifesto: Science, Technology, and Socialist-Feminism in the Late Twentieth Century" in *Simians, Cyborgs and Women: The Reinvention of Nature* (New York: Routledge, 1991), 149–81.

28 In fact we already have such a theory: a compound can change phase without changing from solid to liquid, for instance, but I want to keep the example simple.

is being consistent—must also fail to be justified in any context. This sounds paradoxical. Is there really any such thing as a proposition that is both a necessary truth *and* arbitrary, from the point of view of justification?

In fact, the commitment to implicit conventions that I have attributed to Wittgenstein entails that many propositions that have historically been classified by philosophers as necessary truths are arbitrary in the sense that they lack any justification. Convention, as we saw in Chapter 3, is the mother of normativity[29] in both mathematics and logic. We can, of course, justify new results in mathematics by appealing to old results that we already accept. But the question of whether the laws of addition, for example, can be justified is one that, for Wittgenstein, has no answer—save, perhaps, a pragmatic one (the laws of addition are *useful* to us because ...). Still, in another sense, there is nothing *arbitrary* about our embracing a mathematical convention because—as we have seen before—we have a "deep need for the convention" (RFM I §74). It is not as though we could give up on the transitivity of addition and just carry on our lives as though nothing had happened (though people who had never adopted the convention might not miss it). Similarly, in logic, that a given proposition expresses a tautology or that a rule of inference takes a certain form is, for Wittgenstein, the result of a tacit convention. It is, remember, "*we* that are inexorable in applying these laws" (RFM I 118), we who give them the normative force of laws. Those tacit conventions, like the tacit grammatical norms that govern any language-game, are constitutive of the meanings of the terms they govern, in this case the logical "constants," conjunction, disjunction, etc. So Wittgenstein asserts in a remark from 1944:

> We can conceive the rules of inference—I want to say—as giving the signs their meaning, because they are rules for the use of these signs. So that the rules of inference are involved in the determination of the meaning of the signs. In this sense rules of inference cannot be right or wrong. (RFM VII §30)

If we wanted to use some other set of logical constants and found it useful to do so, we could define them by employing different rules of inference.

Is there textual evidence for thinking that either mathematics or logic is part of the hard rock of the riverbed? That Wittgenstein has propositions of mathematics in mind might be suggested by some later remarks:

29 To modify a *bon mot* of Barry Stroud's.

> The mathematical proposition has, as it were officially, been given the stamp of incontestability. I.e.: "Dispute about other things; *this* is immovable—it is a hinge on which your dispute can turn."
>
> And one can *not* say that of the proposition that *I* am called L.W. Nor of the proposition that such-and-such people have calculated such-and-such a problem correctly. (OC §§655–56)

Mathematical propositions are "hinge" propositions, and to say this is to say something stronger than that they are not in doubt in some specialized context. Although there are contexts in which each of the latter propositions—"that I am called L.W." and "that such-and-such people have calculated such-and-such a problem correctly"—may serve as a norm of representation, they belong to the silt of the riverbed, rather than its hard rock.

This is far from an airtight case for seeing mathematics as hard rock. After all, as we saw in Chapter 4, by Wittgenstein's own lights the concept of number—and therefore, propositions that make use of this concept—is a variable concept with a *history*. Perhaps the ancient Celts could not doubt the fundamental theorem of calculus, but that is because they lacked the requisite concepts. Mathematicians throughout the eighteenth century were acquainted with the theorem and its concepts, but some doubted that it was really a *theorem* until the analytical work of Cauchy and Weierstrass in the nineteenth century.[30]

Remarks about the pancontextual indubitability of logic are difficult to find in *On Certainty*. That is partly because in that collection Wittgenstein defines "logic" as including "everything descriptive of a language-game" (OC §56; see OC §82). Logic, therefore, includes many norms of description that are pertinent only to the specialized contexts of particular language-games. It is roughly what 'grammar' designated in Chapter 3. Nevertheless logic in a less expansive sense is a smaller part of grammar, and, like at least some mathematics, it has the stamp of incontestability for Wittgenstein in 1937:

> Isn't it like this: so long as one thinks it can't be otherwise, one draws logical conclusions. This presumably means: so long as *such-and-such is not brought in question at all.*
>
> The steps which are not brought in question are logical inferences. But the reason why they are not brought in question is not that they 'certainly correspond to the truth'—or something of the sort,—no, it is just this that

30 See Morris Kline, *Mathematics: The Loss of Certainty* (New York: Oxford University Press, 1980), 127–52, 172–77.

> is called 'thinking', 'speaking', 'inferring', 'arguing'. There is not any question at all here of some correspondence between what is said and reality; rather is logic *antecedent* to any such correspondence; in the same sense, that is, as that in which the establishment of a method of measurement is *antecedent* to the correctness or incorrectness of a statement of length. (RFM I §156)

So logic, in a narrower sense than grammar, is a necessary precondition of thinking and speaking and so on. It is not clear that Wittgenstein means here "some logic (grammar) or another," as I proposed in Chapter 3. It seems that in both this passage from the late 1930s and in the riverbed analogy Wittgenstein is telling us that meaning and thought rest on something... *transcendental*!

6.9 BACK TO THE *TRACTATUS*?

The conclusion of the preceding section may seem to take back what I have been insisting is one of the central claims that divides Wittgenstein's later work from his early work—that normativity does not presuppose something transcendent, something that lies beyond the world. Indeed, Wittgenstein himself seems to have been worried about the possibility: "Am I not getting closer and closer to saying that in the end logic cannot be described? You must look at the practice of language, then you will see it" (OC §501).

I shall conclude this chapter by trying to show that the position at which Wittgenstein arrives in *On Certainty* does not constitute a retreat to the extra-worldliness of the *Tractatus*,[31] nor to its cryptic saying-showing distinction.

The first step in making this case is to remember from Chapter 2 that logic in the *Tractatus* is not merely transcendental in the sense that it is a necessary condition for the possibility of meaning, but also *transcendent* in the sense that it lies "outside the world." And the argument that is supposed to persuade us that logic lies outside the world is premised on observing that there could be no value that depended on anything in the world because "all happening and being-so"—everything in the world—"is accidental" (TLP §6.41). So logic, the precondition of sense, is not *just* a necessary condition for sense, but something that is itself absolutely necessary. And that is to say—very roughly—that propositions of logic would be tautologies whether there were any world or not.

---

31 This conclusion has been drawn by some. See, for example, Philip R. Shields, *Logic and Sin in the Writings of Ludwig Wittgenstein* (Chicago: University of Chicago Press, 1993), 19.

For the later Wittgenstein, by contrast, there are no logical propositions unless there are language-users to formulate them or presuppose them in practice. Logical propositions—at least some of them, as I explain below—if they can be formulated at all, must be true, but they could fail to be true if there were no thought or language, because then nothing would be either true or false. There would be no propositions and, so, no logical propositions—no tautologies. (Notice that it does not follow from this that there would be no rocks or trees or nuclear fission, just no true or false propositions about them.)[32]

But even if this means that Wittgenstein is not merely returning to the *Tractatus*, we may well wonder what consequences the pancontextual stability of the laws of logic has for the contention that "it is *we* that are inexorable in applying these laws" (RFM I 118).

I can think of at least five relatively discrete points that need making here. The first point is that the focus of *On Certainty* is on a particular subset of language-games—those in which we claim to know something or attribute knowledge to someone else or deny such attributions. The concern here is with what he called in the *Philosophical Grammar* "true-false games" (PG I V §68; 111), not with *all* forms of language-use.[33] That is why norms of *representation* are at issue. By contrast, the language-game of the builders in the *Investigations* is not concerned with representation, with making true or false claims, or with claims to know anything. It consists entirely in the giving and following of orders. Of course, not just anything can count as successfully carrying out an order, so perhaps this language-game presupposes a "norm of compliance," without which it and similar games would not be played, but there is no automatic reason to try to collapse this norm into a traditional "law of logic."

Second, not *all* the "laws of logic" (or of mathematics) need be pancontextual norms of representation. Some of them may be part of the sandy river-bottom. This is true not only of propositions of logic, construed broadly as "grammar," but of logic more narrowly construed as well. Wittgenstein might plausibly allow that what "is called 'thinking', 'speaking', 'inferring', 'arguing'" (RFM I §156), and so on, is subject to change and development, just as what we call a "game" can change and develop over time. We might take this to be demonstrated by the proliferation of "alternative logics" that have been produced in the last three quarters of a century or so.

32 Recall from Chapter 4 that there is some question whether Wittgenstein thought that tautologies could be true. But even if tautologies are not properly speaking true, they must still be formulated or presupposed by language-users in order to be tautologies.

33 See Michael N. Forster, *Wittgenstein on the Arbitrariness of Grammar* (Princeton: Princeton University Press, 2004), 9 for this point.

Consider, for example, the law of the excluded middle, which holds that every proposition is either true or false; there are no propositions that lack truth-values. This is a commonplace of "classical" logic, but its abandonment has been seriously proposed at one time or another by various thinkers. Aristotle thought that propositions about the future remained indeterminate until the future became the present. Intuitionists about logic and mathematics have thought that only provable propositions should be taken to have truth-values, and Michael Dummett has defined "anti-realism" about a sphere of discourse as the view that propositions belonging to that sphere lack truth-values if they cannot be confirmed or disconfirmed.[34] Some interpretations of quantum indeterminacy have it that there is no fact of the matter concerning the momentum of a subatomic particle until someone tries to measure it. Sorites paradoxes might lead us to say that there is no fact of the matter for *every* collection of sand-grains whether or not it constitutes a heap.

Or consider the position of so-called relevance logicians. They hold that the classical logical rule of inference which says that from a contradiction *everything* follows is a bad rule. We ought to replace it, they say, with the rule that from a contradiction almost *nothing* follows.[35] Other logicians have tried to take a middle way here and suggest a way of reasoning from sets of premises that contain contradictions by finding a principled way of isolating the contradiction.[36]

More dramatically, advocates of some forms of paraconsistent logic have argued that *some* contradictions can be true.[37] This amounts to a rejection of the classical law of non-contradiction, which says that no proposition is simultaneously and unambiguously both true and false. It goes beyond my powers to make a compelling case for this view in a short space (and perhaps even in a long one), but it is not a frivolous view.

Some "laws of logic" can, thus, plausibly be argued to belong to the sand of the riverbed and not to its hard rock, but not all. For example, even if it is correct that some contradictions can be true, no one, to my knowledge, has seriously advocated the view that all contradictions are true,[38] that we should set aside what

34 See Michael Dummett, "Realism" in *Truth and Other Enigmas* (Cambridge, MA: Harvard University Press, 1978), 145–65.

35 See, e.g., Alan Ross Anderson and Nuel D. Belnap, Jr., *Entailment: The Logic of Relevance and Necessity*, Vol. 1 (Princeton: Princeton University Press, 1975), 163.

36 See, e.g., P.K. Schotch, "Paraconsistent Logic: the View from the Right," *Proceedings of the Biennial Meetings of the Philosophy of Science Association*, 2 (1993): 421–29.

37 See, e.g., Graham Priest, "The Logic of Paradox," *Journal of Philosophical Logic*, 8 (1979): 219–41.

38 Hegelians sometimes talk this way, but they do not mean the same thing by 'contradiction' as most logicians do. For Hegel—and for Marx—a contradiction is something more like an historically inevitable instability in some state of affairs, which will lead to the alteration of that state of affairs, as Marx thought capitalism unavoidably sowed the seeds of its own destruction.

Hilary Putnam has called the "minimal" principle of non-contradiction.[39] This weaker principle says that it is not the case that *every* proposition is simultaneously and unambiguously both true and false. That is compatible with what proponents of paraconsistent logic want to say (and maybe even with what some adventurous literary theorists want to say), and it has the look of a proposition that will stand fast in any context.

The third point to be made about the consequences of pancontextual norms of representation for Wittgenstein's conventionalism is this: insofar as there would be no norms of representation at all if there were no representors—no players of true-false games—there is no pragmatic distinction to be drawn between the fabled inexorability of logic and our inexorability in insisting that certain propositions be treated as laws of logic. The laws of logic do not get to be inexorable in any way other than by standing fast in all true-false linguistic contexts. And "standing fast" here, remember, need not mean that we explicitly formulate them. (Who are "we" here? Linguistically competent human beings.) A people who had no interest in abstruse questions about logic might never explicitly formulate the minimal principle of contradiction, but no language-game that they would play would ever call it into doubt. (Of course, if the words 'true' and 'false' and 'proposition' (and the rest) came to mean something different—to occupy different roles in the linguistic proceedings of a people—then the users of those words might well reject instances of the type of sentence, "Not all contradictions are true." But that would not be to call the minimal principle of non-contradiction into doubt.)[40]

This latter, subsidiary point about the tacitness of what stands fast is connected with a fourth feature of Wittgenstein's conventionalism. That is that when Wittgenstein wonders whether he is coming closer to saying that logic cannot be described, he is not committing himself to some mysterious doctrine of showing the ineffable. His point is, rather, that a tautology—a statement of a "law of logic"—is not a *description* of anything, and when I try to represent the logical truths whose tautologousness serves as a norm of representation for all contexts of discussion and inquiry, I succeed only in reminding myself of tautologies. There is no mysticism here, just an acknowledgement of one of the lessons of the discussion of rule-following in the *Investigations*—that if any norms are to be explicit, then some must be implicit. That is, we cannot *learn* a system of norms if they are

39 Hilary Putnam, "There Is at Least One *A Priori* Truth," *Realism and Reason* (Cambridge: Cambridge University Press, 1983), 101.

40 I have been treating immunity from doubt and "standing fast" as though they amounted to exactly the same thing, but it is possible that there is a distinction to be drawn here. Wittgenstein does remark that "It may be for example that all enquiry on our part is set so as to exempt certain propositions from doubt, *if they are ever formulated*" (OC §88; my emphasis).

all explicit to begin with, or we face an infinite regress of rules to interpret rules. The only difference introduced in *On Certainty* is that there is some *one* norm or minimal set of norms that must be implicit.

Fifth, the conclusion that there are pancontextual hinge-propositions on which all true-false games swing (to mix Wittgensteinian metaphors) is closely related to the anti-sceptical argument that we examined in §§6.2 and 6.3 above. Any reason I could have for doubting that, say, the minimal principle of non-contradiction is necessary is a reason for doubting that I understand what 'contradiction' and 'true' and 'false' and 'proposition' and 'language' and 'thinking' mean. As with the arguments against private language and the anti-sceptical argument of *On Certainty*, this argument should not be taken as a knock-down refutation of the possibility of rejecting the minimal principle. Rather, it is an argument that the burden of proof is on someone who contends that "no statement is immune to revision,"[41] or that a viable practice *akin* to true-false games could be established without presupposing something like the minimal principle of non-contradiction.[42]

So do certain low-level logical truths end up being justified after all? The question is apposite because it may seem as though I have just given, on Wittgenstein's behalf, something like a transcendental argument to show that some such principles—the minimal principle of non-contradiction being a perspicuous example—are necessary conditions of the very possibility of meaning and justification. If hinge propositions are not supposed to admit of justification in the contexts for which they are hinges, then some kind of inconsistency seems to be lurking. Even if we see the argument as one that attempts to shift the burden of proof, it still may seem to offer a justification of sorts for a minimal logic.

I think this conclusion can be reasonably rejected. To ask whether or not we should accept the minimal principle of non-contradiction is tantamount to asking whether or not we should continue playing true-false games, whether we should continue making and assessing claims to know things, whether we should believe

41 W.V. Quine, "Two Dogmas of Empiricism" in *From a Logical Point of View*, rev. ed. (Cambridge, MA: Harvard University Press, 1980), 43.

42 Quine himself urges on us a "principle of charity" (*Word and Object* [Cambridge, MA: MIT Press, 1960], 59 n2), which requires that we not attribute to a speaker whose language we are trying to translate a wanton disregard for logical truths. He is no believer in the "myth of... prelogical people" (69). So it is not entirely clear that Quine means it when he says that no statement is immune from revision. Even in "Two Dogmas..." the only logical law he envisions revising is the law of the excluded middle.

that anything is true or false (and not both). These questions in turn have a point only if there is some alternative that we could reasonably consider adopting, but there is no such alternative. This is what human beings do, in a variety of ways, and there is no giving it up. That we *do* play true-false games is no *justification* for a minimal logic.

7

OBJECTIONS AND EXTRAPOLATIONS

In the last four chapters I have been presenting a view of Wittgenstein as committed to a deflationary, therapeutic conception of philosophy. Wittgenstein, I have maintained, is not interested in grand system-building. He explicitly eschews the project of giving deep theoretical explanations of meaning, mind, and knowledge and aims at letting the metaphysical wind out of many of the traditional problems of philosophy.

However, as I noted at the end of Chapter 3, this kind of therapeutic reading of Wittgenstein provokes some disquiet amongst philosophers of many different stripes. Wittgenstein was himself aware that his view of the nature of philosophy could expect a hostile reception:

> Where does our investigation get its importance from, since it seems only to destroy everything interesting, that is, all that is great and important? (As it were all the buildings, leaving behind only bits of stone and rubble.) What we are destroying is nothing but houses of cards and we are clearing up the ground of language on which they stand. (PI §118)[1]

1 Ludwig Wittgenstein, *Philosophical Investigations*, 2nd ed., translated by G.E.M. Anscombe (Oxford: Basil Blackwell, 1968).

Unfortunately, his dismissive response here will not do much to satisfy the worries that he is aware he provokes.

My main task in this final chapter is to address some of the major criticisms of Wittgenstein's conception of the task of philosophy head-on. In the process I hope also to weave into this project some of the loose threads I have left hanging in earlier chapters.

7.1 FAREWELL TO PHILOSOPHY?

If traditional philosophical problems are really just sophisticated illusions that arise from failing to acquire a synoptic view of grammatical conventions, then it may seem that the unmasking of these illusions will bring an end to philosophy. There will, after all, be no further progress to be made in understanding the topics of philosophy, because there will be no science-like inquiry whose theories will admit of further revision and refinement (and, occasionally, replacement).

Wittgenstein may seem to concede as much when he observes,

> It is not our aim to refine or complete the system of rules for the use of our words in unheard-of ways.
>
> For the clarity that we are aiming at is indeed *complete* clarity. But this simply means that the philosophical problems should *completely* disappear.
>
> The real discovery is the one that makes me capable of stopping doing philosophy when I want to.—The one that gives philosophy peace, so that it is no longer tormented by questions which bring *itself* in question.... (PI §133)

And even if Wittgenstein himself continued to practice the activity of philosophy all his life, he certainly did not hesitate to advise young protégés to choose another line of work—preferably some kind of manual labour. Does Wittgenstein think we should give up philosophy altogether?[2]

I find little evidence for thinking that we should interpret the peace that philosophy seeks as something that Wittgenstein thought could be a permanent or lasting peace. If I could stop doing philosophy "when I want to," it would mean

2 Habermas seems to think so as did Russell. See Jürgen Habermas, "Philosophy as Stand-in and Interpreter," 306, translated by C. Lenhardt in *After Philosophy: End or Transformation?*, edited by Kenneth Baynes, James Bohman, and Thomas McCarthy (Cambridge, MA: MIT Press, 1987), 296–315 and Bertrand Russell, *My Philosophical Development* (London: Unwin, 1959), 214, 216–17.

that for me particular problems would lack the interminable character that non-philosophers quickly notice. I could set a problem to one side because I would no longer be driven by a compulsive need to answer a question that has no answer. I would not have to return again and again to the same problem. Philosophy would no longer be called into question because its results would lead neither to an insoluble philosophical scepticism nor to a layperson's scepticism about the futility of philosophical inquiry. But because "Language sets everyone the same traps" (CV 25; *cf.* BT 312),[3] there will never be any shortage of work for philosophers whose task is to "erect signposts at all the junctions where there are wrong turnings, to help people past the danger points" (CV 25; *cf.* BT 312). The city of language is a sprawling metropolis, with many unfrequented side-streets to get lost in, ever growing and changing. *New* philosophical puzzles—and unrecognized, new formulations of old ones—arise with, for example, the advent of new technologies. Think of how many problems philosophers of mind have had to deal with since the invention of the digital computer and the new linguistic practices that have come with it. Because such problems arise with new scientific and technological advances, it looks at first as though they require scientific or even technological solutions that would displace philosophy. If there is a threat to the ongoing practice of philosophy, it comes not from Wittgenstein's therapeutic recommendations, but from the infatuation with scientific and technological models that guides the economic decisions of university administrators and corporate and government granting agencies.

There is, it should be emphasized, nothing in this view to suggest that philosophers are magically invulnerable to "the bewitchment of our intelligence by means of language" (PI §109). People who are drawn to philosophical problems—whether they specialize in philosophy or not—are perhaps the people who are most vulnerable to this kind of "bewitchment." Philosophy, remember, is "work on oneself" (CV 23; *cf.* BT 300). But this is not to say that the non-philosopher is automatically free from confusion. She may make the same kinds of mistakes that the philosopher makes, but for her they do not *look* like problems. So Wittgenstein is not recommending the stance of untutored common sense as a model for philosophers to emulate.

3 Ludwig Wittgenstein, *Culture and Value: A Selection from the Posthumous Remains*, rev. 2nd ed., edited by Georg Henrik von Wright, Heikki Nyman, and Alois Pichler, translated by Peter Winch (Oxford: Blackwell, 1998); Ludwig Wittgenstein, *The Big Typescript TS 213*, edited and translated by C. Grant Luckhardt and Maximilian A.E. Aue (Oxford: Blackwell, 2005).

7.2 ORDINARY LANGUAGE PHILOSOPHY

Other critics of Wittgenstein have charged that at the bottom of his therapeutic view lies a naive privileging of "ordinary language," as though philosophical problems could be dissolved by good old common sense combined with some nitpicking attention to detail. Russell complained that Wittgenstein had "grown tired of serious thinking" (1959, 217) and had "debased himself before common sense as Tolstoy had debased himself before the peasants" (214).[4] This interpretation of Wittgenstein sees him as allied, on the one hand, with G.E. Moore and, on the other, with the ordinary-language philosophy practiced with fierce precision by J.L. Austin and his coterie of Oxonians in the 1950s. According to this view, philosophical problems arise from the *misuse* of words, and the goal of philosophy is to point out how past philosophers have abused their language.[5] Such a view, Russell lamented, left philosophy "at best, a slight help to lexicographers, and at worst, an idle tea-table amusement" (217).

There are, indeed, passages in which Wittgenstein gestures toward ordinary language as being in some way relevant to the dissolution of philosophical troubles. Consider:

> What *we* do is bring words back from their metaphysical to their everyday use. (PI §116)

> When I talk about language (words, sentences, etc.) I must speak the language of every day. (PI §120)

> Here it is easy to get into that dead-end in philosophy, where one believes that the difficulty of the task consists in our having to describe phenomena that are hard to get hold of, the present experience that slips quickly by, or something of the kind. Where we find ordinary language too crude ... (PI §436)

But Wittgenstein's complaint, I think, is not that philosophers *misuse* words and, therefore, create a lot of silly problems that can be fixed by using words correctly. Although norms of correct use have a role to play in Wittgenstein's account (a perspicuous representation of our linguistic practices makes those norms explicit),

4 Eagleton worries, with more sophistication than Russell, that Wittgenstein is trading old-style metaphysics for a metaphysics of common sense. See Terry Eagleton, "Wittgenstein's Friends," *New Left Review* I, no.135 (September-October 1982): 64–90, especially 72–73.

5 Is this a fair account of Austin's view? Maybe not, but my concern here is with how Wittgenstein's views have been portrayed.

Wittgenstein is well aware that norms of linguistic use *change* in many ways, arbitrary and non-arbitrary. There is no automatic objection to be lodged against the explanatorily-minded philosopher who wants to use an old term in a new way. Philosophical difficulties arise only when philosophers and non-philosophers alike attempt to apply a term in a new way without recognizing that they are doing so, as may happen, for example, when we follow psychoanalysis in speaking of unconscious intentional attitudes or vulgar genetics in thinking of DNA as the "blueprint" of life. This is what it is like to wander down a side-street in the city of language.

Far from being a remedy for such problems, ordinary language—together with human frailty—is their source:

> We want to establish an order in our knowledge of the use of language: an order with a particular end in view; one out of many possible orders; not *the* order. To this end we shall constantly be giving prominence to distinctions which our *ordinary forms of language* easily make us overlook. (PI §132; second emphasis mine)

This is not to say, by any means, that philosophy is concerned with repairing some deficiency in ordinary language—the polar opposite of ordinary-language philosophy. The philosopher's task is descriptive, remember, not reformist. "Such a reform for particular practical purposes, an improvement in our terminology designed to prevent misunderstandings in practice, is perfectly possible. But these are not the cases we have to do with" (PI §132). It is not the business of philosophy, as Wittgenstein envisions it, to try to change existing norms of use—for example, by seeking an *ideal* language that is somehow invulnerable to confusion and ambiguity (as Frege proposed). But neither is it the business of philosophy to stand in the way of changes that explicitly serve a practical purpose. Existing norms of use are not sacred. The business of philosophy is to remind us what the norms are, to give us a synoptic overview of them, when we fall into confusion.

Another way of making this complaint is to say that in naively privileging "ordinary" language, Wittgenstein fails to see that it is continuous with the language of philosophy—that philosophy is itself "ordinary," just another language-game, and, therefore, just as authoritative as non-philosophical language. This contention is, of course, beside the point if Wittgenstein is not an ordinary-language philosopher, but it is, in any event, only half-right. Philosophy, like other disciplines, invents and adapts its own terminology that may be either more or less closely related to non-philosophical ways of talking. Philosophers may, for example, adopt for special purposes a stricter use of the verb 'to know' than is applied around the dinner-table or at the nearest clothing store, and they may invent special terms of art like 'quintessence' and 'reliabilism'. This is an intelligible sense in which philosophical discourse is not "ordinary." Wittgenstein himself employs a special terminology that he finds suited to the discipline he practices: 'language-game', 'criterion', 'family-resemblance', etc. If Wittgenstein were naively privileging ordinary language, then he would be caught in a performative inconsistency because, despite his alleged allegiance to ordinary language, he uses special terms of art with the same willingness as Freud spoke of the unconscious or metaphysicians have spoken of tropes and possible worlds, instead of sticking to ordinary, non-philosophical uses of language. But, again, in the absence of any such allegiance there is no objection to such terms of art to be found in Wittgenstein's philosophy, as long as their use is clear.

7.3 QUIETISM AND PESSIMISM

A further objection that was raised in Chapter 3 criticized Wittgenstein's injunction against giving explanations in philosophy as a species of "quietism" or, indeed, a form of reckless pessimism about philosophical problems, which treats them as mysteries that we are simply not capable of fathoming.[6] It may seem, moreover, that Wittgenstein regularly violates his own strictures against giving explanations. Surely the conventionalism that I attributed to Wittgenstein in earlier chapters is itself an attempt to offer an explanatory theory of the nature of necessity, for example.[7]

The charge of pessimism simply misunderstands Wittgenstein's position. It is true that Wittgenstein, as I have portrayed him, takes inspiration for his descriptive, therapeutic view from the apparent intractability of certain longstanding problems in philosophy—the problem of universals, the mind-body problem, the problems of intentional and semantic content, etc.

> We keep hearing the remark that philosophy really does not progress, that we are still occupied with the same philosophical problems as were the Greeks. Those who say this however don't understand why it is so. It is because our language has remained the same & keeps seducing us into asking the same questions. (CV 22; *cf.* BT 312)

6 See, e.g., Crispin Wright, *Truth and Objectivity* (Cambridge, MA: Harvard University Press, 1992), 202–30. Russell's complaints carry a whiff of this, too.

7 See, e.g., Ernest Gellner, *Words and Things: A Critical Account of Linguistic Philosophy and a Study in Ideology* (London: Victor Gollancz, 1959), Chapter III for this kind of complaint.

But it requires a significant amount of philosophical intuition-tutoring for most people to come to believe that these problems admit of eventual *solution*. (If the relationship between mind and body seems to be an exception, then this is largely, I think, because it has been successfully presented to non-specialists as a *scientific* problem.) I find myself struggling with the intuitions of my introductory philosophy students in precisely this way every September in order to put them in a position to take seriously the material I ask them to read. Despite my efforts, I continually read essays in which students remark that there are no right answers in philosophy. Working scientists, similarly, often require little convincing that if philosophical problems admitted of real solutions, they would already be the subject of some special science—as the problems of physics and biology have become. So it seems equally apt to charge critics of Wittgenstein (and of other philosophers who take a deflationary attitude toward the traditional problems of philosophy—Richard Rorty springs to mind) with starry-eyed optimism of the sort enjoyed only by true believers.

The fact that these charges are so easily traded suggests that a more dispassionate assessment is needed, and surely such an assessment must take Wittgenstein's view as a serious competitor. Moreover, Wittgenstein, as I have argued, is not simply recommending that we give up on philosophy. Rather, he offers an alternative and a diagnosis for why so many traditional philosophical problems seem so intractable, and that diagnosis is surely no less plausible than the bald insistence that we just have not tried hard enough yet.[8]

But does Wittgenstein himself fall back into offering explanations, rather than sticking to his vow to give only descriptions? Does his conventionalism offer an explanation of the nature of necessity, as suggested above?

Suppose for the moment that this is so. This backsliding could be as easily seen as confirmation of Wittgenstein's contention that philosophical problems are the result of a deep temptation we feel to appeal to the model of natural science. That even he fails to resist this temptation is merely evidence in favour of this part of his diagnosis of the source of philosophical problems.

However, I think it is more accurate to say that the charge of inconsistency misunderstands Wittgenstein's target. It is true that Wittgenstein's conventionalism attempts to enlighten us about the steadfastness of ostensibly necessary truths, but it does not purport to uncover the mysterious *nature* of necessity. Rather Wittgenstein is better thought of as contending that necessity—like meaning

8 The most serious rival to this view, it seems to me, is the kind of naturalized philosophy that attempts to solve longstanding philosophical problems by an appeal to the special sciences. It is telling that traditional philosophers often accuse naturalists of changing or begging the question.

and truth and knowledge—has no nature, that we best understand necessity by examining the role in our linguistic practices of propositions that have traditionally been classified as necessary truths. When we do this, we see that to call a proposition a necessary truth is to assign to it a particular role in our linguistic proceedings, the role of being a "norm of description" (OC §167)[9] across a broad array of linguistic contexts.

It is true, of course, that Wittgenstein or anyone can misdescribe those linguistic proceedings. Finding a vantage point from which one can give a clear overview of grammatical norms is a difficult task. That claim is central to Wittgenstein's account of the source and character of traditional philosophical problems. But from this it does not follow that Wittgenstein is offering explanatory hypotheses about the nature of necessity, mind, meaning, knowledge, etc. If it seems that he does so—when, for example, he argues against private language, or describes rule-following, or reminds us of the many different kinds of words that we classify as "names"—then that is the result of reading his texts as though there *had to be* such explanatory hypotheses lurking, as though he had to be trying to categorically refute the logical possibility of private language or the results of sceptical arguments, for example. In short, the basis for this charge is very often an artifact of not taking Wittgenstein's remarks about philosophical method seriously enough, of not believing him when he eschews the traditional philosophical project of developing a "theory of X" and then reading him as though he were presenting such theories.

7.4 CONSERVATISM

Wittgenstein's "quietism" and descriptivism have also been interpreted by some as an inherently conservative attempt to discourage critique of linguistic expressions that play the ideological role of misrepresenting the oppressive advantage of the powerful as though it were somehow necessary, inevitable, or just. Critics of this stripe are fond of citing quietest passages like this one:

> Philosophy may in no way interfere with the actual use of language; it can in the end only describe it.
>
> For it cannot give it any foundation either.
>
> It leaves everything as it is.... (PI §124)

9 Ludwig Wittgenstein, *On Certainty*, translated by Denis Paul and G.E.M. Anscombe (New York: Harper Torchbooks, 1972).

Surely, it might be argued, leaving "everything as it is" signifies a slavish devotion to the status quo and a trivializing of the efforts of philosophers who have worked for various liberatory and egalitarian ideals![10]

Wittgenstein's personal attitude toward political questions was mostly disdainful and dismissive, though what anecdotal evidence is available and what few remarks he left in his notebooks suggest as much sympathy for some kind of Marxism "in practice" but not "in theory" (Monk 343)[11] as for any right-leaning political views. But, of course, his personal political views and the practical consequences of his views about philosophical method might well be at odds with each other.[12]

However, I think that closer examination of the passage above suggests that it is poorly understood if it is offered as evidence of the politically conservative nature of Wittgenstein's thinking. In the next breath he goes on to say of philosophy:

> ... It also leaves mathematics as it is, and no mathematical discovery can advance it. A 'leading problem of mathematical logic' is for us a problem of mathematics like any other.
>
> It is the business of philosophy, not to resolve a contradiction by means of a mathematical or logico-mathematical discovery, but to make it possible for us to get a clear view of the state of mathematics that troubles us: the state of affairs *before* the contradiction is resolved. (And this does not mean that one is sidestepping a difficulty.) ... (PI §§124–25)

It would be strange to cite *these* remarks as evidence of political conservatism, and this is not just because disputes in mathematics have, at best, a tenuous connection to disputes about power. The point of these remarks, I think, is that philosophy has no insight into the hidden essence of mathematics, because mathematics *has no* hidden essence. It is, rather, a "network of norms" (RFM VII §67),[13] and understand-

10 See Herbert Marcuse, *One-Dimensional Man* (Boston: Beacon Press, 1964), 170–78, and Eagleton, "Wittgenstein's Friends." Related complaints can be found in Ernest Gellner, *Language and Solitude: Wittgenstein, Malinowski and the Habsburg Dilemma* (Cambridge: Cambridge University Press, 1998), Part II. Some conservatives have looked to Wittgenstein for support. See, e.g., J.C. Nyíri, "Wittgenstein's Later Work in Relation to Conservatism" in *Wittgenstein and His Times*, edited by Brian McGuinness (Oxford: Blackwell, 1982), 44–68.

11 Ray Monk, *Wittgenstein: The Duty of Genius* (London: Jonathan Cape, 1990).

12 I defend Wittgenstein's philosophy from charges of conservatism in greater detail in "Wittgenstein, Pessimism and Politics," *The Dalhousie Review* 80, no.2 (2000): 185–216.

13 Ludwig Wittgenstein, *Remarks on the Foundations of Mathematics*, 3rd ed., edited by G.H. von Wright, R. Rhees, and G.E.M. Anscombe, translated by G.E.M. Anscombe (Oxford: Blackwell, 1978).

ing a philosophical problem in mathematics requires getting a clear view of those norms:

> ... The fundamental fact here is that we lay down rules, a technique, for a game, and that then when we follow the rules, things do not turn out as we had assumed. That we are therefore as it were entangled in our own rules.
>
> This entanglement in our rules is what we want to understand (i.e. get a clear view of).... (PI §125)

And these remarks cast light on the ones that precede them, the ones about not interfering in the actual use of language. Getting a clear view of our entanglement in our rules in mathematics

> ... throws light on our concept of *meaning* something. For in those cases things turn out otherwise than we had meant, foreseen. That is just what we say when, for example, a contradiction appears: "I didn't mean it like that."
>
> The civil status of a contradiction, or its status in civil life: there is the philosophical problem. (PI §125)

Similarly, philosophy has no insight into the hidden essence of *language*, because language has no hidden essence, no foundation. It is a motley collection of practical activities in which certain contingent grammatical conventions are implicit, and these are all that is needed for it to be possible for us to utter noises and make marks that are meaningful (though the implicitness and complexity of some of those conventions makes it possible for us to become entangled in our own rules). In particular, the possibility of meaning does not rest on something big and metaphysical that lies "outside the world," and natural languages do not need to be improved or replaced by an ideal language in the way that Frege thought necessary if misunderstanding is to be avoided.

This, and not a commitment to conservative politics, is why "It is not our aim to refine or complete the system of rules for the use of our words in unheard-of ways" (PI §133). As I argued above, Wittgenstein has no principled objection to attempts to change norms of linguistic use if it suits some practical purpose to do so. He simply believes that the dissolution of traditional philosophical problems typically requires that we make explicit to ourselves what those norms of use are. If there were a way of treating these problems without going through this kind of exercise, he might take it:

> It is not by any means clear to me, that I wish for a continuation of my work by others, more than a change in the way we live, making all these questions superfluous. (For this reason I could never found a school.) (CV 70)

As it is, he sees no plausible way of achieving his end other than working to gain a synoptic overview of the linguistic practices that lead us into confusion. But once we have that synoptic overview, it is up to us what we want to do with it. I say 'want' and 'we' advisedly here, because, although there are special contexts in which authorities can alter norms of use at will ("In the following discussion I shall use the terms 'mind' and 'brain' interchangeably..."), making a substantive, directed difference to norms of use at large is no easy thing—especially if one finds oneself in a position of relative social and political disadvantage within one's linguistic community. However, nothing in Wittgenstein's view of philosophy adds to the burdens of the oppressed.

Indeed, I think that the critics who level such charges have failed to appreciate the radical political potential that lies in both Wittgenstein's hostility toward scientism and his emphasis on the contingency and contextual character of our linguistic practices. Consider these points in order.

Wittgenstein was plainly troubled by the growing cultural supremacy of science, particularly at the end of World War II, when he hoped for "the destruction of a ghastly evil, of disgusting soapy water science" (CV 56), which he feared would, in cooperation with industry, "unite the world" in "infinite misery": "I mean integrate it into a single empire, in which to be sure peace is the last thing that will then find a home. For science & industry do decide wars, or so it seems" (CV 72). It would be simplistic and implausible to see his philosophical work as aiming at bringing about an end to this "ghastly evil," but it is not so implausible to see his work as a challenge to scientism in at least two ways. First, it resists the intrusion of the methods of science into the treatment of philosophical problems, insisting, rather, that this is the "real source of metaphysics" and "darkness" (BB 18).[14] Secondly, it rejects the tendency, promoted since by Quine, to collapse the distinction between hinge-propositions or norms of representation or pieces of instruction, on the one hand, and empirical propositions or hypotheses on the other. That very distinction, in turn, makes it possible to see different epistemic contexts as enjoying a degree of autonomy from each other, rather than as local manifestations of a general scientific inquiry that might one day absorb and thereby justify the worthy, while consigning the unworthy to the rubbish-bin of pseudo-science. This is not to say that particular linguistic practices are immune to external critique, but that some

14 Ludwig Wittgenstein, *The Blue and the Brown Books*, 2nd ed. (Oxford: Blackwell, 1969).

practices are not scientific is not an *automatic* objection to knowledge-claims that they may generate.

The significance of Wittgenstein's emphasis on contingency can be brought out by noticing that it is not just philosophers who have a craving for generality. A similar craving is evinced in the tendency of the powerful to represent their own experience and interests as if they were the experience and interests of everyone, to represent the contingent and local social order that serves their interests as one that is necessary and universal (if not now, then in the future—the "triumph" of capitalism over socialism, the "threat" to a viable society posed by same-sex marriage, the "inevitable" unhappiness of women who eschew child-rearing for a career). If it seems futile or dangerous to resist the necessary or inevitable, then the status quo is that much more stable. This tendency is what Marx described pejoratively as "ideology,"[15] and the required response to it is the critique of ideology, which displays the contingent and local for what they are, and helps us to see whose interests are served by representing the contingent and local as necessary and general.

It strains credulity to suggest that Wittgenstein is showing us how, e.g., Platonism serves the interests of the powerful (it is not clear to me that it does).[16] But his complaint about science and industry uniting the world in "infinite misery" leaves little doubt that Wittgenstein disdained the cultural prominence of science in part because it served *someone's* interests at the expense, potentially, of the interests of a great many others. And his treatment of necessity in terms of norms of description allows that some of what passes for necessary truth may well be the result of sociocultural gatekeeping. This, if accepted, should make us wary of claims of necessity or inevitability.

Likewise, his treatment of concept application in terms of family resemblances discourages any kind of hasty essentialism—a point that has been nicely made by Cressida Heyes.[17] Heyes argues that Wittgenstein's work is especially relevant to recent thorny debates in feminist theory about essentializing applications of the concept "women" (and other gender concepts). In particular, she observes (i) that Wittgenstein's anti-essentialism does not result in a radical nominalism, according

---

15 Marx's remarks on ideology are widely scattered, but a good place to start is with Karl Marx and Friedrich Engels, *The German Ideology*, translated by Roy Pascal (New York: International Publishers, 1970).

16 See James Brown and Glenn Parsons, "Platonism, Metaphor and Mathematics," *Dialogue* 63 (2004): 47–66.

17 See Cressida Heyes, *Line Drawings: Defining Women through Feminist Practice* (Ithaca, NY: Cornell University Press, 2000). Similar suggestions are made in less detail by Hilde Lindemann Nelson, "Wittgenstein Meets 'Woman' in the Language-Game of Theorizing Feminism" in *Feminist Interpretations of Ludwig Wittgenstein*, edited by Naomi Scheman and Peg O'Connor (University Park, PA: Pennsylvania State University Press, 2002), 213–34.

to which the application of the term 'women' is simply arbitrary, and (ii) that his insistence that lines can be drawn around concepts in different ways for different purposes makes it possible to see how the concept "women" might be differently demarcated in different contexts, so that for particular practical purposes it may be perfectly reasonable to insist that the category "women" should not apply to male-to-female trans-sexuals, even while acknowledging that in other contexts the self-identification of such people as "women" is also reasonable.

Critics who find Wittgenstein's work politically conservative must, I think, respond seriously to these arguments before they are entitled to their conclusions.

7.5 HOW GENERAL IS WITTGENSTEIN'S METHOD?

I have already remarked on Wittgenstein's motivation for thinking that traditional problems of philosophy require dissolution instead of solution. His position is controversial but, I think, defensible. However, there is a further question concerning the generality of his view. Are *all* the problems of philosophy the results of sophisticated confusion?

There are reasons to think that this question should be answered negatively. We could, of course, *define* philosophical problems as those that arise from our lacking a synoptic view of grammatical conventions. Perhaps this move is acceptable for certain purposes, but it risks appearing *ad hoc*, having no motivation other than to protect a certain conception of philosophy. Additionally, if such a stipulation is eschewed, it is unclear how the thesis could be established short of an enumerative induction over all known problems of philosophy. Furthermore, such an induction would not consist simply in looking at each problem quickly and offering a 'yes' or 'no' answer. Each one would have to be subjected to careful examination, and reasonable people could continue to disagree about the appropriate verdict in each case.

Here is another reason. A consistent application of Wittgenstein's techniques should keep us open to the possibility that "philosophy," like "number" and "game" and "language" and "women," is a family-resemblance concept.[18] Even if many of the traditional core-questions in philosophy have the illusory character that Wittgenstein claims for them, it may be that there are other questions, still reasonably classified as *philosophical*, that do not conform to this pattern. It may be that what counts as a philosophical question varies from context to context, according to the interests that help define those contexts. (Perhaps "How does one build

18 Phyllis Rooney, in an insightful paper, criticizes Wittgenstein for failing to see this. See her "Philosophy, Language, and Wizardry" in Scheman and O'Connor (eds.), 25–47.

an intuition pump?" should count as a philosophical question in the context of obtaining scarce research grants.) "To repeat, we can draw a boundary—for a special purpose. Does it take that to make the concept usable? Not at all! (Except for that special purpose.)" (PI §69).

But there is a general thesis that might be advanced, consistent with the foregoing caveats. That is that the exercise of obtaining a synoptic view of the grammatical norms implicated in any ostensibly philosophical problem is a necessary step in identifying what *kind* of problem it is and whether it admits of solution or stands in need of dissolution. From this point of view, Wittgenstein's attitude toward philosophical method is *relevant* whenever a philosophical problem arises, whether it proves to be the last word or not.

7.6 WITTGENSTEIN'S SILENCE ABOUT ETHICS

The foregoing considerations may provoke curiosity about a particular set of philosophical problems that Wittgenstein seldom discusses in his later work—the set of philosophical problems concerning ethics. In Chapter 2 we saw that the author of the *Tractatus* regarded the ethical as transcendent and unspeakable because he thought that all grounds of value must lie beyond the world—that the possibility of anything *in* the world (and hence *contingent*) being of value depended on something *necessary*. This is a fundamentally "mystical" (TLP §6.522), religious view of ethics, and I think it is no idle speculation to suppose that the transcendent ground of moral value concerning which Wittgenstein thought nothing could be said is none other than God. "What is Good is Divine too. That, strangely enough, sums up my ethics" (CV 5), he wrote in 1929.

However, I argued in Chapter 3 that Wittgenstein came to reject the *Tractatus*'s demand for transcendent, necessary grounds of value, and this seems to be incompatible with thinking of the "Good" as something "Divine." If there need be no grounds of value beyond the world in order for meaning to be possible, then neither need there be any grounds of moral value that lie beyond the world, and, in particular, there is no need for God. This line of reasoning does not entail that God does not exist, but it does deprive Wittgenstein of the only argument for God's existence consistent with the *Tractarian* doctrine of saying and showing.[19] By the standards of Wittgenstein's later philosophy, God is an idle cog in the mechanism.

19 I say "consistent" here, but what I mean is consistent with the spirit of the *Tractatus*, not with its letter, since *all* arguments for the existence of God end up being nonsense by the reckoning of the *Tractatus*.

So two questions naturally arise: why does Wittgenstein have so little to say about ethics in his later work? What *should* Wittgenstein say about problems in philosophical ethics, given his abandonment of the view that value must lie outside the world? I shall return to the second question in the next section. Let me try to say something here about the first.

Many prosaic reasons might be offered for Wittgenstein's relative silence about ethics in his later work. Not every philosopher feels driven to write about every major topic in philosophy. There is no shortage of academic philosophers who specialize in arcane technical problems in metaphysics, or logic, or epistemology, who never have much to say about ethics (think of Quine and Davidson), just as there are numerous moral philosophers who have little to say about metaphysics, logic, and epistemology (think of Rawls). Perhaps Wittgenstein is just another on this list.

Or maybe Wittgenstein just did not have the *time* to get to questions in ethics. Perhaps he was so busy with the philosophies of language, mind, and mathematics that he just did not get around to taking up ethics. It was only in the last two years of his life that he wrote extensively on problems in epistemology. Ethics might have been next on his list if he had not died at a comparatively young age.

Perhaps there is some truth in these hypotheses, but Wittgenstein's passionate view about ethics at the time of his earlier writings makes it difficult to believe that the subject was of no consequence to him later on, or that it was less important to him than, say, mathematics. So it is tempting to give another answer, which is that giving up on the idea of a transcendent God did not come easily to Wittgenstein and the resulting ambivalence made it difficult for him to say much about moral value that lay within the world.

That Wittgenstein felt such an ambivalence is illustrated by a number of remarks from his notebooks. Consider what he writes in 1937:[20]

> I am reading: "& no man can say that Jesus is the Lord, but by the Holy Ghost." And it is true: I cannot call him Lord; because that says absolutely nothing to me. I could call him "the paragon", "God" even or rather: I can understand it when he is so called; but I cannot utter the word "Lord" meaningfully. Because I do not believe that he will come to judge me; because that says nothing to me. And it could only say something to me if I were to live quite differently. (CV 38)

Someone who can say that Jesus is Lord is someone who takes for granted a series of propositions that Wittgenstein cannot at this point in his life, someone who

20 Thanks to Steven Burns for drawing my attention to this passage.

embodies in his or her life very different norms of representation. These are norms that Wittgenstein can no longer accept. In a passage from 1944 Wittgenstein considers whether he could believe in a miraculous occurrence, such as the trees bowing down at the words of a saint:

> —Now, do I believe that this happens? I don't.
>
> The only way for me to believe in a miracle in this sense would be to be *impressed* by an occurrence in this particular way. So that I should say e.g.: "It was *impossible* to see these trees & not to feel that they were responding to the words." Just as I might say "It is impossible to see the face of this dog & not to see that he is alert & full of attention to what his master is doing." And I can imagine that the mere report of the *words* & life of a saint can make someone believe the reports that the trees bowed. But I am not so impressed. (CV 51–52)

What must be taken for granted if one is to believe in miracles is something that Wittgenstein can see only as a contingent norm of representation, and that is not enough, he hints, to sustain religious belief in him:

> But if I am to be REALLY redeemed,—I need *certainty*—not wisdom, dreams, speculation—and this certainty is faith. And faith is faith in what my *heart*, my *soul*, needs, not my speculative intellect. For my soul, with its passions, as it were with its flesh & blood, must be redeemed, not my abstract mind. (CV 38)

Such certainty is difficult to maintain without believing that value must lie outside the world.

Wittgenstein, it might be argued, could see that his changed philosophical view left no role for God, but he found it difficult to abandon the spiritual perspective to which he had been led as a philosophizing soldier. "I am not a religious man but I cannot help seeing every problem from a religious point of view," he told his student Maurice Drury in 1949.[21] "The trouble with you and me, old man," Theodore Redpath reports him saying on more than one occasion, "is that we have no religion!" Redpath describes visiting Little St. Mary's Church in Cambridge with Wittgenstein, who remarked when a woman came in to pray, "*That* is what

---

21 Maurice Drury, "Some Notes on Conversations with Wittgenstein" in *Recollections of Wittgenstein*, edited by Rush Rhees (Oxford: Oxford University Press, 1984), 79.

a church is for!"[22] And when Redpath asked him—as late as 1940—why he never expressed any political views in his lectures, Wittgenstein's response was that "he *could* not do so but that one day he would give a lecture or talk explaining *why* he could not" (Redpath 94). To my knowledge, no such lecture ever materialized.

However, there is more to the story of Wittgenstein's changed attitude towards religious belief than this, for it appears that, like meaning and moral value, the divine or the sacred is itself to be brought into the world, stripped of the transcendent trappings that it wears in Wittgenstein's earlier writing.[23] This move amounts to seeing religious or spiritual discourse as rooted in its own primitive language-games that give sense to the terms applied in these contexts.[24] "No *opinion* serves as the foundation for a religious symbol" (RFGB 123),[25] writes Wittgenstein in 1931. Only a practice could do that:

> Kissing the picture of one's beloved. That is *obviously not* based on the belief that it will have some specific effect on the object which the picture represents. It aims at satisfaction and achieves it. Or rather: it *aims* at nothing at all; we just behave this way and then we feel satisfied. (RFGB 123)

Such rituals lie on a continuum with the complex rituals of an organized religion like Christianity, and—it is tempting to read Wittgenstein as saying—we misunderstand the discourse of Christianity and other monotheisms when we suppose that their adherents must interpret prayer as an attempt to *affect* the will of an all-powerful being or that they must think of God as an *explanation* for the origins of the cosmos or of the ostensible order that we find throughout the universe. This is to be misled by "certain analogies between the forms of expression in different regions of language" (PI §90) in just the sort of way that Wittgenstein warns us against.

In a discussion of these matters, Peter Winch describes an encounter with a woman whose child suffered from a degenerative disease that promised to take the child's life. The woman told Winch that "she firmly believed that one day,

---

22 Theodore Redpath, *Ludwig Wittgenstein: A Student's Memoir* (London: Gerald Duckworth & Co., 1990), 43–44.

23 I am indebted to Béla Szabados for this point.

24 This is not to say, as Brian Clack rightly points out, that religion is itself a language-game. As we saw in Chapter 4, language-games are simple linguistic exchanges, interwoven with actions, that we might use to teach a child the use of a certain kind of word. See Bernard R. Clack, *An Introduction to Wittgenstein's Philosophy of Religion* (Edinburgh: Edinburgh University Press, 1999), 87.

25 Ludwig Wittgenstein, "Remarks on Frazer's *Golden Bough*," in *Philosophical Occasions 1912–1951*, edited by James Klagge and Alfred Nordmann (Indianapolis: Hackett Publishing, 1993).

after death, the whole family would be together again and that her afflicted child would be there as a whole, normal human being" (Winch 1987, 65).[26] It would be a mistake, says Winch, to interpret the woman as *merely* expressing an attitude, e.g., her love for her child, her compassion for her child's suffering, or even her disappointment that she cannot see her child live a long, healthy, fulfilling life. Such expression is a part of what she is saying, and it explains why it would be thoughtless and disrespectful to challenge what she says, but there is more here than just the expression of an attitude. However, it would equally be a mistake, he contends, to suppose that in addition to this expression of attitude, the woman holds a belief that entails some ontological commitment to a life beyond her natural life, to suppose that she is making a *prediction* about events yet to come (66). "We will be reunited after death" means just what it says in the sense that it cannot be reduced to or replaced by something else, and yet we are not to think of it as a prediction, because prediction is not part of the religious language-game. "We speak of understanding a sentence in the sense in which it can be replaced by another which says the same; but also in the sense in which it cannot be replaced by any other" (PI §531).

Winch contends that the "picture" of reunion is not used the same way by religious speakers as it is in the context in which I long to be reunited with my lover after a long absence. "If I say," of a man who says that the eye of God sees everything, "he used a picture, I don't want to say anything he himself wouldn't say" (LC 71).[27] Bearing in mind Winch's contention that we should not take religious utterances *merely* to be expressions of attitudes, I think we must assume that by "picture" Wittgenstein means "metaphor" or some kind of figurative language, which resists easy paraphrase much in the way that poetic metaphors do. (We could think of this as a moderation of Wittgenstein's earlier view, discussed in Chapter 2, that ethical and religious expressions "*seem*, prima facie, to be just *similes*" (LE 42),[28] but cannot be paraphrased at all.) So I may say with conviction that we will be reunited after death without merely expressing my fondness for you *and* without making a prediction, much as a poet may say, with great sincerity, "... the things I hold/ Together with my sight will fall apart/ If someone else so

26 Peter Winch, "Wittgenstein: Picture and Representation" in *Trying to Make Sense* (Oxford: Blackwell, 1987), 64–80.

27 See Ludwig Wittgenstein, *Lectures and Conversations on Aesthetics, Psychology and Religious Belief*, edited by Cyril Barrett (Berkeley: University of California Press, 1967), 70–71.

28 Ludwig Wittgenstein, "Lecture on Ethics" in *Philosophical Occasions: 1912–1951*, edited by James Klagge and Alfred Nordmann (Indianapolis: Hackett Publishing, 1993), 37–44.

much as looks at them,"[29] without being committed to an extraordinary ontology of special optical powers.

Would religious believers accept this sort of figurative, metaphysically deflationary treatment of their own discourse? Perhaps some would, but I suspect that many would feel as though something vital had been left out. If it is a misunderstanding to interpret the belief of the woman in Winch's story as a prediction, or to interpret prayer as an attempt to affect God's will, or to interpret the belief in God as offering an explanation of the universe, then I think that it is a misunderstanding that many religious people are themselves in the grip of. Religious fundamentalists who oppose the teaching of evolution by natural selection in high-school science classes or who think that by martyring themselves they will enter heaven or who believe that they have a God-given right to occupy a particular plot of land surely would not be satisfied with a metaphorical interpretation of their convictions. Neither would people who believe in the "power" of prayer or in faith-healing. Indeed, a great many believers who are given neither to fanaticism nor to thinking that God intervenes in the course of nature would have a hard time recognizing their own religious faith with the metaphysics drained from it.

However, this does not show that the interpretation is incorrect, any more than the fact that many mathematicians are platonists shows that there is anything wrong with Wittgenstein's metaphysically deflationary treatment of our talk of numbers. It is entirely possible that when they try to reflect on their own discourse and practice, religious believers are prone to philosophical puzzlement. One may be able to carry out the practical activity of putting a room in order but be unable to describe correctly the arrangement of the room (z §119),[30] as we saw in Chapter 3.

Does this show us that an ethics based on Wittgenstein's later philosophy must still be a religious ethics, even if it has been stripped of its metaphysical pretensions? I am not convinced that it does. If mixing religious talk with explanatory or predictive talk threatens us with misunderstanding, then it seems to me that we have comparable grounds for worrying that mixing religious talk with *moral* talk threatens us with misunderstanding too.

It is worth noting that this deflationary treatment of religious discourse did nothing to alleviate Wittgenstein's own ambivalence about religious belief:

---

29 Ward McBurney, "Ode to a Tape Gun," 15 Aug. 2007, Story Ward. 21 Mar. 2008. <http://storyward.blogspot.com/2007_08_15_archive.html>.

30 Ludwig Wittgenstein, *Zettel*, 2nd ed., edited by G.E.M. Anscombe and G.H. Von Wright, translated by G.E.M. Anscombe (Oxford: Basil Blackwell, 1981).

> Suppose someone said: "What do you believe, Wittgenstein? Are you a sceptic? Do you know whether you will survive death?" I would, really, this is a fact, say "I can't say. I don't know", because I haven't any clear idea what I'm saying when I'm saying "I don't cease to exist," etc. (LC 70)

7.7 ETHICAL CONCEPTS AND FAMILY RESEMBLANCES

Although a good deal more could be said about Wittgenstein's later attitude toward religion, I shall not attempt to defend my suggestion that religious and ethical discourse should be thought of as largely distinct from each other. I shall, nonetheless, assume it in what follows. With this in mind, I want to return to my second question from §7.6 above: What *should* Wittgenstein have had to say about philosophical problems in ethics, given his abandonment of transcendent grounds of value?

As I remarked above, Wittgenstein was not *completely* silent about this. In a passage I quoted in Chapter 4 from his 1932–33 lectures, before he had taken up the terminology of "family resemblances," he tells us that the word 'good' does not have a "general meaning":

> I am not saying it has four or five different meanings. It is used in different contexts because there is a transition between similar things called "good", a transition which continues, it may be, to things which bear no similarity to earlier members of the series. (WLC II 33)[31]

In short, Wittgenstein's metaethical view is that goodness has no hidden essence, no nature. But if this is true, then it suggests that long-standing disputes between consequentialists and deontologists concerning the nature of moral goodness (happiness? a good will?) *are* the result of philosophical confusion—of failing to command a clear view of the grammar of morality.

Such a picture is suggested by Wittgenstein's 1938 Lectures on Aesthetics, which he begins by suggesting that philosophy should "distinguish far more parts of speech than an ordinary grammar does" (LC 1).[32] Words used to describe personal experience, for example, would constitute their own category:

---

31 Ludwig Wittgenstein, *Wittgenstein's Lectures, Cambridge, 1932–35*, edited by Alice Ambrose (Amherst, NY: Prometheus Books, 2001).

32 Thanks to Béla Szabados for drawing my attention to this discussion.

> You would have another chapter on numerals—here there would be another kind of confusion: a chapter on 'all', 'any', 'some, etc.—another kind of confusion: a chapter on 'you', 'I', etc.—another kind: a chapter on 'beautiful', 'good'—another kind. (LC 1)

In almost the next breath, Wittgenstein reminds us of his method of language games:

> One thing we always do when discussing a word is to ask how we were taught it. Doing this on the one hand destroys a variety of misconceptions, on the other hand gives you a primitive language in which the word is used. Although this language is not what you talk when you are twenty, you get a rough approximation to what kind of language game is going to be played. (LC 1–2)

Language-games, as "*objects of comparison*" (PI §130), cast light on our actual, complicated practices, and they remind us that speaking is embedded in a situation of acting so that "We are concentrating, not on the words 'good' or 'beautiful' ... but on the occasions on which they are said" (LC 2).

So if we want a philosophical account of goodness, we do not need an explanatory theory, but a survey of how the word 'good' and its cognates could be taught and learned without designating some unified, abstract form of goodness, and of how, within that set of practices, moral goodness could be separated from other forms of goodness. So connected with the thought that 'good' and its cognates are family resemblance terms is a certain picture of elementary moral education. How could I learn to use the term 'good'?

Consider the sorts of language-games that might be employed to teach a term like this. Perhaps it is, at first, a term of praise: "Good boy!" I am told when my behaviour meets with or exceeds my caregivers' expectations. I learn to apply such praise to others—my siblings, other children, family pets—and I learn also to extend praise to the deeds that I and others perform—"That's good!", "Good work!" I'm presented with examples to which I am trained to apply the term, much as I learn to apply diverse terms like 'block', 'slab', 'red', 'two' to particular examples. These examples will include cases of both moral and non-moral goodness, which I learn to differentiate in the course of learning a whole array of other, subtler, moral vocabulary ('politeness', 'sharing', 'fairness', 'cooperation', etc.). My moral concepts get extended with new examples that stand in various resemblance relations to earlier examples in a way that is similar to the extension Wittgenstein identifies of mathematical concepts, such as "number."[33]

I am gesturing, then, at an account of moral concepts that does not require that there be any set of necessary and sufficient conditions justifying the application of moral terms. But the point is not just a meta-ethical one. It also suggests something about normative ethics—namely, that it ought to invoke something like legal reasoning, starting with a series of clear paradigms and judging new cases according to their similarities with past ones. "[A]esthetic discussions [are] like discussions in a court of law," Moore reports Wittgenstein saying.[34] "What we really want, to solve aesthetic puzzlements, is certain comparisons—grouping together of certain cases" (LC IV §2). We might say the same thing about ethical puzzlements. Over time, maybe we get to start drawing some tentative generalizations, but any moral rules or principles that we settle on are going to be constantly open to revision in the light of new cases that seem to be relevantly similar to established paradigms, but which incorporate novel aspects hitherto unnoticed or unappreciated.[35]

---

33 For a development of the analogy between moral vocabulary and mathematical vocabulary see Cora Diamond, "Wittgenstein, Mathematics, and Ethics: Resisting the Attractions of Realism" in *The Cambridge Companion to Wittgenstein*, edited by Hans D. Sluga and David G. Stern (Cambridge: Cambridge University Press, 1997), 226–60.

34 G.E. Moore, "Wittgenstein's Lectures in 1930–33" in *Philosophical Occasions: 1912–1951*, edited by James Klagge and Alfred Nordmann (Indianapolis: Hackett Publishing, 1993), 106. For more on the analogy with legal reasoning see Roger Shiner, "On Giving Works of Art a Face," *Philosophy* 53 (1978): 307–24; Steven Burns, "The Place of Art in a Reasonable Education" in *Reason in Teaching and Education*, edited by William Hare (Halifax: Dalhousie School of Education, 1989), 23–40; and Stephen Toulmin, *Return to Reason* (Cambridge, MA: Harvard University Press, 2001), Chapter 8.

35 There is some convergence here with Peter Winch, *Ethics and Action* (London: Routledge & Kegan Paul, 1972), and Susan Hekman makes some related points (and some that go well beyond what I have said) in "The Moral Language Game" in Scheman and O'Connor (eds.), 159–75, though I would take issue with her reading of many of the passages from Wittgenstein that she cites in support. A similar view of moral reasoning takes inspiration from psychological prototype theory (which itself is inspired in part by Wittgenstein's work—see E. Rosch and C.B. Mervis, "Family Resemblances: Structures in the Internal Structure of Categories," *Cognitive Psychology* 7 [1975]: 573–605). See Mark Johnson, *Moral Imagination: Implications of Cognitive Science for Ethics* (Chicago: University of Chicago Press, 1993), 8–9, 189–92. Nalini Bhushan offers a good sketch of Wittgenstein's importance to Rosch's work, though I think she errs in reading Wittgenstein as a relativist. See "Eleanor Rosch and the Development of Successive Wittgensteinian Paradigms for Cognitive Science" in Scheman and O'Connor (eds.), 259–83. In *Wittgenstein and Moral Philosophy* (London: Routledge, 1989), Paul Johnston takes seriously the idea of applying Wittgenstein's method to ethics, but he sees a sharper divide between a "Wittgensteinian investigation of ethics" and a "Wittgensteinian investigation of concepts" (18) than I do, though he is surely right to emphasize that ethical concepts are relevant to "a whole area of our lives" (18) in a way that some concepts are not.

Of course, one of the respects in which there is a significant difference between ethical concepts and other concepts is that disagreement about the application of moral concepts can have serious practical consequences. People do not typically come to blows over disputes in mathematics (PI §240), as Wittgenstein reminds us, but in cases of moral disagreement they may at times do just that. What are we to say about such controversies?

I suspect that the sources of moral controversy are many. Some disagreements are likely the result of our being "entangled in our own rules" (PI §125), and a necessary step in their resolution will then be attempting to get a clear view of what norms are latent in our moral practices and what they seem to commit us to in particular cases. Philosophers working in the fields of practical ethics make regular contributions to this task. One of the results of getting such a synoptic view, I think, may well be the recognition that existing moral practices acknowledge competing sources of value—good consequences *and* good intentions, for example. Realizing that our practices commit us to competing sources of value does not, of course, tell us how to resolve conflicting demands that may arise from such sources. It may be that in some cases clarity about moral norms will help us to see that the conflict is merely apparent, but there is no guaranteeing this in every case. At such times we are faced with very real practical problems, and I believe that there may be no strictly philosophical remedy, whatever clarity and insight might be contributed by philosophers. What is needed in such cases is *good judgment* and the negotiation of a settlement amongst interested parties.

Now, this suggestion that some moral controversies lack a "philosophical solution" may provoke the worry that ethical debate in the end reduces to a power struggle—a worry that may be exacerbated when we consider that sometimes the norms themselves, and not just their application to particular cases, may be objects of controversy. (Think of recent feminist criticisms of such liberal notions as equality and autonomy.) Does the view I am gesturing at threaten to reduce ethical debate to a power struggle? Does it entail some kind of normative ethical relativism, according to which what is morally right or wrong (and not merely what is *called* "right" or "wrong") varies from culture to culture or time to time?

The view I have been considering does make it possible that members of different communities will select different moral paradigms when it comes to teaching children the application of moral vocabulary. Indeed, cultural variation makes this likely. But from this it does not follow that radically different moral norms are likely. Or, better, it does not follow that radically different moral *principles* need be at work, even if there is variation concerning particular judgments, and local rules.

I think the situation in ethics is analogous to the situation with respect to grammatical norms. There *can* be variation here, but it does not follow from this that moral standards are simply arbitrary, that just *any* proposition could express a moral norm. I quote again a passage I have already had recourse to more than once: "to the *depth* that we see in the essence there corresponds the *deep* need for the convention" (RFM I §74). The *kind* of creatures that human beings are—for all their diversity and variation—places constraints on what is morally possible for us. I do not mean by this that we are incapable of doing terrible things to each other. That is obviously false. My point, rather, is that some kinds of moral principles are more naturally plausible and relevant to us. A moral principle that advises us to maim and kill as we please is not a principle that can be contemplated by a person of moral seriousness. To vary the point, *whatever* particular interests I might have, there are certain conditions that are necessary for my pursuing those ends (John Rawls calls them "primary goods"; David Braybrooke calls them "course of life needs"),[36] and to the extent that the satisfaction of those interests depends upon the cooperation and tolerance of others, principles that help to secure that cooperation and tolerance are of special interest to me.

Of course, in the world of practice negotiations about ethical principles and their application do *involve* power-struggles, even if they do not *reduce* to them. (Think about disagreements over the morality of abortion.) But this fact cannot be made to go away by any theory of the nature of moral goodness or by any particular conception of moral reasoning. We moral agents are stuck with it.

7.8 WITTGENSTEIN AND QUINE

I began this book with a survey of some traditional views about the relation between science and philosophy. Most of those views predated or were contemporary with Wittgenstein's, but the last of them, Quine's, came to prominence only after Wittgenstein's death. In the course of my discussion I have made occasional remarks concerning what I take to be significant differences between Wittgenstein and Quine, but something more systematic would be desirable, especially given that Wittgenstein's view might be thought of as a "naturalistic" view in the sense that it rejects any form of "supernaturalism" about norms. 'Naturalism', of course, is a term that has been championed by Quine and his followers.

36 John Rawls, *A Theory of Justice* (Cambridge, MA; Belknap Press, 1971), 62; David Braybrooke, *Utilitarianism: Restorations; Repairs; Renovations* (Toronto: University of Toronto Press, 2004), 151.

In one sense this is a desire that cannot be satisfied here. Quine's work is too difficult, substantial, controversial, and influential to compare or contrast satisfactorily with Wittgenstein's (which is, likewise, difficult, substantial, controversial, and influential) in such a short space. But a few points can be made without becoming irretrievably mired in a vast swamp.[37]

First, a number of features of Quine's philosophy are clearly in conflict with a number of features of Wittgenstein's. His strict behaviourism, though inconsistently applied, will find no home in Wittgenstein's practices that embody implicit norms. Indeed, Quine's behaviourism prompts him to say that an implicit norm cannot be distinguished from the absence of any norm whatsoever.[38]

Second, the radical holism about meaning and confirmation that Quine expresses in "Two Dogmas of Empiricism" is not compatible with Wittgenstein's contextualism about meaning and justification, nor with his correlative insistence that some "propositions of the form of empirical propositions" (OC §401) have a special role to play as norms of representation. The closest Quine comes to this is to speak of certain beliefs or statements as being closer to the "interior of the field" (TDE 42).[39] We are reluctant to revise them, he says, because we have a "natural tendency to disturb the total system as little as possible" (TDE 44). But such talk says nothing about the *role* played by such propositions, and Quine's prevailing image is of a single, unified body of statements with an interior and a periphery, not of a motley of interconnected systems for which different propositions serve as norms of representation.[40]

Third, Quine's rejection both of *a priori* knowledge and of the analytic-synthetic distinction in "Two Dogmas..." is of ambiguous significance for Wittgenstein's view. Even propositions that belong to the hard rock of the riverbed of thought are not propositions that we *know*, according to Wittgenstein, because we have

37 I have tried to say more in "Internal Relations and Analyticity: Wittgenstein and Quine," *Canadian Journal of Philosophy* 26, no.4 (1996): 591–612 and in Chapter 2 of *Philosophy and Its Epistemic Neuroses* (Boulder, CO: Westview Press, 2000). I have found instructive Chapter 7 of P.M.S. Hacker, *Wittgenstein's Place in Twentieth-Century Philosophy* (Oxford: Blackwell, 1996) and many of the essays in *Wittgenstein and Quine* edited by Robert Arrington and Hans-Johann Glock (London: Routledge, 1996). Jane Heal's *Fact and Meaning: Quine and Wittgenstein on Philosophy of Language* (Oxford: Blackwell, 1989) also wants examination, though I suspect her Wittgenstein is closer to her Quine, than my Wittgenstein is to my Quine.

38 W.V. Quine, "Truth by Convention" in *Philosophy of Mathematics Selected Readings*, edited by Paul Benacerraf and Hilary Putnam (Englewood Cliffs, NJ: Prentice-Hall, 1964), 344.

39 W.V. Quine, "Two Dogmas of Empiricism" in *From a Logical Point of View*, 2nd ed. (Cambridge, MA: Harvard University Press, 1980), 20–46.

40 There are, it should be acknowledged, interpretations of Quine that emphasize the later moderation of his holism and make a plausible case for treating him as a contextualist. See Roger Gibson, "Quine, Wittgenstein and Holism" in Arrington and Glock (eds.), 80–96.

no justification for them, and we cannot say what it would be like for them to be false. But for Quine the *a priori* is simply that which is not subject to rational revision, so it looks as though on Wittgenstein's view, there ends up being at least one *a priori* truth (for reasons much like the ones adduced by Putnam in "There Is at Least One *A Priori* Truth").[41] However, such a view is little comfort, I think, to philosophers who hope to establish significant results *a priori*—for example, the way Descartes or Kant thought was possible.

As for the analytic-synthetic distinction, Wittgenstein has no fondness for such terminology, but there is a sense of 'analyticity' that is compatible with Wittgenstein's contention that hinge-propositions are partly *constitutive* of the meanings of their terms and the terms of propositions that "swing" on these hinges. In this sense an analytic proposition is such that one does not understand it (or one prefers a different interpretation of its terms) if one doubts it to be true. This *epistemic* conception of analyticity, I contend, is immune to Quine's arguments in "Two Dogmas ...," which are directed at what Paul Boghossian has called a *metaphysical* conception of analyticity,[42] according to which an analytic proposition is one that is true *in virtue of* what its constituent terms mean—as though meanings were independently existing entities that, in proper combination, could bestow truth on a proposition. For Wittgenstein, by contrast, that we hold a certain proposition unshakeably true determines what we mean by its constituent terms.

Finally, Quine's philosophical outlook is shaped by a fixation on the methods and authority of natural science, especially physics. This scientistic faith is manifest in his behaviourism and in his proposal that philosophers abandon questions about whether or not knowledge-claims can be justified in favour of scientific explanations of how organisms acquire particular beliefs (behaviourally represented) as the result of sensory excitation by their physical environments.[43] (It is unclear that this project is consistent with the holism about confirmation advocated in "Two Dogmas ...," unless, improbable though it may seem, Quine can give an account of confirmation in behaviouristic terms.)

All this is plainly in conflict with Wittgenstein's anti-scientistic outlook. Whatever points of convergence may be found between Quine and Wittgenstein,

41 See Hilary Putnam, "There Is at Least One *A Priori* Truth," *Realism and Reason* (Cambridge: Cambridge University Press, 1983), 98–114.

42 See Paul Boghossian, "Analyticity Reconsidered," *Noûs* 30, no.3 (1996): 360–91.

43 See W.V. Quine, "Epistemology Naturalized" in *Ontological Relativity and Other Essays* (New York: Columbia University Press, 1969), 68–90.

there remain deep differences, for whereas Quine sees science and philosophy as partners in a shared endeavour, Wittgenstein urges us to question the cultural pre-eminence of science. For him philosophy aims not at new knowledge, but at complete clarity.

BIBLIOGRAPHY

Bibliographical abbreviations used in the text are noted below in **bold face**.

Ackermann, Robert. *Wittgenstein's City*. Amherst: University of Massachusetts Press, 1988.

Albritton, Rogers. "On Wittgenstein's Use of the Term 'Criterion'" in *Wittgenstein: The Philosophical Investigations*, edited by George Pitcher. Garden City, NY: Doubleday, 1966.

Anderson, Alan Ross and Nuel D. Belnap, Jr. *Entailment: The Logic of Relevance and Necessity*, Vol. 1. Princeton: Princeton University Press, 1975.

Anscombe, G.E.M. *An Introduction to Wittgenstein's Tractatus*, 3rd ed. London: Hutchison & Co., 1967.

——. and G.H. von Wright. Editors' Preface to Ludwig Wittgenstein, *Zettel*, 2nd ed., edited by G.E.M. Anscombe and G.H. von Wright, translated by G.E.M. Anscombe. Oxford: Blackwell, 1981.

Armstrong, D.M. *A World of States of Affairs*. Cambridge: Cambridge University Press, 1997.

——. *Universals: An Opinionated Introduction*. Boulder, CO: Westview Press, 1989.

Arrington, Robert and Hans-Johann Glock, eds. *Wittgenstein and Quine*. London: Routledge, 1996.

Austin, J.L. *How to Do Things with Words.* New York: Oxford University Press, 1965.

Ayer, A.J. "Can There Be a Private Language?" in *Wittgenstein: The Philosophical Investigations*, edited by George Pitcher. Garden City, NY: Doubleday, 1966.

Baker, Gordon. "Criteria: A New Foundation for Semantics," *Ratio* 16, no.2. 1974.

——. and P.M.S. Hacker. *Scepticism, Rules and Language*. Oxford: Blackwell, 1984.

Bambrough, Renford. "Universals and Family Resemblances," *Proceedings of the Aristotelian Society* 61. 1960–61.

Beardsley, Patrick. "Augustine and Wittgenstein on Language," *Philosophy* 58. 1983.

Bhushan, Nalini. "Eleanor Rosch and the Development of Successive Wittgensteinian Paradigms for Cognitive Science" in *Feminist Interpretations of Ludwig Wittgenstein*, edited by Naomi Scheman and Peg O'Connor. University Park, PA: Pennsylvania State University Press, 2002.

Black, Max. *A Companion to Wittgenstein's "Tractatus"*. Ithaca, NY: Cornell University Press, 1964.

Boghossian, Paul. "Analyticity Reconsidered," *Noûs* 30, no.3. 1996.

——. "The Rule-Following Considerations," *Mind* 98. 1989.

Brandom, Robert. *Making It Explicit.* Cambridge, MA: Harvard University Press, 1994.

Braybrooke, David. *Utilitarianism: Restorations; Repairs; Renovations.* Toronto: University of Toronto Press, 2004.

Brown, James and Glenn Parsons. "Platonism, Metaphor and Mathematics," *Dialogue* 63. 2004.

Burns, Steven. "The Place of Art in a Reasonable Education" in *Reason in Teaching and Education*, edited by William Hare. Halifax: Dalhousie School of Education, 1989.

Canfield, John V. "The Community View," *The Philosophical Review* 105. 1996.

——. "Private Language: The Diary Case," *Australasian Journal of Philosophy* 79, no.3. 2001.

——. *Wittgenstein, Language and World.* Amherst: University of Massachusetts Press, 1981.

Carnap, Rudolf. "The Elimination of Metaphysics Through Logical Analysis of Language," translated by Arthur Pap, in *Logical Positivism*, edited by A.J. Ayer. Glencoe, IL: The Free Press, 1959; Originally published as "*Überwindung der Metaphysik durch Logische Analyse der Sprache*," *Erkenntnis* 2. 1932. **EM**

——. "Intellectual Autobiography" in *The Philosophy of Rudolf Carnap*, edited by P.A. Schilpp. LaSalle, IL: Open Court, 1963.

Cavell, Stanley. "The Availability of Wittgenstein's Later Philosophy" in *Must We Mean What We Say?* Cambridge: Cambridge University Press, 1976.

——. "Declining Decline: Wittgenstein as a Philosopher of Culture" in *This New Yet Unapproachable America: Lectures after Emerson and Wittgenstein.* Albuquerque, NM: Living Batch Press, 1989.

Chomsky, Noam. *New Horizons on Language and Mind.* Cambridge: Cambridge University Press, 2000.

Clack, Bernard R. *An Introduction to Wittgenstein's Philosophy of Religion.* Edinburgh: Edinburgh University Press, 1999.

Coffa, J. Alberto. *The Semantic Tradition from Kant to Carnap: To the Vienna Station*, edited by Linda Wessels. Cambridge: Cambridge University Press, 1991.

Collins, Harry and Trevor Pinch, *The Golem: What Everyone Should Know about Science.* Cambridge: Cambridge University Press, 1993.

Conant, James. "Elucidation and Nonsense in Frege and Early Wittgenstein" in *The New Wittgenstein*, edited by Alice Crary and Rupert Read. London: Routledge, 2000.

——. "Must We Show What We Cannot Say?" in *The Senses of Stanley Cavell*, edited by Richard Fleming and Michael Payne. London and Toronto: Associated University Presses, 1989.

Crary, Alice and Rupert Read, eds. *The New Wittgenstein*. London: Routledge, 2000.

Davidson, Donald. "On Saying That" in *Inquiries into Truth and Interpretation.* Oxford: Clarendon Press, 1984.

——. "What Metaphors Mean" in *On Metaphor*, edited by S. Sacks. Chicago: University of Chicago Press, 1978.

Descartes, René. *Discourse on the Method*, in *The Philosophical Writings of Descartes*, Vol. I, translated by John Cottingham, Robert Stoothoff, and Dugald Murdoch. Cambridge: Cambridge University Press, 1984.

——. *Meditations on First Philosophy*, in *The Philosophical Writings of Descartes*, Vol. II, translated by John Cottingham, Robert Stoothoff, and Dugald Murdoch. Cambridge: Cambridge University Press, 1984. **MED**

——. *Objections and Replies* in *The Philosophical Writings of Descartes*, Vol. II, translated by John Cottingham, Robert Stoothoff, and Dugald Murdoch. Cambridge: Cambridge University Press, 1984.

Devitt, Michael. *Realism and Truth*, 2nd ed. Princeton: Princeton University Press, 1997.

Diamond, Cora. "Ethics, Imagination and the Method of Wittgenstein's *Tractatus*" in *The New Wittgenstein*, edited by Alice Crary and Rupert Read. London: Routledge, 2000.

——. "Throwing Away the Ladder: How to Read the *Tractatus*" in *The Realistic Spirit: Wittgenstein, Philosophy, and the Mind*. Cambridge, MA: MIT Press, 1991.

——. "Wittgenstein, Mathematics, and Ethics: Resisting the Attractions of Realism" in *The Cambridge Companion to Wittgenstein*, edited by Hans D. Sluga and David G. Stern. Cambridge: Cambridge University Press, 1997.

Drury, Maurice. "Some Notes on Conversations with Wittgenstein" in *Recollections of Wittgenstein*, edited by Rush Rhees. Oxford: Oxford University Press, 1984.

Dummett, Michael. "Realism" in *Truth and Other Enigmas*. Cambridge, MA: Harvard University Press, 1978.

Eagleton, Terry. "Wittgenstein's Friends," *New Left Review* I, no.135. September-October 1982.

Ebbs, Gary. *Rule-Following and Realism*. Cambridge, MA: Harvard University Press, 1997.

Edmonds, David and John Eidinow. *Wittgenstein's Poker*. London: Faber and Faber, 2001.

Engelmann, Paul. *Letters from Ludwig Wittgenstein with a Memoir*, translated by L. Furtmüller, edited by Brian McGuinness. Oxford: Blackwell, 1967.

Everett, Daniel. "Cultural Constraints on Grammar and Cognition in Pirahã," *Current Anthropology* 46. 2005.

Forster, Michael N. *Wittgenstein on the Arbitrariness of Grammar*. Princeton: Princeton University Press, 2004.

Frege, Gottlob. "On Sense and Reference" in *Logicism and the Philosophy of Language: Selections from Frege and Russell*, edited by Arthur Sullivan. Peterborough, ON: Broadview Press, 2003.

—. "The Thought: A Logical Inquiry" in *Logicism and the Philosophy of Language: Selections from Frege and Russell*, edited by Arthur Sullivan. Peterborough, ON: Broadview Press, 2003.

Gasking, D.A.T. and A.C. Jackson, "Wittgenstein as a Teacher" in *Ludwig Wittgenstein: The Man and his Philosophy*, edited by K.T. Fann. New York: Dell, 1967.

Gellner, Ernest. *Language and Solitude: Wittgenstein, Malinowski and the Habsburg Dilemma*. Cambridge: Cambridge University Press, 1998.

—. *Words and Things: A Critical Account of Linguistic Philosophy and a Study in Ideology*. London: Victor Gollancz, 1959.

Gibson, Roger. "Quine, Wittgenstein and Holism" in *Wittgenstein and Quine*, edited by Robert Arrington and Hans-Johann Glock. London: Routledge, 1996.

Goldfarb, Warren. "Kripke on Wittgenstein on Rules," *Journal of Philosophy* 82. 1985.

Habermas, Jürgen. "Philosophy as Stand-in and Interpreter," translated by C. Lenhardt, in *After Philosophy: End or Transformation?*, edited by Kenneth Baynes, James Bohman, and Thomas McCarthy. Cambridge, MA: MIT Press, 1987.

Hacker, P.M.S. *Insight and Illusion*. Oxford: Clarendon Press, 1972.

—. "Was He Trying to Whistle It?" in *The New Wittgenstein*, edited by Alice Crary and Rupert Read. London: Routledge, 2000.

—. *Wittgenstein: Meaning and Mind*, Part II. Oxford: Blackwell, 1993.

—. *Wittgenstein's Place in Twentieth-Century Philosophy*. Oxford: Blackwell, 1996.

Hahn, Hans, Otto Neurath, and Rudolf Carnap, "The Scientific Conception of the World: The Vienna Circle," translated by P. Foulkes and M. Neurath, in *Otto Neurath: Empiricism and Sociology*, edited by M. Neurath and R.S. Cohen. Dordrecht: D. Reidel, 1973.

Halett, Garth. *A Companion to Wittgenstein's* Philosophical Investigations. Ithaca, NY: Cornell University Press, 1977.

Haraway, Donna. "A Cyborg Manifesto: Science, Technology, and Socialist-Feminism in the Late Twentieth Century" in *Simians, Cyborgs and Women: The Reinvention of Nature*. New York: Routledge, 1991.

Heal, Jane. *Fact and Meaning: Quine and Wittgenstein on Philosophy of Language*. Oxford: Blackwell, 1989.

Hekman, Susan. "The Moral Language Game" in *Feminist Interpretations of Ludwig Wittgenstein*, edited by Naomi Scheman and Peg O'Connor. University Park, PA: Pennsylvania State University Press, 2002.

Heyes, Cressida. *Line Drawings: Defining Women through Feminist Practice*. Ithaca, NY: Cornell University Press, 2000.

Hume, David. *An Enquiry Concerning Human Understanding*, edited by Eric Steinberg. Indianapolis: Hackett Publishing, 1977.

Hutto, Daniel. "Two Wittgensteins Too Many: Wittgenstein's Foundationalism" in *The Third Wittgenstein*, edited by Danièle Moyal-Sharrock. Aldershot: Ashgate, 2004.

Hymers, Michael. "Going around the Vienna Circle: Wittgenstein and Verification," *Philosophical Investigations* 28, no.3. 2005.

——. "Internal Relations and Analyticity: Wittgenstein and Quine," *Canadian Journal of Philosophy* 26, no.4. 1996.

——. *Philosophy and Its Epistemic Neuroses*. Boulder, CO: Westview Press, 2000.

——. "Putnam and the Difficulty of Renouncing All Theory," *International Studies in Philosophy* 35, no.4. 2003.

——. "Wittgenstein, Pessimism and Politics," *The Dalhousie Review* 80, no.2. 2000.

Janik, Allan and Stephen Toulmin. *Wittgenstein's Vienna*. New York: Simon and Schuster, 1973.

Johnson, Mark. *Moral Imagination: Implications of Cognitive Science for Ethics*. Chicago: University of Chicago Press, 1993.

Johnston, Paul. *Wittgenstein and Moral Philosophy*. London: Routledge, 1989.

Kant, Immanuel. *Critique of Pure Reason*, translated by Norman Kemp Smith. New York: St. Martin's Press, 1965.

——. *Metaphysical Foundations of Natural Science* in *Philosophy of Material Nature*, translated by James W. Ellington. Indianapolis: Hackett Publishing, 1985. **MFNS**

Kitcher, Philip. *The Nature of Mathematical Knowledge*. Oxford: Oxford University Press, 1983.

Kline, Morris. *Mathematics: The Loss of Certainty*. New York: Oxford University Press, 1980.

Kripke, Saul. *Naming and Necessity*. Cambridge, MA: Harvard University Press, 1980.

——. *Wittgenstein on Rules and Private Language*. Cambridge, MA: Harvard University Press, 1982. **WRPL**

Kuhn, Thomas. *The Structure of Scientific Revolutions*, 2nd ed. Chicago: University of Chicago Press, 1970.

Lakoff, George and Rafael Núñez. *Where Mathematics Comes From: How the Embodied Mind Brings Mathematics into Being*. New York: Basic Books, 2000.

Langton, Rae. "Speech Acts and Unspeakable Acts," *Philosophy and Public Affairs* 22, no.4. 1993.

Locke, John. *An Essay concerning Human Understanding*, abridged and edited by A.D. Woozley. New York: Meridian, 1974. **ECHU**

Lugg, Andrew. "Wittgenstein's *Tractatus*: True Thoughts and Nonsensical Propositions," *Philosophical Investigations* 26, no.4. 2003.

Luntley, Michael. *Wittgenstein: Meaning and Judgment*. Oxford: Blackwell, 2003.

Lycan, W.G. "Noninductive Evidence: Recent Work on Wittgenstein's 'Criteria,'" *American Philosophical Quarterly* 8, no.2. 1971.

Marcuse, Herbert. *One-Dimensional Man*. Boston: Beacon Press, 1964.

Martin, Robert M. *The Meaning of Language*. Cambridge, MA: MIT Press, 1987.

Marx, Karl and Friedrich Engels. *The German Ideology*, translated by Roy Pascal. New York: International Publishers, 1970.

McBurney, Ward. "Ode to a Tape Gun," 15 Aug. 2007, Story Ward. 21 Mar. 2008. <http://storyward.blogspot.com/2007_08_15_archive.html>.

McDowell, John. "Criteria, Defeasibility, and Knowledge," *Proceedings of the British Academy* 68. 1982.

——. "Wittgenstein on Following a Rule" in *Mind, Value and Reality*. Cambridge, MA: Harvard University Press, 1998.

McGinn, Marie. *Sense and Certainty: A Dissolution of Scepticism*. Oxford: Blackwell, 1989.

McGuinness, Brian. "Preface" in Friedrich Waismann, *Wittgenstein and the Vienna Circle*, edited by Brian McGuinness, translated by Joachim Schulte and Brian McGuinness. Oxford: Blackwell, 1979.

Menger, Karl. "Memories of Moritz Schlick" in *Rationality and Science*, edited by Eugene T. Gadol. New York: Springer-Verlag, 1982.

Miller, Alexander. *Philosophy of Language*. Montreal and Kingston: McGill-Queen's University Press, 1998.

Millikan, Ruth. *Language, Thought, and Other Biological Categories*. Cambridge, MA: MIT Press, 1984.

——. "Truth Rules, Hoverflies and the Kripke-Wittgenstein Paradox," *Philosophical Review* 99, no.3. 1990.

Monk, Ray. *Ludwig Wittgenstein: The Duty of Genius*. London: Jonathan Cape, 1990.

Moore, G.E. "Moore's Paradox" in *G.E. Moore Selected Writings*, edited by Thomas Baldwin. London: Routledge, 1993.

——. *Selected Writings*, edited by Thomas Baldwin. London: Routledge, 1993.

——. "Wittgenstein's Lectures in 1930–33" in *Philosophical Occasions: 1912–1951*, edited by James Klagge and Alfred Nordmann. Indianapolis: Hackett Publishing, 1993.

Moyal-Sharrock, Danièle. "Introduction" in *The Third Wittgenstein*, edited by Danièle Moyal-Sharrock. Aldershot: Ashgate, 2004.

——. "*On Certainty* and the Grammaticalization of Experience" in *The Third Wittgenstein*, edited by Danièle Moyal-Sharrock. Aldershot: Ashgate, 2004.

——. *Understanding Wittgenstein's* On Certainty. New York: Palgrave Macmillan, 2004.

Nelson, Hilde Lindemann. "Wittgenstein Meets 'Woman' in the Language-Game of Theorizing Feminism" in *Feminist Interpretations of Ludwig Wittgenstein*, edited by Naomi Scheman and Peg O'Connor. University Park, PA: Pennsylvania State University Press, 2002.

Nelson, John O. "Is the Pears-McGuinness Translation of the *Tractatus* Really Superior to Ogden's and Ramsey's?" *Philosophical Investigations* 22, no.2. 1999.

Nietzsche, Friedrich W. *Beyond Good and Evil*, translated by Walter H. Kaufmann. New York: Vintage Books, 1966.

Nozick, Robert. *Philosophical Explanations*. Cambridge, MA: Belknap Press, 1981.

Nyíri, J.C. "Wittgenstein's Later Work in Relation to Conservatism" in *Wittgenstein and His Times*, edited by Brian McGuinness,. Oxford: Blackwell, 1982.

Priest, Graham. "The Logic of Paradox," *Journal of Philosophical Logic* 8. 1979.

Putnam, Hilary. *Reason, Truth and History*. Cambridge: Cambridge University Press, 1981.

——. "There Is at Least One *A Priori* Truth" in *Realism and Reason*. Cambridge: Cambridge University Press, 1983.

Quine, W.V. "Epistemology Naturalized" in *Ontological Relativity and Other Essays*. New York: Columbia University Press, 1969.

——. *From a Logical Point of View*, 2nd ed. Cambridge, MA: Harvard University Press, 1980.

——. *Ontological Relativity and Other Essays*. New York: Columbia University Press, 1969. **OR**

——. "Truth by Convention" in *Philosophy of Mathematics Selected Readings*, edited by Paul Benacerraf and Hilary Putnam. Englewood Cliffs, NJ: Prentice-Hall, 1964.

——. "Two Dogmas of Empiricism" in *From a Logical Point of View*, 2nd ed. Cambridge, MA: Harvard University Press, 1980. **TDE**

——. *Word and Object*. Cambridge, MA: MIT Press, 1960.

Ramsey, Frank P. Critical Notice of L. Wittgenstein's *Tractatus Logico-Philosophicus*, *Mind* 32, no.128. 1923.

——. "General Propositions and Causality," *Philosophical Papers*, edited by D.H. Mellor. Cambridge: Cambridge University Press, 1990.

Rawls, John. *A Theory of Justice*. Cambridge, MA: Belknap Press, 1971.

Redpath, Theodore. *Ludwig Wittgenstein: A Student's Memoir*. London: Gerald Duckworth & Co., 1990.

Rhees, Rush. "Can There Be a Private Language?" in *Wittgenstein: The Philosophical Investigations*, edited by George Pitcher. London: Macmillan, 1966.

Rilke, Rainer Maria. *The Notebooks of Malte Laurids Brigge*, translated by Stephen Mitchell. New York: Vintage International, 1990.

Rooney, Phyllis. "Philosophy, Language, and Wizardry" in *Feminist Interpretations of Ludwig Wittgenstein*, edited by Naomi Scheman and Peg O'Connor. University Park, PA: Pennsylvania State University Press, 2002.

Rorty, Richard. "Wittgenstein and the Linguistic Turn" in *Philosophy as Cultural Politics*. Cambridge: Cambridge University Press, 2007.

Rosch, E. and C.B. Mervis. "Family Resemblances: Structures in the Internal Structure of Categories," *Cognitive Psychology* 7. 1975.

Russell, Bertrand. *Analysis of Mind*. London: George Allen & Unwin, 1921.

——. "Descriptions" in *Logicism and the Philosophy of Language: Selections from Frege and Russell*, edited by Arthur Sullivan. Peterborough, ON: Broadview Press, 2003.

——. "Introduction" in *Tractatus Logico-philosophicus* by Ludwig Wittgenstein, translated by C.K. Ogden. London: Routledge & Kegan Paul, 1922.

——. *My Philosophical Development*. London: George Allen & Unwin, 1959.

——. "On Denoting" in *Logicism and the Philosophy of Language: Selections from Frege and Russell*, edited by Arthur Sullivan. Peterborough, ON: Broadview Press, 2003.

——. "On the Nature of Truth and Falsehood" in *Philosophical Essays*, rev. ed. London: George Allen & Unwin, 1966.

——. "On Scientific Method in Philosophy" in *The Collected Papers of Bertrand Russell*, Vol. 8, edited by John G. Slater. London: George Allen and Unwin, 1983. **OSMP**

——. "The Philosophy of Logical Atomism," Lecture II in *The Collected Papers of Bertrand Russell*, Vol. 8, edited by John G. Slater. London: George Allen & Unwin, 1983.

——. *The Problems of Philosophy*. Indianapolis: Hackett Publishing, n.d.

Ryle, Gilbert. *The Concept of Mind*. Harmondsworth: Penguin, 1963.

Schlick, Moritz. "The Turning Point in Philosophy," translated by David Rynin, in *Logical Positivism*, edited by A.J. Ayer. Glencoe, IL: The Free Press, 1959. **TPP**

Schotch, P.K. "Paraconsistent Logic: the View from the Right," *Proceedings of the Biennial Meetings of the Philosophy of Science Association*, 2. 1993.

Searle, John. "Proper Names," *Mind* 67. 1958.

Shanker, Stuart. *Wittgenstein's Remarks on the Foundations of AI*. London: Routledge, 1998.

Sheffer, Henry. "A Set of Five Independent Postulates for Boolean Algebras, with Applications to Logical Constants," *Transactions of the American Mathematical Society* 14. 1913.

Shields, Philip R. *Logic and Sin in the Writings of Ludwig Wittgenstein*. Chicago: University of Chicago Press, 1993.

Shiner, Roger. "On Giving Works of Art a Face," *Philosophy* 53. 1978.

——. "Wittgenstein and Heraclitus: Two River-Images," *Philosophy* 49. 1974.

Stern, David G. "A New Exposition of the 'Private Language Argument': Wittgenstein's 'Notes for the "Philosophical Lecture"'," *Philosophical Investigations* 17, no.3. 1994.

——. "The Uses of Wittgenstein's Beetle: *Philosophical Investigations* §253 and Its Interpreters" in *Wittgenstein and His Interpreters: Essays in Memory of Gordon Baker*, edited by Guy Kahane, Edward Kanterian, and Oksari Kuusela. Oxford: Blackwell, 2007.

——. *Wittgenstein on Mind and Language*. Oxford: Oxford University Press, 1995.

——. *Wittgenstein's Philosophical Investigations: An Introduction*. Cambridge: Cambridge University Press, 2004. **WPII**

Stoppard, Tom. *Rosencrantz and Guildenstern Are Dead*. London: Faber and Faber, 1967.

Strawson, P.F. *Individuals*. London: Methuen, 1959.

Stroll, Avrum. "Wittgenstein's Foundational Metaphors" in *The Third Wittgenstein*, edited by Danièle Moyal-Sharrock. Aldershot: Ashgate, 2004.

Stroud, Barry. "Wittgenstein and Logical Necessity" in *Wittgenstein: The Philosophical Investigations*, edited by George Pitcher. London: Macmillan, 1966.

——. "Wittgenstein's 'Treatment' of the Quest for 'a language which describes my inner experience and which only I myself can understand'" in *Meaning, Understanding, and Practice: Philosophical Essays*. Oxford: Oxford University Press, 2000.

Suits, Bernard. *The Grasshopper: Games, Life and Utopia*. Peterborough, ON: Broadview Press, 2005.

Szabados, Béla. "Wittgenstein on Mistrusting One's Own Belief," *Canadian Journal of Philosophy* 11, no.4. 1981.

Toulmin, Stephen. *Return to Reason*. Cambridge, MA: Harvard University Press, 2001.

Waismann, Freidrich. *Wittgenstein and the Vienna Circle*, edited by Brian McGuinness, translated by Joachim Schulte and Brian McGuinness. Oxford: Basil Blackwell, 1979.

Watkins, Eric. "Kant's Philosophy of Science" in *The Stanford Encyclopedia of Philosophy*. Winter 2003 Edition, edited by Edward N. Zalta. <http://plato.stanford.edu/archives/win2003/entries/kant-science/>.

Waugh, Alexander. *The House of Wittgenstein: A Family at War*. New York: Doubleday, 2008.

Williams, Meredith. "Blind Obedience, in *Meaning Scepticism*, edited by Klaus Puhler. New York: Walter de Gruyter, 1991.

Williams, Michael. *Problems of Knowledge*. New York: Oxford University Press, 2001. **PK**

——. *Unnatural Doubts: Epistemological Realism and the Basis of Scepticism*. Princeton: Princeton University Press, 1996. **UD**

Winch, Peter. *Ethics and Action*. London: Routledge & Kegan Paul, 1972.

——. "Wittgenstein: Picture and Representation" in *Trying to Make Sense*. Oxford: Blackwell, 1987.

Wittgenstein, Ludwig. *The Big Typescript TS 213*, edited and translated by C. Grant Luckhardt and Maximilian A.E. Aue. Oxford: Blackwell, 2005. **BT**

——. *The Blue and the Brown Books*, 2nd ed. Oxford: Blackwell, 1969. **BB**

——. *Culture and Value: A Selection from the Posthumous Remains*, rev 2nd ed., edited by Georg Henrik von Wright, Heikki Nyman, and Alois Pichler, translated by Peter Winch. Oxford: Blackwell, 1998. **CV**

——. *Last Writings on the Philosophy of Psychology*, Vol. I, edited by G.H. von Wright and Heikki Nyman, translated by C.G. Luckhardt and Maximilian A.E. Aue. Oxford: Blackwell, 1990.

——. "Lecture on Ethics" in *Philosophical Occasions: 1912–1951*, edited by James Klagge and Alfred Nordmann. Indianapolis: Hackett Publishing, 1993. **LE**

——. *Lectures and Conversations on Aesthetics, Psychology and Religious Belief*, edited by Cyril Barrett. Berkeley: University of California Press, 1967. **LC**

——. *Notebooks 1914–1916*, 2nd ed., edited by G.H. von Wright and G.E.M. Anscombe, translated by G.E.M. Anscombe. Chicago: University of Chicago Press, 1979.

——. "Notes for Lectures on 'Private Experience' and 'Sense Data,'" translated by David G. Stern, in *Philosophical Occasions 1912–1951*, edited by James Klagge and Alfred Nordmann. Indianapolis: Hackett Publishing, 1993.

——. *On Certainty*, translated by Denis Paul and G.E.M. Anscombe. New York: Harper Torchbooks, 1972. **OC**

——. *Philosophical Grammar*, edited by R. Rhees, translated by A.J.P. Kenny. Oxford: Blackwell, 1974. **PG**

——. *Philosophical Investigations*, 2nd ed., translated by G.E.M. Anscombe. Oxford: Blackwell, 1968. **PI**

——. *Philosophical Remarks*, edited by R. Rhees, translated by R. Hargreaves and R. White. Oxford: Blackwell, 1975. **PR**

——. "Remarks on Frazer's *Golden Bough*" in *Philosophical Occasions 1912–1951*, edited by James Klagge and Alfred Nordmann. Indianapolis: Hackett Publishing, 1993. **RFGB**

——. *Remarks on the Foundations of Mathematics*, 3rd ed., edited by G.H. von Wright, R. Rhees, and G.E.M. Anscombe, translated by G.E.M. Anscombe. Oxford: Blackwell, 1978. **RFM**

——. "Some Remarks on Logical Form" in *Philosophical Occasions 1912–1951*, edited by James Klagge and Alfred Nordmann. Indianapolis: Hackett Publishing, 1993.

——. *Tractatus Logico-philosophicus*, translated by C.K. Ogden. London: Routledge & Kegan Paul, 1922. **TLP**

——. *Tractatus Logico-philosophicus*, translated by David Pears and Brian McGuinness. London: Routledge and Kegan Paul, 1975.

——. *Wittgenstein's Lectures, Cambridge, 1930–1932*, edited by Desmond Lee. Chicago: University of Chicago Press, 1982. **WLC I**

——. *Wittgenstein's Lectures, Cambridge, 1932–1935*, edited by Alice Ambrose. Amherst, NY: Prometheus Books, 2001. **WLC II**

——. *Zettel*, 2nd ed., translated by G.E.M. Anscombe. Oxford: Blackwell, 1981. **Z**

Wright, Crispin. "Kripke's Account of the Argument Against Private Language," *Journal of Philosophy* 81. 1984.

——. *Truth and Objectivity*. Cambridge, MA: Harvard University Press, 1992.

INDEX